Good Choices Good Life

Good Choices
Good Life

Becoming The Person You Were Intended To Be

Second Edition

Michael L. Nelson

Copyright © 2022 by Michael L. Nelson

All rights reserved. No part of this book may be reproduced or transmitted in any form or by any means, electronic or mechanical, including photocopying, recording, or by information storage and retrieval systems, without the written permission of the publisher, except by a reviewer who may quote brief passages in a review.

ISBN 978-0-98168760-5 Hardcover
ISBN 978-0-9996589-2-5 Paperback (second edition)
ISBN 978-0-9996589-3-2 eBook

Library of Congress Control Number: 2008941416

Second paperback edition 2022

Manufactured in the United States of America
25 24 23 22 21 20 19 18 17   1 2 3 4 5

GOOD CHOICES GOOD LIFE

To my grandchildren ... Natalie, Matthew, and Michael
May your choices be good ones.

I believe, and firmly so, that each of us has a special purpose for being here. I believe that we each have certain interests, abilities and feelings that collectively define that purpose. I believe that by paying close attention to these qualities and supporting them with good choices, we can become the person we were intended to be. This book was written to help you do exactly that.

Contents

About This Book xiii

Chapter 1 — Learning How to Live   1

Life Doesn't Just Happen 1
A Life Is Built with Thoughts and Deeds 5
Some Misunderstandings About Life 6
What Was Intended for You? 11
It's All Up to You…and the Choices You Make 16

Chapter 2 — We Are Who We Choose To Be   19

No Matter What, We Have Choices 19
Poor Choices Are All Around Us 21
You Can't Wait for the World to Change 24
Our Choices Define Us 25
Self-Control Improves Our Choices 27
Things That Influence the Choices We Make 29
Good Choices Are Not Always Easy 37

Chapter 3 — Developing Understanding   41

Good Thinking, Good Choices 41
How Good Is Your Thinking? 44
Experience vs. Understanding 46
Developing Understanding – House Rules and
Personal Rules 47
Recognizing Our Need for Understanding 53
The Folly of Not Understanding 56

Chapter 4 — Being Honest   59

You Are What You Say and Do 59
Why Are People Dishonest? 61
Honesty Is a Character Test 64
Do Our Little White Lies Make Us Dishonest? 67
Being Honest 69
Honesty Is a Perishable Condition 73
What Will Honesty Do for You? 76

Chapter 5 — Becoming Who You Are   81

The Opportunity…of a Lifetime 81
Living in the Middle 83
So, Where Do You Live? 84
Understanding Your Basic Needs 88
Distractions from Becoming "Who You Are" 91
How Do I Become Myself? 100
To Be (Yourself), or Not to Be 106

Chapter 6 — Acting on Faith — 109

- The Role of Faith 109
- What is Faith? 111
- The Components of Faith 117
- Developing Faith 121
- Developing Faith in Yourself 124
- Is Developing Your Faith Worth It? 128

Chapter 7 — Giving to Others — 131

- "Getting It" 131
- Our Self-Centered World 139
- The Foundation of Giving is Respect 142
- Respect – Feeling It vs. Showing It 143
- Respect – The Chicken or the Egg 147
- Level I Giving – The Little Things 148
- Level II Giving – Your Time and Your Money 154
- Level III Giving – Yourself and Your Life 160
- What Will You Give? 164

Chapter 8 — Developing Friendships — 165

- The Importance of Friendships 165
- A Few Points About Friendship 166
- The Development of Friendships 169
- Positioning Ourselves for Friendship 173
- A Friend is a Friend is a Friend…or Maybe Not 176
- Close Friends vs. Good Friends 177

Chapter 9 — Letting Love into Your Life   181

   Bingo!.. 181
   Responding to Love When It Appears 188
   Letting Love Lead You.. 193
   Where Does Love Come From? 198

Chapter 10 — Discovering Your Gifts   203

   Our Gifts 203
   The Gift Discovery Process 205
   Where Do Our Gifts Come From?.............................. 207
   How Many Gifts Do We Have? 210
   Never Assume It's Not a Gift......................................211
   Your Gifts Evolve with Your Choices 213
   As You Think About Your Gifts................................... 217
   The Realities of Gift Discovery 220
   Some Closing Thoughts About Gifts 224

Chapter 11 — Tending to Your Body   227

   The Unhealthy Truth 227
   My, That Was Big of You.. 229
   We Say, "We Exercise!" 238
   A Society of Pill Poppers 244
   Other "Sins of the Body"... 245
   Our Choices Are Killing Us 250
   Now, Three Questions for You................................... 252

Chapter 12 — Establishing Goals and Taking Risks   257

Lots of Ways to Live It 257
Why Establish Personal Goals? 259
Goal Setting Is a Thinking Process 262
Start by Looking Inside Yourself 267
What Do You Want to Accomplish? 270
Please Note: Goals Have an Immediate Impact on Your Life 279
What Role Does Risk Taking Play in All of This? 280
Anytime Is a Good Time for Goal Setting 283

Chapter 13 — Making the Effort   293

Empty Promises and Empty Efforts 296
Making the Effort for Others 298
Becoming the Person We Were Intended to Be 302
We Shall Overcome...Someday 304
Where Effort Counts the Most 307

Chapter 14 — Your Choices, Your Life   317

What Will You Accomplish With Your Life? 317
Don't Settle for Being Average 320
A Few Choice Reminders 322

Closing Comments   331

My Thanks to Others   332

References   333

INTRODUCTION
ABOUT THIS BOOK

*"It isn't how much you do that counts,
but how much you do well and how often you decide right."*

WILLIAM FEATHER
American Publisher and Author

Good Choices Good Life was never intended to be a "how to" book because I don't believe someone can tell another person exactly how to live. That's something each of us must work out for ourselves. Rather, I'd categorize it as a "things to think about" book because it contains points, quotes, and examples that I believe are worth considering if you want to improve the choices you are making in your life.

Initially, this was going to be a short writing just for my grandchildren. With so many bad influences in the world today, I wanted them to understand that they could make their own choices and become the person they want to be regardless of what others around them were saying or doing. Somewhere along the way, the project took on a life of its own, and now here is the book you are about to read.

Writing this book caused me to think through many of my beliefs about life and living. There's a clarifying benefit to putting what you feel and believe down in writing. As a result, I would say that I wrote *Good Choices Good Life* as much for myself as for those who will now read it.

I must tell you that I believe that writing *Good Choices Good Life* was something I was intended to do. First, I was blessed to have the time to devote to the research and writing of the book. Second, I truly enjoyed the many hours of diligent work that were required to complete it. Finally, when I revisited certain sections that had sat idle for several months, I was often amazed by some of the words I found there. I knew that I had written them, but it was apparent to me that I had some help and inspiration along the way.

In parts of the book, I've acknowledged the potential role that our "inner voice" can play in our lives. While I can't explain exactly how spiritual guidance works, I do believe that there is a presence within us—the Spirit of Goodness, if you will—that, if we pay attention to it, will guide us in many of the choices we make.

If this book reminds you of the fundamental importance of the choices you make and helps you think more carefully about the choices you are making in your life, it will have been a worthwhile effort. Good luck to all of us as we learn, grow and work to make better choices in our lives.

Michael L. Nelson

CHAPTER 1

LEARNING HOW TO LIVE

*"Our own life is the instrument with which
we experiment with the truth."*

THICH NHAT HANH
Vietnamese Buddhist Monk

Life Doesn't Just Happen

Let's start with a very important question. What determines the quality of your life and its ultimate impact on those around you? Some believe it's your family's influence and your educational experiences that make the primary contributions to this result. Others think that it's your level of intelligence and how smart you are that "allows" you to succeed. Maybe it's the genes you were born with that over time "construct" the person you turn out to be. Or, is it simply a matter of luck that determines the person you become and what you accomplish with your life? Something plays <u>the</u> <u>primary</u> <u>role</u> in defining the outcome of your life. But what is it?

In spite of the importance of this question, many of us don't give much serious thought to the answer. We prefer to go with the flow and let our lives work out in their own way. Granted, it's much easier to let life happen and not be personally on the line for actual results. However, life doesn't just happen. You or another person chooses what the next comment or activity will be. Whether you let someone make these selections for you or you elect to make them for yourself, you develop as an individual according to the choices that guide your life.

Yes, people come into this world subject to certain pre-existing conditions – where you were born, the color of your skin, your basic physical characteristics, the guidance you received in early childhood, and your general health are all things that helped form the early you. But at a very young age, your choices start to override these factors. The 3-year old little girl makes her choice concerning which doll she will take to bed at night. The 7-year old boy chooses what he will do after school and who his friends will be. The 12-year old decides how long he will study, which sports he will play, and what he will do in his spare time. By the time we are 15 or 16 years old, each of us has almost total control over our choices about what we think, what we say, and what we do. Beyond these early years we continue to control our lives by making such important choices as the level of education we'll attain, who we'll marry, and what we'll do with our lives.

> *Steve and Thomas were twins and just entering their senior year in high school. Although identical in size and appearance, they chose to live in very different ways. Steve chose to study and to volunteer for special projects at school. Thomas, on the other hand, skipped classes, never studied very much, and spent most of his time thinking about what he would do after school each day.*

As a result of his choice to enter the high school science fair, Steve developed an interest in learning more about the impact of foods on cardiovascular disease. After the fair, Steve spent lots of time reading about cardiovascular research on the Internet and wrote several of his high school papers on the subject. One day, as he was reading a particularly interesting article about heart surgery and viewing the detailed schematics that it included, "the bug" bit him. He suddenly realized that he wanted to devote his life to this field of medicine and help others lead more comfortable lives.

Thomas, on the other hand, was feeling the need for pocket money for beer and cigarettes. As a result, he chose to go to work on a construction site after school. It wasn't long before Thomas needed even more money, so he chose to drop out of high school and work at his construction job full time.

Ten years later, "Dr. Steve" was standing by his patient's hospital bed reviewing the successful open-heart procedure he'd performed the previous day. "You'll be good as new and able to go back to work in a couple of weeks," he explained. Steve really loved helping people like this!

Thomas was now in Alaska having discovered that jobs paid better up there. He didn't really like what he was doing, but he had plenty of money for beer and cigarettes.

Two brothers, identical in looks, and alike in many ways, but very different in the choices they made – and in the way their lives worked out.

So, one facet of living we all need to understand is that, regardless of our initial circumstances, <u>we define our lives through the choices we make</u>. Some of these choices we make independently and others we make by simply going along with the preferences of others. In either event, you are the one who decides. You can be polite or impolite. You can work hard or just get by. You can decide what you want to do with your life or just accept whatever comes your way. These – and hundreds of other choices – define you as an individual and determine the life experience you'll have. When you recognize the role that your choices play in defining who you are, you can start to see that the outcome of your life is something that you determine.

Granted, you are a one-of-a-kind combination of physical characteristics, mental abilities, personal interests, and emotional feelings that collectively define you as an individual. However, it's not simply possessing this unique "package of capabilities" that will determine the enjoyment and effectiveness of your life. <u>It's how you choose to use it</u>. Therefore, developing an understanding of the role that choices play in defining who you are, and ultimately who you become, is a fundamentally important step in your ability to develop the life you have been given.

Although we receive advice on this important subject from our parents, teachers, and friends, learning how to live is something that each of us must work out for ourselves. There isn't a course you can take that outlines the exact steps you should follow, nor is there any one person who can explain everything to you. Although you may benefit from the experiences of others, the choices concerning how you live your life are yours, and yours alone, to make.

> *"Life's greatest achievement is the
> continual remaking of yourself so that
> at last you know how to live."*
>
> WINFRED RHODES
> Author

A Life Is Built with Thoughts and Deeds

Life is a self-building process. The outcome of your life is dependent, first of all, on the way you think – the kind of thoughts you have about other people, about yourself, and about what you expect to accomplish with your life. The process starts in your head. When you look for good things in other people and make an effort to think well of them, you create a positive context for your own life. When you think of your life as an opportunity to help others, you establish a positive environment for interacting with the people your life touches. When you think about worthwhile goals for your life, you have a positive mental reference for the choices you make. So, the "process of living" starts with your thoughts and, more specifically, how well you think.

Another reality of this self-building process is that your actions affect you as much as they do other people. Not only does the new neighbor appreciate the flowers you brought, but you gain a certain sense of satisfaction from having done so. Her life was made a little happier as a result of your actions, but your life was made happier, too. Similarly, the person who steals from another is, in effect, robbing his own opportunity to feel good about himself and at the same time is choosing to live a life that will mean little to other people. It's a mistake to believe that our words and our actions only affect others. In reality, we are on the receiving end of what we say and what we do as well.

So, you build your life thought by thought and deed by deed. It is through a lifetime of thoughts and deeds that you create your self image and display your character to those around you. These thoughts and deeds are, in reality, choices that you make about the way you'll feel or act. As a result, it's not something that happens to you but rather how you think and what you do that determines the type of person you'll be and the level of happiness you'll ultimately achieve. If you choose your thoughts and deeds wisely, you are, in effect, taking advantage of the opportunity you have to live a happy and rewarding life.

> *"Watch your thoughts; they become your words. Watch you words; they become you actions. Watch your actions; they become your habits. Watch your habits; they become your character. Watch your character for it will become your destiny."*
>
> UNKNOWN

Some Misunderstandings About Life

The world around us is constantly trying to influence us in some way. In many instances, we can easily identify the influence as being good or bad and react accordingly. However, there are other influences that we don't even try to evaluate but simply accept under the logic that "it's the way things are done now." For example, when I was growing up not one couple that I knew, in high school or college, lived together without being married. Today, it's a common practice to do otherwise and, in many instances, to have children without officially tying the knot.

If we are not careful in both our thinking and the choices we make, we can allow, often unknowingly, the "ways of the world" to become indications of how we should live our lives. We have the tendency to accept something because "everyone is doing it." When we do so, we reveal our misunderstanding of how life should be lived. Life is never great if we live it in a "copy cat" fashion. Life is much more rewarding when we allow our individuality to develop so that we, in our own special ways, can contribute something good and positive to the world and those who live in it.

There are dozens of misunderstandings about how life should be lived. If you stop and think about it, I'm sure you can easily identify some of them. If you observe how those around you are living their lives, you will likely identify many more. Here are just a few, three to be exact, that I believe are very important as you think about how you are choosing to live your life.

Misunderstanding #1: An Active Life is a Meaningful One

Many of us are so busy with our jobs, our families, and other activities that we fail to take the time to assess who we really are and what is fundamentally important. Our lives, to a great extent, are controlled by our "to do" lists...drive the kids to school, attend the meeting at work, get the grocery shopping done, pay the bills, go to the ball game, plan the weekend…the list goes on and on.

We move from activity to activity and readily accept most of this busy work as an integral part of our lives. In fact, you might think that the more activities you handle, the better the job you're doing with your life. You may even feel a sense of pride from the hustle and bustle of your life and view your ability to juggle things as a skill that's envied by others. Unfortunately, you could be confusing a busy life with a meaningful one. While a meaningful life certainly has its share of activities associated with family, work, and friends, a well-lived life is determined <u>not by your level of activity but by whether you're living up to the potential that your life represents</u>.

In today's world, it's easy to lose sight of the fact that time is a precious commodity and that no one has an endless supply of tomorrows. Take a close look at yourself and determine if you're on the road to developing a special life or simply living a very busy one. There's nothing to be gained from delaying your answer to this self-assessment. For the sooner you make the distinction between <u>being busy</u> and <u>achieving your potential</u>, the sooner you can begin to create an exceptional life.

> *"It is not enough to be busy; so are the ants.*
> *The question is: What are we busy about?"*
> HENRY DAVID THOREAU

Misunderstanding #2:
What Other People Think About You Is Important

I'm not talking about the times when someone close to you provides knowledgeable and experienced advice concerning what you should do or how you should handle a situation in your life. There are "learning moments" in every life and we all want to make sure we pay attention when they occur. What I'm talking about here are the times when we actually make choices, not based on what we should or really want to do but rather based on how others will view us and what they will think as a result of our actions.

The truth is many of us conduct much of our living under the influence of what others think. Are we dressed right for the party? What will our friends think about our house when they come to see us? Can other people "see" that we are successful? By succumbing to this need for recognition, you can actually raise the stress level in your life and make some very important choices solely because you want others to think well of you. As a result, many of us live to meet the expectations of other people, not the expectations that we've consciously developed and adopted for ourselves.

> "The eyes of other people are the eyes that ruin us.
> If all but myself were blind, I should want neither
> fine clothes, fine houses, nor fine furniture."
>
> BENJAMIN FRANKLIN

Misunderstanding #3:
It Will All Just Work Out Someday

Whether our primary, day-to-day activities involve school, work, or family – or a combination thereof – it's easy for us to be swept along by the flow of life believing that if we just do our best things will work out favorably at some point. Many of us feel that if we work hard and "keep our nose clean" at some point we will have a life that provides much happiness and personal satisfaction. Well, I hate to burst the bubble, but this simply is not true. It really depends on the focus of your efforts. Someone once said that "80% of the people in the world are working on the solution to the wrong problem." Likewise, if you are spending most of your time "working on life" in the wrong way, you are not likely to achieve the true potential that you possess regardless of how long you take or how much effort you devote to it.

Unfortunately, many of us live for ourselves. We want to "be successful" and enjoy the finer things that this world has to offer believing that they will make us happy. As such, we tend to be the primary focus of our choices and most of our efforts are aimed at improving our own circumstances, not the circumstances of others. If we never break out of this self-centered perspective and live our lives making choices in this self-focused way, we may never experience the true "rewards" that life has to offer.

Satisfaction in life comes from accomplishing something worthwhile not for yourself, but for others. Whether it is managing the development of a child into a productive young adult, the help and assistance provided to clients and fellow employees, or your long-term dedication and loving support of a close friend, life works out well only when you focus your efforts on helping others. To achieve such requires careful thought concerning how you live your life and a willingness to make choices that focus your abilities on improving the life of another person. It is the focus of your choices that determines if things eventually work out well for you...or if they don't.

> *"The life of every man is a diary in which he means to write one story, but often writes another. His humblest hour is when he compares the volume as it is with what he intended it to be."*
>
> JAMES M. BARRIE

What Was Intended for You?

Here's another important question. Were you brought into this world with certain intentions for your life, or were you just delivered here and left to work things out on your own? Without taking the time to reflect on this question and answering it for yourself, you run the risk of never really understanding why you're here. If you refuse to think about the potential of an intended purpose for your life, you may never understand what your role was supposed to be. If you just want to "be happy" and live one day at a time, you may miss the opportunity to use your life to accomplish something important over the long term. However, if you pay attention to the signals that come into your life, you don't have to stretch very far to believe that your life has a specific purpose and that you, in fact, came pre-equipped to fulfill it.

One of the first indications of how we should conduct our lives is the feeling we get from doing something good for someone else. We are called to action by the needs of other people. The better job we do at responding to those needs, the more enjoyable our lives become. We simply feel better when we do something good for someone else. Whether it is something as simple as slowing our car to let a complete stranger into the traffic flow, or spending months taking care of a sick relative, we feel better as a result of helping others. These good feelings, a direct result of making helpful choices, are really "signals" that indicate we were intended to conduct our lives in a helpful way.

Other signals come our way via the interests we develop. As we live our lives, we find ourselves motivated to do certain things or to learn more about certain subjects. These interests direct our lives in more specific ways and, when supported by good choices, often lead to the development of special skills and abilities. Some of us enjoy math, while others prefer history. Some want to be farmers and others want to work in government. Some are great speakers, while others want to do things in a quiet and unnoticed way. It is through the careful interpretation of our interests that our intended lives are revealed to us.

Love is another signal that communicates and defines the life that we were intended to live. Love is not under your control – it's not something you can go out and find or cause to happen. Instead, love finds you and can set your life in motion in almost unbelievable ways. When love enters your life, you suddenly become energetic about things you want to do, people you want to be with, or projects that you want to complete – all important indications of how your life should be lived. By letting love guide your choices, you are, in effect, living the life that was intended for you.

> Jordan's grandfather had been a firefighter for more than 30 years. Jordan's dad was also a firefighter, and everyone in the family expected him to follow in his dad's footsteps. His mother often said, "Jordan, you're going to make lots of people very proud when you put on that blue uniform."
>
> When Jordan was a child, he received a new fire truck every Christmas, each one bigger and redder than the one before. The trucks were nice, but Jordan seldom played with them for very long. Instead, he loved to draw, sketching for hours all by himself. Jordan drew many things, but houses with lots of trees and flowers seemed to be what he enjoyed the most.
>
> In high school, Jordan got a summer job working for a local builder to save money for his first car. He began by stacking bricks and hauling concrete for the bricklayers. Eventually, he joined the framing crew and loved spending time talking with his fellow workers about the angles in the roofline or how the deck should be positioned. He spent many evenings at home roughing out ideas for a house or working on a kitchen layout to make it more functional.
>
> At dinner one night, Jordan's dad told the family how his station had contained a major fire at a local chemical plant that day. "Just think, Jordan,"

his mom said, "it won't be many years before you'll be putting out fires just like your Dad!"

Jordan looked at his parents. He took a deep breath. "I know you want me to be a firefighter like Dad and Granddad," he said. "But that's not what I want to do. I've decided to be an architect. I love building houses and working on new house plans. I can feel it...designing houses is what I want to do."

His mom and dad were very surprised. They had never thought of Jordan as anything other than a firefighter. After some silence, his father replied, "Jordan, at some point every person has to choose how they will live their life. We know you've enjoyed your construction jobs, and we should have encouraged you to consider other possibilities. So, if becoming an architect is what you really want to do, you can count on us to help you as much as we can."

After worrying about this moment for some time, Jordan was relieved. He had explained his choice to his parents, and, although somewhat of a surprise to him, they were supporting his decision. He loved his mom and dad and didn't want to disappoint them. However, he knew "in his bones" that being an architect was what he was meant to do. He knew this choice was the right one for him.

Our intended life speaks to us in many ways. The challenge for us, however, is to be able to recognize these signals and have the faith to follow the path they define for us.

> "Man's main task is to give birth to himself,
> to become what he potentially is."
>
> ERICH FROMM
> Man for Himself

An interesting aspect of this overly simplified explanation of "how life works" is that you're not in charge of the signals that communicate your intended life to you. The feelings that come from doing good things for other people develop within you without your influence or control. Your interests in certain areas of work or study expose themselves unexpectedly as a byproduct of your activities. The love you develop for certain people or projects enters your life without prior request. So the signals that can potentially frame and define your life aren't things that you simply dream up, but rather they come to you as you live your life.

One has to wonder where these signals come from. While I can't fully explain this, I do believe that there is something very important "going on" inside each and every one of us. Some of us refer to these feelings as our conscience, some consider it a spiritual presence and, as many others, I see it as God "at work" in us. I believe that God motivates us through the good feelings that come from helping others, the loves that enter and direct our lives, and the unique interests and abilities that make us the individuals we are. I believe that God presents these "suggestions" to us and works in this world through our adoption and development of them.

> *"God gave man individuality of constitution and a chance for achieving individuality of character. He puts special instruments into every man's hands by which to make himself and achieve his mission."*
>
> JOSIAH G. HOLLAND
> Doctor, Teacher and Editor

It's All Up to You...and the Choices You Make

This is not to say that you should sit quietly and wait for a magic signal to tell you what to do. Instead, you must be aware of your inner feelings and be willing to make choices based on them. To maximize your life experience, you must be aware of this spiritual guidance and work to develop the life that you have been given. You must respect your individuality, follow your own good judgment, and make the kind of choices that allow you to become the person you were intended to be.

If you acknowledge that many of your inner feelings are really insights into the life you are intended to live, you can start to think more carefully about what your "inner voice" is saying to you. If you can somehow come to believe that your life has an intended purpose, you can start to make choices that you feel are right for you regardless of what others are doing. If you can start to see that you are here to accomplish specific things – both for yourself and for others – your life takes on a new and special meaning. If there is a secret to living a meaningful and rewarding life, it must be working to confirm the intended purpose for your life and then making the choices required to fulfill it.

My impression, and to a great extent my own experience, is that many of us don't give adequate time and thought to how life, in general, should be lived or, more specifically, what we should do with our own. We prefer to enjoy life as much as we can, not thinking too much about the needs of others or our opportunities in this regard. Then one day we suddenly realize that we're not as happy as we had been pretending to be. Please don't waste your life just going through the motions. You can surface the intended life that lives within you if you will give it some careful thought and use good judgment in the choices you are making.

CHAPTER 2

WE ARE WHO WE CHOOSE TO BE

"Life is the sum of all of your choices."
ALBERT CAMUS
Nobel Prize Winner in Literature

No Matter What, We Have Choices

The quality, meaning, and results of our lives are dependent upon the choices we make about what we think, what we say, and what we do. Regardless of our circumstances, the enjoyment we experience, as well as the impact we have on others, is totally dependent upon the choices we make about the way we live our lives. If we make good choices, we'll have a good life. If we make bad choices, we won't. It's as simple as that.

One could argue that some people are in circumstances that will not change no matter what choices they make. Certainly, the man sentenced to prison, the young boy growing up without a father, and the woman fighting a life-threatening disease are examples of circumstances where someone can't simply "make a choice" and change things. However, even in extreme conditions, we still have the opportunity to make choices that define the person we are. The prisoner can choose to help other inmates learn and benefit from his mistakes. The young boy can choose to earn good grades even without a father there to help him. The woman with health concerns can choose to maintain a positive and loving attitude in spite of the odds against her. It's not your circumstances that define you, but rather how you choose to live your life in reaction to them.

> Mattie Stepanek died of muscular dystrophy at the age of 13. He spent most of his life in a wheelchair and, in his last few years, required supplemental oxygen and blood transfusions on a regular basis. His three older siblings died from the disease and his 44-year old mother was experiencing the adult version of the same condition when he died. By any definition, Mattie was dealt a bad hand.
> But, Mattie chose to play his hand to the best of his ability, and he did so brilliantly. He maintained a positive attitude, always smiled, and always showed enthusiasm to those around him. He wrote poetry and published five books including the New York Times best-seller <u>Heartsongs</u>. He appeared on many national TV shows and was the National Goodwill Ambassador for the Muscular Dystrophy Association. Jerry Lewis said, "With Mattie, there was always a silver lining. Life threw its worst at him, and he responded by seeing the good."
>   I don't know how many people will be at your funeral or at mine, but there were more than 1,300 at Mattie's. Oprah Winfrey spoke and described how Mattie had impacted her life. In his eulogy,

President Jimmy Carter made the observation, "I have traveled to more than 120 countries, met many kings and queens, but Mattie was the most extraordinary person I have ever met."

We're not all like Mattie, but we can all learn to make good choices like he did.

The collective result of all of the choices you've made is the person you are today. Additionally, the choices you make in the future will further define who you are and, ultimately, the quality of the life you'll live. By being aware of the role that choices play in your life and by trying to make choices that are appropriate for you, you develop, over time, into the person you were intended to be. Through your choices, you create your life and determine the extent to which your life will impact other people and the world in which you live.

Poor Choices Are All Around Us

Stop and take a serious look at life in America today. You'll see an ever-increasing level of violence on television. You'll see less discipline, lower expectations, and deteriorating results in many schools. You'll see business leaders whose ethics impair corporate reputations and cost people their jobs. You'll see people elected to important roles in government make choices that help no one but themselves. You'll hear songs filled with hateful lyrics and four-letter words. You'll see lives and neighborhoods destroyed by the drug culture. You'll see teenage pregnancies, abortion, crime, and divorce at all-time highs.

Almost everywhere you look, our poor choices seem to be increasing.

Why are Americans making so many poor choices? Why don't we understand that our choices have implications within our lives? Simply stated, we've moved from doing what _is_ good to doing what _feels_ good. In other words, we've moved from doing what we _ought_ to do to doing what we _want_ to do. We've come to believe that "feeling good" – instead of taking the often more difficult route of doing the right thing – will lead us to a meaningful life. This is the result of discarding many of the personal values that have influenced people's lives for many, many years. Our personal choices reflect what we value. As our values deteriorate, so do the choices that we make. In fact, according to a recent Gallup Poll, Americans don't feel that our personal or moral values are very strong; and in most people's opinion, these values are likely to deteriorate even more in the future. Shown below are some of the poll's results:

How would you rate the overall state of moral values in this country?

Moral Value Ratings	% Respondents
Excellent	1%
Good	16%
Fair	39%
Poor	44%
Total	100%

Source: Gallup Poll

Do you think moral values in this country are getting better or getting worse?

State of Moral Values	% Respondents
Getting Better	11%
Getting Worse	82%
Other	7%
Total	100%

Source: Gallup Poll

You Can't Wait for the World to Change

This moral decline is not likely to improve any time soon. Therefore, you should recognize that following the crowd is not going to lead you to a full and happy life. Instead, you and I must live our way through this world day-by-day and choice-by-choice. If we are to achieve our true potential, we must learn to focus on what is important in our own lives. We must cultivate a choice-making ability that will not only prevent us from being unduly influenced by other people, but will also allow us to realize the unique potential that we all possess. We must learn to <u>make choices based on good values</u> – not based on what feels good – if we want to do something special with our lives.

Don't be misled by people who think they know everything. You simply have too much to lose. As I've already stated, I believe there is a great life inside every one of us. Regardless of your age or circumstances, there is much you can accomplish with the life you have been given. More importantly, there is a definite contribution you can make to the people around you. Making the right choices – the ones that will allow you to fully realize the potential that lies within you – are the steppingstones which lead to such a life.

> *"Not armies, not nations, have advanced the race; but here and there, in the course of the ages, an individual has stood up and cast his shadow over the world."*
>
> THE REV. EDWIN H. CHAPIN
> Minister and Preacher

Our Choices Define Us

Some of us make the mistake of believing that our current circumstances dictate, to a great extent, how we'll live our lives. "My parents didn't have the money to send me to college, so I just lost interest in finishing my education," the high school dropout says as he tries to justify his jobless state to his friend. Without question, there are factors that determine our initial lifestyle – who our parents are, where we live, and the experiences we have early in our lives, to name a few. However, <u>it's not these factors, but how we react to them</u>, that determine the lives we will ultimately live. Many people have social handicaps or other disadvantages but overcome them and go on to lead very rewarding and successful lives. On the other hand, some have every advantage in the world – great family, good financial resources, and the opportunity for a wonderful education – but turn out lives that are great disappointments to the people around them. Therefore, it's not "the factors" we were born into that determine the lives we will lead, but how we react to them and, subsequently, the choices we make as we form a life of our own choosing.

> *Paul Revere Williams was born in 1894 as the son of a head waiter who worked at the Peabody Hotel in Memphis, TN. Before the age of five he moved with his family from Memphis to southern California. Shortly thereafter, he became an orphan when both of his parents died of tuberculosis.*
>
> *Paul's foster parents discovered that he loved to draw. As a five-year-old, he began to carry a sketchbook and pencil as his toy of choice. That artistic love grew during his high school years and upon graduation he decided to pursue a career in architecture. Being an architect in Los Angeles and Beverly Hills sounds wonderful, but it was 1912 and Paul Williams was black. Nevertheless, he worked his way through the Los Angeles School of Art and Design and the University of Southern California and went on to realize his dream of being a successful architect.*
>
> *Over his 50+ year career, Williams designed over 3,000 projects including homes for well-know celebrities Lucille Ball, Tyrone Power, Frank Sinatra, Za Za Gabor, and an important participant in this story, Danny Thomas. He became the first African American member of the American Institute of Architects. In 1960, Williams designed, free of charge, the blueprints for a children's research hospital which was Danny Thomas' dream and stands today as St. Jude Children's Research Hospital in Memphis, TN.*

> *In 1972, Paul Williams attended the St. Jude 10-year anniversary reception at the Peabody Hotel in Memphis where his father, Chester, had been the head waiter many years before. He had come full circle – from Memphis to L.A. and back to Memphis. I'm sure he was very proud of "the trip" his life had made.*

Granted, there are circumstances that we can do little or nothing about. However, it's not those circumstances that define our lives, but rather how we choose to respond to them. The young woman raised in the wrong part of town by an uneducated single mother has the odds stacked against her, but, if she so chooses, she can go to college and make something of herself. The young man, experiencing pressure from his friends to try marijuana for the first time, can choose to say "no" to these influences and live a drug-free life. The father, although anxious to have a successful career, can choose not to have a drink after work but go home to spend that time with his wife and children. Therefore, it's not our circumstances, but rather the choices we make in response to them that determine the type of person we will be and the kind of life we will live.

> *"My own view of history is that human beings do have genuine freedom to make choices. Our destiny is not predetermined for us; we determine it for ourselves."*
>
> ARNOLD TOYNBEE
> English Economic Historian

Self-Control Improves Our Choices

The benefits of self-control are often overlooked, but it's exactly this ability that allows us to make better decisions. Without self-control, an individual tends to rush into things with little or no thought about the consequences of his choice. With self-control, a person gains the opportunity and the time to think through the choice he is about to make. In fact, studies have shown that individuals with greater self-control go on to live better and more effective lives.

> *In a classic experiment, psychologist Walter Mischel left a succession of four-year-olds in a room with a bell and a marshmallow. They were told that if they rang the bell, he would come back and they could eat the marshmallow. If, however, they didn't ring the bell and waited for him to come back on his own, they could then have two marshmallows.*
>
> *In videos of the experiment, the children squirmed, kicked, and hid their eyes trying to exercise self-control so they could get two marshmallows. Some broke down and rang the bell within a minute; others lasted more than 15 minutes.*
>
> *The study followed these children for many years and found that the children who waited longer earned higher SAT scores, got into better colleges, and had, on average, more successful adult lives. The children who rang the bell the quickest received worse teacher and parental evaluations and were more likely to have drug problems and other dependencies.*

> *This experiment reveals that self-control is essential. Young people who learn to delay gratification can sit through sometimes boring classes to earn a degree. They can perform rote tasks in order to master a language, and they can avoid drugs and alcohol. Individuals lacking self-control experience a series of failed ordeals. For them, life is a parade of foolish decisions: teen pregnancy, drugs, gambling, truancy, and crime.*

So, is self-control something you are born with or is it a skill or ability you can acquire? Subject to the job we do as parents, children can learn self-control at a relatively early age. According to *The Whole Child* by Joanne Hendrick, PhD: "By setting limits for children, you help them learn self-regulation, that is, how to set limits for themselves. This process of learning self-control begins in infancy as babies begin to develop their sense of self." Okay, but what about us older folks? What can we do if we know that we need to develop more self-control? With a view toward making choices, there are at least three things we "older ones" can do to improve our self-control:

- Stop and think. Before you rush into any important choice, stop and think about it. If it's an important choice, you might take days, weeks or even months to arrive at your decision.
- Perform an information check. By this I simply mean ask yourself: Do I have all of the information I need to make this choice? If the answer is no, then take whatever time you need to become fully informed before you decide.

- Talk it over with someone. Sometimes just thinking about it and getting more information is not enough. Sometimes you need to verbalize your options with another person and obtain their input and guidance before you can properly choose what to do.

Things That Influence the Choices We Make

Each of us is different. We have different backgrounds, different faiths, and different political beliefs. We sound different when we speak. We come in different shapes, different sizes, and different colors. Some of us are tall, while others are short; some are fast and some are slow. However, in spite of these differences, there are at least <u>five</u> <u>things</u> <u>common</u> <u>to</u> <u>all</u> <u>of</u> <u>us</u> that influence the choices we make. The more we are aware of these influences, the better job we can do with the choices we make.

Our Need to Be Accepted

Many of the poor choices we make happen because of our perceived need to be accepted or approved by those around us. Most of us want social acceptance and will go to great lengths to get it because we feel that it "validates" us in some way. When others like us, we think we're okay. This belief is probably more prevalent when we're young, but for many of us it continues throughout our lives. This happens because we have not properly valued our independence and instead place a higher value on the opinions of others than our own. We invite this circumstance when we focus on <u>*who*</u> likes us instead of <u>*what*</u> we can be doing with our lives. By making more choices that focus on _what_ we are becoming and fewer choices based on _who_ likes us today, we learn to validate ourselves instead of relying on others to do it for us.

> "I was part of that strange race of people aptly described as spending their lives doing things they detest, to make money they don't want, to buy things they don't need, to impress people they don't like."
>
> BENJAMIN FRANKLIN

Our Appearance

We miss the mark when we define who we are by the way we look. First impressions may be important, but they are quickly overshadowed by the information we can share with others and the way we make other people feel when we're with them.

> *Martin was probably the sharpest member of his college graduating class. An above average student, he always dressed "to the nine's," maintained his hair in the latest style, and looked like a successful businessman even though he was still in college. However, Martin also had "an air" about him and the fact he thought he was better than most folks was not hard to see. Three months and 27 interviews after his college graduation, Martin could not understand why he hadn't received one single job offer.*

Many of us place a high value on the way we look. Otherwise, fad diets, the latest fashions, and cosmetic surgeries wouldn't be in such demand. You might wonder, "What's wrong with wanting to look good?" The problem is not in trying to look nice, but in giving these activities too high a priority in your life. The qualities and attributes that define the type of person you really are can't be seen. Therefore, you make a mistake when you try to define yourself and others primarily by what is visible to the eye.

> *"The lie is in the surrender of the man to his appearance;*
> *as if a man should neglect himself*
> *and treat his shadow on the wall*
> *with marks in infinite respect."*
>
> Ralph Waldo Emerson
> The Conduct of Life

Our Interests and Skills

Each of us has personal interests which lead us to participate in certain activities, study particular subjects, or work in a selected field. Some of us believe that these interests are God-given, some believe they develop through our associations with other people, and some consider them to be simply the byproduct of our experiences. Regardless of their source, we do know that one of the great opportunities we have as individuals is to pursue the things that interest us.

One of the keys to living a meaningful life is to recognize these "seeds" of interest. It is up to you to discover them, nurture them, and allow them to grow. These interests may lead you to be a teacher, a farmer, an engineer, a firefighter, or a restaurateur. Other interests may lead you into gardening, painting, writing, tennis, or other enjoyable activities. Still others may motivate you to dedicate your life to an important cause, devote years to medical research, or even travel to another country to help others build their way of life.

Discovering and identifying these interests isn't a matter of luck, for those who leave such choices to chance are often disappointed with their lives. It's a matter of being willing to listen to "the voice" inside of you. It's a matter of searching and working to evaluate activities of potential interest to you. It's a matter of believing and knowing that you were meant to do or to accomplish certain things with your life.

> *"The line you succeed in will be of your own finding. The Davids in life do not slay the Goliaths of difficulty and temptation in another man's armor, even though it be the king's, but with their own self-made weapons, though they be nothing more formidable than a sling and a stone.*
>
> G. E. BISHOP
> Forbes Book of Quotations

Our Basic Values

You cannot determine who a person really is just by looking at him. Instead, over time, that person becomes known based on the values he possesses and practices. To a great extent, your personal values – such as honesty, concern for others, and a willingness to work hard – determine how you'll view almost every situation you face and, in most instances, the choices that you'll make. Your values are your internal reference points; they determine many of your actions, most of your feelings and set the course for the type of life you live. Your choices will, over time, align themselves with the personal values that are active in your life.

There is an important distinction here – it is the difference between personal values <u>that you believe in</u> and the personal values <u>that you practice</u>. In short, just because you believe in a certain value doesn't mean that your life will reflect it. For example, your friend may tell you he believes that honesty is an important value. However, when adding up his golf score on that horrendous hole, he stated he had "a 6" when he really had an 8. Obviously, <u>believing</u> and <u>practicing</u> are two entirely different things.

> *Randy Pausch was a professor of computer science at Carnegie Mellon. His specialty was human-computer interaction and he was recognized as a pioneer in virtual reality research. He co-founded the Entertainment Technology Center, a joint initiative between the School of Computer Science and the College of Fine Arts at Carnegie Mellon.*
>
> *In September, 2006 at the age of 45 he was diagnosed with pancreatic cancer. As devastating as the news was, Randy made the choice to make the time he had remaining count for something and hopefully to help others as well. He worked to organize a message to give to others so that they would benefit from his experience. Titled "Really*

Achieving Your Childhood Dreams" but dubbed "The Last Lecture" he presented it to his class at Carnegie Mellon on September 18, 2007 and it soon went viral on the Internet. The talk was viewed by thousands of people and later published in a book titled "The Last Lecture" which became a bestseller and remains so today.

Randy Pausch died on July 25, 2008 only ten months after giving his lecture. He had made this point: "Obstacles serve a purpose, they give us a chance to show how badly we want something." He had also reminded his audience, "It's not about how to achieve your dreams, it's about how to lead your life. If you lead your life the right way, the karma will take care of itself...the dreams will come to you."

To practice your values, you must convert these beliefs into a code of conduct that you consciously adopt and apply to your life. For example, you may decide that one of your personal values is honesty and that this value will apply to all of your interactions with family, friends, business associates and, yes, even strangers. However, you can't stop there. This personal value must be converted into a practice – a "value in action," if you will. These are instructions or guidelines that you establish for yourself in simple, easy-to-understand terms so that the actions you take will indeed reflect your values. Your personal value of honesty might become the value in action of "I will always tell the truth, no matter what the circumstances." Therefore, it is the practice – not the value itself – that reflects

We Are Who We Choose To Be

who you really are, what you believe, and what you deem to be important.

> "Slow me down, Lord, and inspire me to send my roots deep into the soil of life's enduring values that I may grow toward the stars of my greater destiny."
>
> AN ANONYMOUS PRAYER

Where do personal values come from? Personal values typically come from one of four sources. A value could become a part of your life because of your family – the way you were raised or the examples set by your parents, family members, or a caring neighbor. It could have come from your friends – a schoolmate who influenced you in some way or an associate whose business ethics have made an impression on you. It could come from your personal experience such as an important lesson you learned from a mistake you made or a "near miss" you had while growing up. Or, fourth and finally, it could result from conscious self-development – your choice to think about the way you want to live, to think carefully about the importance of practicing good values, and to adopt certain values for your life.

> *Brian was raised by his grandparents in a small Midwestern town. He frequently rode with his grandfather in his pickup truck and especially enjoyed the times when his grandfather took him fishing. One day, as they were out "touring," his grandfather stopped the truck in front of a rather dilapidated*

house on a dirt road just outside of town. As Brian discovered, this was the home of an old man his grandfather had known for many years. Brian took particular notice of how his grandfather was concerned about the man's health and well being. He was also touched when his grandfather, who had little money himself, reached into his pocket, gave the old man $20 and said, "Earl, get yourself some more food when you go to town today." Now, some 40 years later, as Brian wrote his check to the local charity, he couldn't help but think about his grandfather and what he did for that old man that day.

Our Goals for Our Lives

The self-fulfilling prophecy – that things usually turn out the way we expect them to – certainly applies to making good choices. Individuals who set important goals and objectives for themselves find it much easier to make choices that are consistent with those goals. On the other hand, individuals who have no real goals in life – no expectations that they can do something special with the life they've been given – are much more likely to make poor choices and to simply drift along as they manage their lives without any real targets or hopes for their futures.

> "It is not enough that we do our best;
> sometimes we have to do what is required."
>
> WINSTON CHURCHILL

Good Choices Are Not Always Easy

Understanding the need to make more effective choices is one thing, but actually doing so can prove to be difficult. The forces of the world will frequently move against your desire to be a better person or to accomplish something that you really want to do. In addition, you may have responsibilities, desires, or established routines that cause you to act or think in certain ways. Granted, it's a lot easier to yield to such influences and not make a special effort to adjust or change the way you've been living. But make no mistake about it, you have the power to choose and to change yourself or your circumstances if such is needed. If you truly want to make life-changing choices, you can do it.

It takes a real effort to develop and maintain a meaningful and worthwhile life. The actual process of living begins with the realization that there is a major difference between the life that is lived "by choice" and the one that is lived "by chance." The latter is easy: you just get up every morning and see what happens to you. On the other hand, to live by choice requires careful study, insightful thinking, establishing goals, taking risks, making diligent efforts, and often taking a road that is different from those around you.

*"A man can do what he ought to do;
and when he says he cannot, it
is because he will not."*

J. A. FROUDE
History Professor

There will be many important "moments of choice" in your life. At every one of these moments your inner character and ability to think will be tested as you struggle to determine the action that's best for you. And, making the right choice is just half of the process. You must also have the will to follow through and actually execute the choice you've made. Many a person has mentally made one choice, only to go out into the world and execute another.

Moreover, you must be willing to invest in good choices over an extended period of time if you want to make something special out of your life. No great athlete wins without months and often years of making the right choices to prepare. No businesswoman becomes a successful executive without investing years of making the right choices for her customers and her employees. No physician becomes a highly competent and respected practitioner without devoting years or even a lifetime of making the right choices for his patients. And, so it is with you and me…we must be willing to make good, although sometimes very difficult choices, year in and year out, if we want to fully develop the special lives that are inside each of us.

> *I slept and dreamed that life was joy.*
> *I awoke and saw that life was duty.*
> *I acted and behold, duty was joy.*
>
> RABINDRANATH TAGORE
> Nobel Laureate and Indian Poet

I know this seems too simple – <u>make</u> <u>better</u> <u>choices</u> and <u>have</u> <u>a</u> <u>better</u> <u>life</u>. "You don't understand some of the things I have to deal with," may be one of your thoughts right now. Maybe I don't. But, given all of the bad things that are going on in the world these days and the fact that the problems in almost every community are getting worse, we need a clearer understanding of what's required to live effectively and how to create a better life for ourselves and those around us. We can't just continue to hope that things will get better. We've got to take some action, starting on a personal level, if we want to make the world a better place. That action, in my way of thinking, can only take place through the choices we make. The improvement process must start with you and me – making better choices so that, in our own special and unique ways, we can contribute to a better future for everyone.

CHAPTER 3

Developing Understanding

"If you think education is expensive, try ignorance."
Bumper Sticker

Good Thinking, Good Choices

One of the major reasons people make poor choices is the lack of understanding about the potential repercussions of a decision they are about to make. Sometimes we really don't understand what we're doing, but we "do it" anyway. Sometimes we do understand, but refuse to acknowledge or think about the potential downside of our actions. In either event, without a reasonable amount of information and a fundamental willingness to be realistic about the possible outcome, the odds are your choice will prove to be a poor one. If you want to improve your choice making skills, you must take the time to gather the information you need and to think about the choice you're about to make.

None of us will ever be smart enough or lucky enough to only make great choices in our lives; that's just not realistic. However, you can significantly improve the quality and effectiveness of the choices you make by developing an understanding of the circumstances involved. You can avoid major mistakes by taking more time, using the information that's all around you, and considering the advice of other people to arrive at a better or more informed choice. You can do your homework so that you improve your understanding of the potential implications of a decision you're about to make, thus increasing the odds that your choice will be a good one.

Good choices take place in our minds. Granted, other things come into play – our love for others, the desire to pursue personal interests, or the motivation to achieve something we deem to be important may all be factors in the choices we make. However, the more the mind is absent from the decision process, the more likely you are to follow some urge or desire that stimulates you to make a choice without really understanding its future impact on your life. "Just because I want to" is seldom sufficient justification for making an important choice. We all need to be good thinkers if we expect to make good choices in our lives.

> *You say "I think" ten times a day Or fifteen times, or twenty And even more, well, anyway... You sure repeat it plenty. But pause and ponder half a wink And start your brain cells clinking; "I think" you say, but do you think Or only think you're thinking?*
>
> BERTON BRALEY
> Author, Writer and Editor

Our schools teach us math, English, science, and history, but very little about the fundamentals of good thinking. Our parents urge us to "make good grades" and "do your best," but provide limited instructions concerning how to think through

Developing Understanding

a choice we're about to make. Our friends, although untrained in making good choices themselves, readily offer their suggestions about where we should go, what we should do, and even what we should think. Therefore, until we personally take the initiative to become better thinkers, we are more likely to yield to our feelings, make snap judgments, or head off in some direction with no real thought as to how the trip may impact our life.

> *Rhonda was 18 and very excited about attending her senior prom. Her mom had bought her a beautiful dress, and she'd spent the afternoon getting her hair and nails done. As she got dressed, she couldn't help but think about her new friend, Ben. Although this was only their third date, she was already thinking that he just might be the one for her.*
>
> *Rhonda and Ben had a great time at the prom and quickly hurried off to the hotel where the post-prom dance was being held. The beer flowed freely, and Ben, ever the gentleman, was making sure that Rhonda was getting her fair share. Later, when Ben told her he'd gotten a room at the hotel so they could "get away from the crowd," Rhonda grinned and happily accompanied him out of the ballroom.*
>
> *Less than two months later, Rhonda was sitting with her mother in the kitchen of their home discussing the fact that there was a strong possibility that Rhonda was pregnant. Her mother listened as Rhonda lamely explained: "Somehow it just*

> *happened." Her mother sat there for a few minutes just looking at her daughter and then quietly asked: "Rhonda, what in the world were you thinking?"*

How Good Is Your Thinking?

Few of us spend much time assessing our own ability to think. We think about lots of things relating to our family, friends, and personal circumstances, but spend little time on how well we can think through something and develop a course of action that most people would consider logical and correct. However, if we rely solely on our luck, and never on our logic, we can be assured that our choices will not produce the life we'd hoped to achieve.

Our ability to think is something that we typically gauge by how things work out. If everything works out okay, we consider our choice to have been a good one. If not, we tend to justify the outcome in all sorts of ways. Seldom do we admit that the reason for the poor choice was simply poor thinking in the first place.

After-the-fact assessments are helpful, but certainly not as beneficial as making the right choice in the first place. Just ask the young woman who made the choice to skip college to marry her heart-throb, and who is now divorced with two children and no degree. Her after-the-fact assessment tells her she made a very bad choice and should have gotten her degree before she got her marriage license. However, there's no reset button that will rewind her life. She has to live with the choice she made.

If you want to make good choices, you must be a good thinker or have a "good thinking process" that you follow. Here are three questions that might help you in this regard:

Have you stopped to think about it?

Just stop and think. This sounds too simple, but not taking the time to do so is probably the most frequent reason for the bad choices we make. We feel pressure from our friends and the world around us and often yield to it, making an important choice before we're actually ready to do so. In almost every case, taking the time to think through things will help you make a better choice. "Stop and think" really means "take as much time as you need" to evaluate your circumstances, identify the alternatives that you have, and make sure you understand the implications of the choice you're about to make.

Do you have all of the information you need?

While stopping and thinking will help improve your choice making process, you'll often need to take it one step further. Many times you will find yourself in situations where you don't have the knowledge to make a certain choice, no matter how long you think about it. In those instances, you must go and gather more information in order to develop the understanding you need. Typically, the better your information, the better your thinking, and, therefore, the better your choice will be.

How will this choice impact the goals you have for your life?

According to Socrates, one of the most important aspects of a human being's life is to know yourself. Although he lived more than 2,000 years ago, the Greek philosopher knew that thinking is much easier if you can do so in context with the goals that you have. If you know what you want to do with your life and what kind of person you want to be, you can think about your choices with these objectives in mind. When your life has a sense of direction, it's much easier to determine if a pending choice will help or hinder the journey you have planned.

Experience vs. Understanding

You don't have to "do wrong" in order to know how to "do right." Bad experiences are not the best way to learn how to make a good choice. For example, you can learn how to avoid a car wreck without the experience of having lived through one. You can learn how to drive safely without the insights gained from several accidents. By listening to those around you and watching the fatalities on the 6 o'clock news, you can get all of the experience necessary to understand the need to be a careful driver. Likewise, you don't have to make every possible mistake to learn how to avoid them and to understand the benefits of an "accident-free" life.

Good choices do not depend on first-hand experience. You don't have to live through something to experience it. If you take the time to do the homework that an important choice deserves, you can develop the level of understanding needed to make the choice that's right for you.

The majority of us do become significantly better thinkers as we move through life. The reason for this isn't necessarily age or maturity but rather the fact that we have more input on which to base our choices: more information, more knowledge, and more observations of the world around us. However, we can waste much of our lives if we wait for this to happen naturally. The challenge for each of us, no matter what our age, is to learn how to use the information that is all around us to become better thinkers <u>now</u>. If you learn how to think effectively, you can develop a reasonable level of understanding about any choice you are about to make without relying on actual experience to be your only teacher.

> *"Better to be unborn than untaught,
> for ignorance is the root of misfortune."*
>
> PLATO
> Greek Philosopher

Developing Understanding – House Rules and Personal Rules

The term "understanding," as it applies to making choices, implies that we have a reasonable perception of the impact of some decision that we are about to make. This perception is based in part on <u>facts</u> and in part on the <u>goals</u> we have for our lives. The facts come from the world around us and are, in effect, "house rules" that apply to all of us – touch the fire, you get burned, no exceptions. Goals, on the other hand, create "personal rules" which develop based on the plan we have for our lives. One person may want to be a chef while another wants to be a teacher – therefore, their personal rules will differ. As you combine the <u>facts</u> determined by the world with the <u>goals</u> you've established for your life, you begin to understand what "fits" you and where you are going. By considering both the facts of the world and the personal goals you have for your life, you can better see the potential impact of a choice you're about to make and thus increase the odds that it will be a good one.

Facts: The First Half of Understanding

In trying to understand "understanding" as it applies to making choices, you need to see the relationship between gathering information, developing knowledge and achieving understanding. There's a definite chronology among these three. Starting with nothing, you gather information pertinent to a question or topic. By studying the information you've gathered, you increase your knowledge of that subject. In effect, you become informed. Once your knowledge reaches a certain level, you achieve an understanding of the subject or choice at hand. Too frequently, we act – and make a choice – with little information, limited knowledge, and no understanding of what we are about to do…circumstances that significantly increase the risk that our choice will be a poor one.

> *Daniel, Jacob, and Ethan were very close friends. They went to the same school, had the same classes, played the same sports, and spent almost all of their free time together. They talked about girls together, started drinking beer together, and smoked their first cigarettes as a threesome. Their personal experiences, although not the best for young men wanting to achieve success in life, were running almost exactly on the same track.*
>
> *As they stood beside Daniel's car one afternoon, Ethan suddenly pulled out a small piece of folded*

paper. He unfolded it, revealing a white powder. "Guys, I got this from a buddy of mine," he said. "It's some really good cocaine, and we can try it together. Let's go somewhere a little more private. It's no big deal...we'll just see what it's like... just give it a try. There's a first time for everything, right?"

Jacob wasn't sure what he should do. He'd done so much with Daniel and Ethan over the years. This was just another experience they could share together; as Ethan said, 'it's no big deal.' But, after a few moments of thinking about it, Jacob decided he needed to know more about the effects of cocaine before he made this decision. From what he'd heard, this seemed to be a much bigger deal than just smoking a cigarette. He thought for a few seconds and said: "I really need to get home. I'll see you guys tomorrow."

When Jacob got home, he performed several searches on the Internet. Over the next few hours, he read dozens of articles and statistical reports about cocaine. He discovered that more than 60 percent of those who tried cocaine became addicted, and almost half of those required professional assistance to get off of the drug. He found that more than 80 percent of college freshman who considered themselves "casual users" of cocaine never graduated from college. And, he found that marriages in which one or both partners used cocaine had a divorce rate twice the national average. In a short

> *period of time, he gained clarity about the effects of this increasingly popular drug.*
>
> *In less than two hours, Jacob had gathered information, increased his knowledge, and developed an understanding about the effects of cocaine, allowing him to make an informed choice. "It's a good thing that I took the time to come and look this up," he thought as he turned off his computer knowing exactly what he was <u>not</u> going to do.*

Hopefully, you can now see how to move from gathering information to having knowledge. But what constitutes crossing the bridge to achieving understanding as far as making choices is concerned? You can gather information from lots of places… newspapers, TV, friends, family members, the Internet, books, and magazines. You selectively store this information, making yourself knowledgeable in a given area. This knowledge becomes understanding only when you have enough information to see how a choice might affect the direction or outcome of your life. Many times, we have a certain level of knowledge about something, but not enough to create an understanding of how it might affect our lives.

For example, when Jacob was standing in the parking lot talking to his friends, he obviously had some knowledge of the effects of cocaine; after all, he was a 16-year-old. But, at that moment, his knowledge wasn't sufficient to help him understand the actual repercussions of trying cocaine. It was only after spending two hours working his way through the information he found on the Internet that his knowledge increased to a level that allowed him to understand the potential outcome of the choice he had been asked to make.

If we want to continue to manage our lives effectively, we must be willing to encounter an endless cycle of gathering information, developing knowledge and achieving understanding. For example, the surgeon who has performed hundreds of operations and understands what must be done to save a patient's life will continue to gather information, increase her knowledge and develop an even greater understanding of how to treat her patients. Likewise, the mother and father who successfully raised their 10-year old son to be a decent young man will likely have to gather more information, develop additional knowledge, and further cultivate their understandings in order to manage the process until the young man becomes 21.

> *"Men are admitted to heaven not because they have curbed or governed their passions, but because they have cultivated their understandings."*
>
> WILLIAM BLAKE
> English Poet and Painter

Goals: The Other Half of Understanding

If we don't have goals and objectives for our lives, it will be very difficult for us to achieve understanding. We have to establish what kind of person we want to be, what we want to accomplish with our lives, and which values we will respect while accomplishing these goals before we can fully develop understanding and have it guide our choices.

Granted, we may not be able to be precise with our goals and objectives at this very moment. As a result, understanding is not always totally clear but often develops in stages if we work toward it. The high school student may not know where or how she'll go to college, but she can fully understand the importance of studying hard and making good grades as she starts to envision "a successful life." When she enters college, she may not know exactly what her career choice will be, but she can fully understand the importance of getting that degree. When she accepts her first job, she may not know if she wants to devote her entire life to this career, but she can fully understand the importance of performing well in order to be eligible for future promotions. As she moves through each stage of her life, she is able to achieve a level of understanding at each point that allows her to make the choices that position her life for even better things in the future.

It's important to remember that developing understanding is a specific choice that only you can make. You can make choices with little understanding of the potential outcomes, relying on luck or the influence of your friends to fashion the outcome for you. Or, you can spend the time and effort to gather the information you need, improve your knowledge, and achieve a reasonable level of understanding about how a pending action will impact in your life. The development of understanding requires a special effort. Those who are willing to make that effort will enjoy the benefits of making better and more rewarding choices as they live their lives.

> "Life is like music, it must be composed by ear, feeling and instinct, not by rule. Nevertheless, one had better know the rules for they guide us in doubtful situations."
>
> SAMUEL BUTLER
> The Way of All Flesh

Recognizing Our Need for Understanding

Most people would readily agree that stopping and thinking, obtaining needed information, and developing understanding are good things, especially in preparation for making an important choice. But recognizing the merit of these activities isn't enough. You must also be able to recognize the moment of need when you actually lack the understanding you need relative to a choice that you're about to make. You're busy. You're involved in many things every day. Nevertheless, you must be careful and not rush past the moment when a better understanding is needed to guide you and help you make the right choice.

> *Christopher was 14 years old and, although his mom loved him very much, she never had the money to buy him clothes like many of the other kids wore. He had wanted a pair of the most popular basketball shoes for more than a year now and had asked his mother at least a dozen times if she would get him a pair. She always said the same thing: "I'd love to buy a pair of those shoes for you, but I just can't afford the $120. Anyway, it's not shoes, but doing the right thing, that makes you a man, Christopher."*
>
> *Christopher had been selected as the manager of the school basketball team. He enjoyed the game and loved to be around the coaches and players. And, of course, he loved being near all of those colorful basketball shoes...especially the brand he liked so much. Every time he saw one of the guys*

wearing those shoes, he wanted a pair for himself even more. He wasn't sure how, but one of these days he was going to have them.

One afternoon while the team and coaches were on the court in the middle of a scrimmage, Christopher was in the locker room cleaning up when the shoe sales representative walked in with an armload of boxes. Christopher couldn't believe his eyes – they were his favorite in various sizes. And he really couldn't believe it when the rep said, "Hey, I'm in a big hurry. I wanted to drop off these shoes for some of the guys to try. How about taking these, and I'll check back with Coach Alexander in a week or two."

"Glad to," Christopher replied as he took the shoe boxes from the rep, who quickly turned and hurried out of the locker room.

Christopher couldn't believe his luck. The manufacturer gave these shoes away and the rep never seemed to keep track of what he dropped off. No one would ever know how many shoes the rep brought today because they were all out on the practice floor. All he had to do was slip a pair in his bag. He was thinking about his girlfriend's reaction to seeing him in those shoes when he seemed to hear his mother's advice, "…it's not shoes, but doing the right thing, that makes you a man, Christopher."

As Christopher stopped and thought for just a moment, he couldn't help but recall what his mother taught him about doing what's right. "Christopher," she would say, "if you want to be a successful man someday you must do the right things while you are young. Sometimes you're going to think you can take a short-cut to success, but you can't. You can only get there by doing what is right every day." Christopher's goal was to be a college basketball coach, take a team to the Final Four, and win it. He certainly didn't want to jeopardize his goal for doing that. As he reflected on his mother's teachings, he understood what he should do.

Christopher chose not to take the basketball shoes that day. If he had, he would have been in serious trouble because the manufacturer had cracked down on unauthorized deliveries. Coach Alexander had already signed the papers for those eight pairs to be delivered. One missing pair would have pointed the finger directly at Christopher. Instead of yielding to his wants and desires, Christopher had stopped and thought about what his mother had said and about his desire to be a winning coach someday. By taking the time to think through things, he had developed an understanding of the implications of his potential actions. More importantly, he used that understanding to guide the choice that he made.

And so it is with us. When we are faced with the opportunity to "get a free pair of shoes," we must be able to recognize our need for understanding… to think and reason beyond the moment, relying on what we have learned from other sources and the goals we have established for our lives, to make the choice that is right for us.

The Folly of Not Understanding

In spite of being uninformed, many of us still exhibit great conviction about our position or point of view. Frequently, we act like we know when we really don't. There are many times when we forge right ahead and make some choice or explain "how it is" when, in reality, we have given little thought and no study of the point we are making. We often want the appearance of being knowledgeable, even though we are not.

There are millions of books, and certainly none of us has read them all. There's an abundance of information in this world, but no one understands all of it. And, there's lots of "street sense" being passed around, but certainly no one person knows all of it. In spite of the impossibility of knowing everything, many of us make our choices knowing very little. Many of us try to live a productive life without the benefit of true knowledge and a fundamental understanding of the implications of a choice we are about to make.

The folly is in making an important choice when we don't have the understanding to do so. The folly is not in saying, "I don't know whether I should do that," but in not taking the time to get the information you need to make an informed decision. The folly is not in admitting to ourselves and to others that, at the moment, we are not "qualified" to make a certain choice; the folly is in plowing ahead when you have a limited understanding of the consequences. It takes a certain level of maturity, regardless of your chronological age, to admit that you don't know what you should do; but acknowledging that reality is the first and most important step in achieving the understanding that you need.

I don't think it's proper to ever refer to someone as "being a fool." Possibly it is more acceptable to simply refer to him as "being foolish." However you elect to label it, making choices, especially important ones, without being knowledgeable and having an understanding of what you're doing is a foolish mistake. When it's your life you are dealing with and the consequences of a poor choice are potentially damaging, it will always be a wise investment of your time to collect the information you need to make an informed choice. Just ask yourself...do I understand what I'm doing? If the answer is "no," do what you have to do to develop your understanding before your choice is made.

> *"Nothing in all the world is more dangerous than sincere ignorance and conscientious stupidity."*
>
> THE REV. MARTIN LUTHER KING

CHAPTER 4

BEING HONEST

"There is no twilight zone of honesty – a thing is either right or it's wrong."

JOHN F. DODGE
Automobile Manufacturing Pioneer

You Are What You Say and Do

Honesty is the foundation of a good choice. Without honesty – complete honesty – we are subject to making choices that don't reflect our true feelings or, even worse, that lead us into unethical or unlawful conduct. There are two parts of honesty that are important. First, we must be honest with ourselves if we expect to "decode" the possibilities that our life represents. Second, we must be honest with others if we want to build and maintain close, lifelong relationships. Honesty is a choice. While you may not be as smart, as pretty, or as wealthy as you would like to be, you can be as honest as you choose to be.

Unfortunately, many people act in a dishonest way in spite of the opportunity to do otherwise. They somehow believe that they can gain something even when the method by which they obtained it was wrong. They fool themselves into thinking that their lives will be better as a result of having something as opposed to having the knowledge that they conducted themselves in an honest and ethical way.

- Shoplifting. According to the National Association for Shoplifting Prevention, there are 23 million shoplifters in the U.S. today who take more than $10 billion worth of goods from retailers each year.
- Occupational Fraud. Unethical acts committed by executives and employees cost U.S. corporations more than $400 billion annually as reported by the Association of Certified Fraud Examiners. Men commit nearly 75% of these offenses, and most abuses occur in organizations with less than 100 employees.
- Lying. You might remember the story about the young newspaper reporter who tossed away a great career opportunity because he lied about where he got his facts. While there are no reliable statistics to support how many of us do similar things in a smaller way, we have all experienced situations in which we knew someone was not being truthful with us.
- Cheating. More than 70 percent of college-bound students admit to having cheated on tests at some point in their academic career, according to studies conducted by the Center for Academic Integrity.
- Exaggerating. According to a report in USA Today, a survey of 7,000 resumes revealed that 48 percent of the applicants exaggerated their past compensation and 71 percent misstated the number of years in a previous job.

Every individual who has ever been involved in one of the dishonest acts referenced above had a choice. It was their choice – not their circumstances at the moment or any other reason they may have used to "justify" their actions – that determined their honesty. The same is true for you and me. Each day, as we live our lives, we have choices. It is the choices that we make, what we actually say and do, that determine whether we are honest or not.

> *"Stupid is as stupid does."*
> FORREST GUMP

Why Are People Dishonest?

There are several reasons why people make the bad choices we characterize as dishonest behavior. The biggest reason is the mistaken belief that there will be no consequences for their actions. "I don't think one hit of marijuana will hurt me." "If I copy this answer off of my friend's paper, the teacher will never know." "I'm out of town on business; my wife will never find out." These explanations are examples of how, with no one looking, we mentally justify certain choices to ourselves. However, if we offered one of these explanations to a friend, it's unlikely that he would agree with our logic.

Sometimes dishonesty is simply the result of following the crowd and letting others make our choices for us. Some people make the mistake of believing that if other people are doing something, then it is okay for them to do it, as well. For example, the teenage boy who decides to stay out past his curfew because none of his friends have to be home is using this misguided logic. The job applicant who inflates her salary history because she believes everyone does it is yet another example. Crowd behavior does not make your behavior right. It's your sins, not someone else's, that will "find you out."

> Haley is a junior in college and is having a difficult time paying her way through school. She works every day after classes, as well as most weekends. She barely gets by and frequently skips a meal due to a lack of money. Her family can't afford to buy her a car, and most of her clothes would be classified as anything but the latest in fashion. She often feels bad when she sees some of the more affluent students drive by on their way to their sorority and fraternity houses.
>
> One day, Haley was approached by a friend's older brother. He said that he understood that she could use some extra cash, and he could help her get it. All she had to do was deliver a few packages to some people around the campus each week, and he'd pay her three times what she was making. Intuitively, Haley suspected that the packages contained drugs, but the brother assured her: "No one will ever find out. Come on Haley, it'll be easy." It would be fantastic to have three times the money and her weekends free. At last, some extra money and time for dating, too, she thought. Clearly, this was a big temptation for Haley. What should she do?
>
> For one thing, Haley should remember that honesty is a perishable value and that she can throw away years of hard work with one stupid mistake. Secondly, she should remind herself that it's her

willingness to work hard, not this extra money, that will improve her life over the long term. And, third, whether anyone found out or not, this "first step" can only lead to greater risks and bigger problems ahead. Like most potentially unlawful situations, if Haley will only take the time to consider the repercussions of her decision, it should be easy for her to say: "I could use the money, but no thank you!"

People commit dishonest acts out of greed simply to gain some personal benefit. They are willing to compromise their ethics and risk their reputation in return for what they consider to be important at the moment. Interestingly, most of these poor choices stem from a lack of something, perceived or otherwise: the bank robber from a lack of money, the cheating student from a lack of willpower to study, the drug user from a lack of judgment. It is our inability to deal with the things that we believe are missing in our lives that positions us for dishonest behavior. Without the understanding that our lives are much better in the long run when honestly lived, the more immediate, ill-gained "reward" may be too enticing for some individuals to pass by.

> "Dishonesty is a forsaking of permanent for temporary advantage."
>
> CHRISTIAN BOVEE
> Thoughts, Feelings and Fantasies

Honesty Is a Character Test

Other than an occasional speeding ticket, most of us consider ourselves to be law-abiding citizens. It's important to note, however, that living within the rule of law isn't all there is to being an honest person. Our level or degree of honesty is also determined by how we deal with ourselves, and by our willingness to do the right thing even when it runs counter to our personal preferences. Being an honest person is not confined to such things as driving within the speed limit, but is constructed, to a great extent, by the decisions you make each day.

> *Bill is Vice President of Computer and Technology Services for his company. Under pressure to obtain a faster server to alleviate suddenly slow response times in the engineering department, he calls his long-time equipment vendor.*
> "*Sally, do you have a T-5400 in stock?*"
> "*Yes, Bill, but we only have one left.*" *the vendor rep replies.*
> "*How quick can you get it to me?*"
> "*We can overnight it, and you'll have it in the morning,*" *Sally responds.*
> "*How much?*"
> "*$25,000 including shipping costs.*" *Sally replies.*
> "*Is that your best price?*" *Bill wants to know.*
> "*Yes, Bill. That price reflects your volume discount.*"
> "*I'll take it. Go ahead and ship it. I'll sign the papers later.*"

As he watches the box containing the new T-5400 being rolled into the computer room the next morning, Bill answers a call on his cell phone.

"Bill, this is Tom Smith with National Computer here in Atlanta."

"Hi, Tom. I'm a bit busy at the moment. What's up?"

"Bill, are you still thinking about a new T-5400 for the engineering group?"

"Yes, in fact I'm getting ready to install one this afternoon."

"We just reduced them 20 percent. $20,000 for the one you need." Tom says.

"And," Tom continues, "we could deliver within the hour."

What should Bill do? He can save his company $5,000 by taking Tom's special deal. He could still make his 6:00pm installation deadline. He hadn't signed any papers, so there's no written contract governing the transaction. He does so much business with Sally's company that the last-second cancellation would make little difference to them. While these facts are accurate, there's one more fact that is even more important. Bill had given his word. He had said, "_I'll take it. Go ahead and ship it. I'll sign the papers later._"

Remember, the truth exists whether we choose to acknowledge it by our actions or not. In this case, the truth was that Bill had made and confirmed his deal with Sally. His word was, in effect, the "contract" until the paperwork could be signed.

> *There's no question about this one. Bill should not even hesitate. He should honor his commitment and move ahead with his original plans. And if his management wants to build a company that's respected by its customers, they should support Bill's decision 100 percent.*

Every time you think, say, or do something, you are, in effect, participating in a character test. You can conduct yourself according to the truth, or you can distort the facts so that things appear to be more in your favor. You can tell the story as it actually happened, or you can "explain things" to put yourself in a more favorable light. You can stand up and do what you know you should do, or you can give in to what may be a more popular thing to do. As we go about our lives, we have opportunities to make many seemingly insignificant choices. However, in making these we reveal whether we are an honest person…or not.

> *Stephen was a great salesman and was recently presented the Excellence Award by his company as its top performer. He was an attentive husband and went out of his way to spend extra time with his children on weekends. His elderly neighbor thought Stephen "hung the moon" because he'd come over to her house to fix things so many times. Without question, Stephen was one nice guy.*
>
> *Tonight Stephen sat in his home office, papers and receipts everywhere, trying to finish his taxes so he could make tomorrow's filing deadline. After many hours, the tax software program was*

indicating that he still owed $485. "No problem," he thought, "I can just bump up my donations to makeup the difference." And he did it.

Stephen may have been a nice guy, even characterized as "a great guy" by his friends, but he certainly wasn't an honest one.

It's important to understand that truth exists whether we choose to acknowledge it or not. The truth is not subject to your opinion or even to your explanation, no matter how effective your argument may be. In the example above, the truth was that Stephen owed an additional $485 in taxes. However, for some reason, probably because he thought he'd never get caught, he could not align his actions with that truth. Although he knew the truth, he made a choice inconsistent with that truth and, as a result, was a dishonest man.

Do Our Little White Lies Make Us Dishonest?

Robbing a bank clearly qualifies someone as being a dishonest person. But what about the little things you say that have small elements of untruth mixed in them? For example, Sue told her friends that she was going to redo her house, although she had no specific plans or the money to do so. Dan told his boss that he believed his customer would order next month, although he knew the customer had no intention of doing so. Jane told her friend that her son was "an honor student," although she knew he missed the honor roll by one point. If it really doesn't hurt anyone, aren't these little fibs okay?

Most of us have a desire to feel special. We want to do important things, have terrific children, live in nice houses, and be viewed by our friends and neighbors as successful. As a result, we have a tendency to exaggerate things at times to put ourselves in a more favorable light. While this practice may not lead to major problems, it is, in fact, dishonest. Any time you don't tell the truth, and nothing but the truth, you are exposing yourself to other difficulties. The problem created by the little white lie is that you have not only stretched the truth with others, you have also been dishonest with yourself. It's only by being honest with yourself that you create the individual that you are proud to be.

Another problem with the little white lies is that, with practice, we get better and better at telling them. Once we've begun, it gets harder and harder for us to distinguish between the little lie and the big one. In effect, the practice of telling "the little ones" conditions us for even greater difficulties in times ahead.

We're taking a step into fantasy land when we tell a white lie. We're avoiding the truth and as a result, hampering the opportunity to deal with reality. Sue would be much better served to have told her friends, "We don't have the money now, but, when we do, we're going to redo our house." Or Dan to his boss, "I don't think the customer will order next month, so I'm going to have to find some other way to make my number." Or Jane to her friend, "My son is doing well in school, but he missed the honor roll by one point." Call it what you will, but the more you deal in the absolute truth, the better your choices and your life will be.

David Casstevens of the Dallas Morning News tells a story about Frank Szymanski, a Notre Dame

center in the 1940's who had been called as a witness in a civil suit in South Bend, IN. The judge asked him, "Aren't you on the Notre Dame football team this year?"
"Yes, Your Honor," Szymanski replied.
"What position?"
"Center, Your Honor."
"How good a center are you?"
Syzmanski squirmed in his seat, but firmly replied, "Sir, I am the best center Notre Dame has ever had."
Coach Frank Leahy, who was in the courtroom, was very surprised. Syzmanski had always been modest and unassuming. So when the proceedings were over, he took Syzmanski aside and asked why he had made such a statement.
Szymanski blushed. "I hated to do it, Coach," he said. "But, after all, I was under oath."

DAVID CASSTEVENS
Chicken Soup for the Soul

Being Honest

Have you ever stopped what you were doing and seriously thought about whether you are an honest person or not? If you were questioned about this you would likely say, "Why of course, I'm an honest person." But, are you? Are you truthful with yourself about who you really are and what you want to accomplish with your life? Are you fair minded and forthright in your dealings with other people? Do the individuals you work, play, or go to school with consider you to be a person of integrity – someone they can really trust? Whether right or wrong, we all have a tendency to justify what we say and do. Therefore, it is beneficial, from time to time, to thoughtfully consider just how honest you are being – with yourself and with others.

Being Honest with Yourself

The starting point for all honest behavior is the way you interact with yourself. If we're not able to be honest with ourselves and act accordingly, we can waste a lot of time believing that – somehow, someway – we'll live a happy and successful life. If we continually fool ourselves about a problem we have or are creating, we may never have the opportunity to resolve it. If we aren't willing to acknowledge that our words and actions may be making others feel bad, we can miss the opportunity to develop friendships that, otherwise, we would have enjoyed. Lack of personal honesty, the inability to shoot straight with ourselves, can turn moments of opportunity into a lifetime of regret and unhappiness.

> *Carley was one of those people who could not – or would not – fully explain why she did something wrong. Although she had been influenced or motivated by something when she made her poor choices, her mom and dad frequently heard the explanation: "I don't know why I did that."*
>
> *The truth was that the explanation was distasteful and it put Carley in a bad light. She avoided admitting this to herself because she did not want to see herself as the type of person she really was. If she wasn't going to admit this to herself, she*

certainly wasn't going to admit it to her parents...or to others.

Today, Carley is grown and will soon be 40 years old. She had been married once, but her husband moved on many years ago and she never heard from him again. When her friend asked her about him one day, Carley replied, "I really don't know why Sam left...just tired of being married, I guess."

The ability to perform accurate self-assessments, even when you don't like what you see, can be the single most important ingredient in developing a meaning and worthwhile life. No one is perfect and most of us are quick to acknowledge this fact. However, moving beyond this general statement, we must be willing to honestly assess our weaknesses and our strengths. It is through such a process that we identify areas that we need to work on or bad habits that we need to change. It is by listening with "an honest ear" to our interests and our motivations that we find the life that we were intended to live. It is through honest evaluation that we determine if we are living a selfish life, focused primarily on ourselves, or a life oriented toward the happiness and well-being of others.

> "I count him braver who overcomes his desires than him who conquers his enemies.
> The hardest victory is the victory over self."
>
> ARISTOTLE

Being Honest with Others

Most of us are very familiar with the Golden Rule – "do unto others as you would have others do unto you" – but how many of us have consistently practiced it? How many of us actually treat others like we want to be treated in return? How many of us go out of our way to do or say something that will make someone else's life more enjoyable? You may believe in honest actions toward others, but if you don't practice them, you'll never experience the positive feelings that such actions produce.

Each of us has a circle of people with whom we interact. This circle includes family relationships with children, parents, grandparents, siblings, and others. It includes friends who range from people we've known forever to the new neighbors who just moved in down the street. Associates with whom we work or go to school would be in this circle as well. Suffice it to say that the degree of friendship with members of our circle varies from exceptionally strong to almost nonexistent. We are close to some, not so close to others. As a result, it is difficult to offer a suggestion that would improve "the connection" you have with every member of this group.

The one exception is the practice of honesty. If a wife can honestly tell her husband why she feels a certain way, most men are caring and concerned enough to adjust their behavior to improve the situation. However, without an honest exchange, the problem will likely continue to exist. If a parent can honestly explain to a child why he isn't allowed to do something, the child will, over time, develop an understanding about why he shouldn't be doing this. However, without this honest explanation, the child may never understand why he's being corrected. If a friend can honestly explain to another the reasons behind his concern for his friend's behavior, they have the opportunity to exchange information that might improve both of their understandings. When we make the choice to be honest with everyone around us, we maximize our opportunities to develop close and meaningful relationships.

> "An honest man is the noblest work of God."
>
> ALEXANDER POPE
> An Essay on Man

Honesty Is a Perishable Condition

It's important to note that honesty is a perishable condition. For example, a person can live many years in an honest way. Then one day he makes the wrong choice and does something that is dishonest. That one choice can change everything. It doesn't seem fair, but in reality, we can taint a lifetime of honesty with one dishonest act. Dishonesty remains the one thing that can end a friendship or business opportunity on a moment's notice. When people detect dishonesty in an individual, their normal reaction is: "If I can't trust you on this, how can I trust you on anything?" This is a valid concern. And, once trust is lost, it is very difficult to re-establish it in any type of relationship.

> *Ralph had performed well in his company for over 10 years and was now being considered, along with several others, for a newly created position in the*

sales department. He really wanted this promotion and, therefore, was looking for every opportunity to present himself in a good light. Unfortunately, Ralph made a poor choice one day and it changed everything.

One of Ralph's business associates was Willie Benson, and they had worked together on several sales projects over the past few years. Willie, who was very creative and always seemed to have a good idea, had applied for the new position as well, but Ralph was not aware that he had done so. One afternoon, as they were talking, Willie said, "I think what the company needs is a special sales history report that would help our sales force project each customer's needs for the coming year."

After listening to more of the details, Ralph responded, "That's a great idea, Willie. It would certainly make our sales forecasts more accurate... and help our customers plan better, too"

A few days later when Ralph was in the interview for the new position, he explained to the VP of Sales, "The first thing I would do if I get this new job is to create a new sales history report that would help our sales force develop more accurate forecasts."

"That's very interesting, Ralph," the VP replied as he thought how similar Ralph's idea was to the one Willie had sent to him in a memo a few days before.

Ralph had presented Willie's idea as though it were his own. Although he thought it would

> increase his chances of getting the new job, it created some real doubts in the mind of the VP who had quickly recognized what was happening.
>
> Willie's promotion was announced the next day. When the VP mentioned to him that "Ralph had the same suggestion that you did about the sales history report," Willie knew that Ralph had tried to steal his idea. As a result the friendship came to a screeching halt, and Willie never trusted Ralph again.

What can you do if you've broken trust with someone and now feel bad about what you've done? Well, honesty works both ways. If you honestly regret what you said or what you did, you can use this feeling as a springboard for making something positive out of the situation. Again, the choice is yours to make. Should you decide to try to repair the relationship, the only "tool" that will allow you to accomplish this is honesty itself. You must be honest in your regret, honest in your apology, honest in your explanation, and honest in all of your future dealings with this individual. It may take some time for the other person to believe you again, but total honesty, and nothing else, will do the trick.

> *"A fair reputation is a plant delicate in its nature, and by no means rapid in its growth. It will not shoot up in a night, but it may perish in a single moment."*
>
> JEREMY TAYLOR
> Clergyman in the Church of England

What Will Honesty Do for You?

The payback for honesty is tremendous. Every time you are honest in your comments and conversations with others, you reveal "the goodness" that you are working to cultivate in your life. Every time you take "the high road" and do the responsible thing, you show yourself and others that you have character and a certain amount of inner strength. Every time you stand up for what you know is right and work to ensure the happiness and well-being of others, you prove that your life has value to more than just yourself. Over time, your honest words and deeds not only endear you to others but form the foundation upon which you can build a life of value and importance.

Honesty Makes You Feel Better

No matter what our justification for being dishonest, we never feel right when we fail to tell the truth or when we do something we know is not honest. Honesty eliminates the need for you to remember who you told what, or to worry that someone may "find you out." Honesty is, in effect, a way of ensuring that you'll be able to look back and feel good about what you did even when things didn't work out the way you hoped they would. When based on dishonest words or actions, winning the argument is never worth the price.

Honesty Builds Trust

In business, marriage, and friendships, there are many qualities that endear one person to another, including humor, intelligence, thoughtfulness, and a positive attitude. However, no quality is more fundamental in building trust and close relationships than honesty. If you're honest in your business dealings, you'll have more customers. If you're honest in your marriage, you'll have a closer bond with your spouse. If you're honest in your friendships, you'll have more friends. Interestingly, it's not so much the information involved, but the actual act of honesty that builds trust between people. People don't expect you to be perfect or to have all of the answers, but they will trust you if you tell them the truth.

Honesty Helps You Resolve Problems

You've surely known people who just can't seem to be clear about things, especially when it involves unpleasant or questionable circumstances. Such people want to talk around the problem and do not face it directly. Refusing to accurately clarify situations in our lives or in the lives of others is a form of dishonesty which simply postpones the opportunity to resolve the issue. Honesty about a situation allows it to be addressed sooner rather than later, and be rectified sooner, as well.

Honesty Helps You Find Your Place in this World

One of the most important benefits of being honest with yourself is that it gives you the ability to assess the interests and motivations that are at work in your life. I believe that there is an intended life in each and every one of us – that we are here for a purpose and that, to some degree, that purpose has been pre-defined. The signals concerning this intended life might be reflected in our basic interests and abilities, the way we feel about certain people or activities, the type of work we believe we want to do, or an important project or cause in which we want to become involved. We must be able to recognize and interpret these signals successfully if we are going to find the intended direction for our lives. It is only by being completely honest with ourselves that we are able to do so.

How does honesty help you do this? As I stated earlier the truth exists whether we acknowledge it or not. The truth is you have special abilities, unique ways of doing things, and certain motivations about what you want to accomplish with your life. The challenge for you is how to engage these personal ingredients and give them power within your life. You will never accomplish this if you allow other people to make choices for you or unduly influence the type of person you turn out to be. It is through the daily practice of being honest about your "hopes and dreams" that you free yourself from such influences and allow your personal qualities to blossom into the person you were intended to be.

> *"The truth is more important than the facts."*
> FRANK LLOYD WRIGHT

Without honesty our other values are of little consequence. For example, the next chapter deals with the quality of "being yourself." However, how could any of us ever be ourselves without the ability to be totally honest? When it comes to your career, how will you ever find that special interest deep inside of you if you cannot be totally honest in your self assessments? When it comes to your marriage or other special friendships in your life, how can you ever create a close relationship if you are not honest in your dealings? Honesty should be an omnipresent value…you need to take it with you wherever you go.

CHAPTER 5

BECOMING WHO YOU ARE

*"Almost every man wastes part of his life
in attempts to display qualities which he does not possess,
or to gain applause which he cannot keep."*

SAMUEL JOHNSON
The Rambler

The Opportunity...of a Lifetime

We live in a world of influences – some are good, and some are bad. If we aren't careful, these influences can modify our thinking, and in some instances, change us into someone we were never intended to be. The choice to become who you are frees you from the stress of trying to become the person "the world" expects you to be. When you make the choice to become who you are, you have decided that you will no longer be controlled by the expectations of others or by the task of making yourself acceptable to everyone around you. You've decided that you are now the one in charge and the one who calls the shots about your life. With this choice, you transfer the responsibility for your life's outcome from the people and circumstances around you to yourself. It is now your life and you have full responsibility for its outcome.

Your most important task is to develop the life you've been given. You have this fantastic opportunity to live a life...what are you going to do with it? How will you utilize the skills and interests that you have? How will you use your life to improve the lives of others? What do you want to achieve during your lifetime? What kind of person do you ultimately want to be? These are questions that each of us must answer one way or another, and you have two basic choices in this regard. You can give careful thought to the person you want to be and work to utilize your individuality in the life that you live. Or, you can give little thought to your personal qualities, simply follow the crowd, and allow the world to shape you however it would like.

As you think about your possibilities, it is important to note that your life comes to you pre-equipped in certain ways. You have special interests, motivations, and feelings that are pre-existing and, if developed properly, will further define the person you become. Many of these qualities are simply the "seeds" or beginnings of an interest or ability. It is up to you to identify the ones you possess and to develop them within your life. If you do a good job at this, you, in effect, become who you are and not the person who others think you should be.

If asked, most of us would say that we want to have a feeling of contentment in our lives and to experience joy from living. Granted, such feelings are important, but we often mistake the route we should take to achieve them. We think that doing fun things, living without pressures or problems, and having all of the money we need are the keys to this result. However, genuine contentment does not come from these things. It comes from utilizing your personal qualities to make your life count for other people. The route to happiness is not simply to be a good and honest person but, in addition, to become who you are by identifying and developing the personal qualities that you possess.

Living in the Middle

Most of us live our lives somewhere between trying to be the person we believe the outside world wants us to be and our desire to be individuals doing things that are personally important to us. We live somewhere between the influence of others and the independence of our own minds. Our desire to be accepted and have the approval of others, to some degree, determines how we conduct our lives. Yet, in spite of these influences, most of us want to develop our individuality and to realize the unique potential that belongs to each of us.

From birth, your associations with other people help you to learn, to grow, and to develop your understanding of the world around you. Many of these relationships – especially those with family members and close friends – provide a fundamental direction to your life. Because you grow up with these influences, it's easy to become conditioned to believing that the evaluations of other people are more important than your own. However, as you grow, you must learn to filter out the influences that aren't good for you and develop the ability to think and choose for yourself. If you don't, you fall prey to a sort of "psychological dictatorship" which can limit your ability to develop into the person you really can be.

For the most part, we all learn to live with this struggle between external and internal direction. As a result, we move back and forth on this imaginary line between influence and independence. Our position varies depending upon the person with whom we're dealing, our circumstances at that time, and our sense of personal direction as an individual. For example, a dominant friend may try to control our thinking even though we have interests that are very different from hers. However, if we're able to recognize such influence, we can better determine what choices we need to make in order to go out and do something personally important with our lives.

> *"Each of us, in effect, strikes a series of deals or compromises between the wants and longings of the inner self and our outer environment that offers certain possibilities and sets certain limitations."*
>
> MAGGIE SCARF
> Secrets, Lies, Betrayals: The Body/Mind Connection

So, Where Do You Live?

An important task in being yourself is to determine where you are on the scale between influence and independence. Are you living under the influence of others, trying to make them happy with your performance, or are you making your own path in your journey through this world? Granted, you want beneficial guidance and suggestions from others, but you also want to develop your life to its fullest potential. You want to be open to new ideas, but you don't want to be influenced to the extent that you lose your individuality. That's why it's important to understand that you live somewhere on this scale between influence and independence. The challenge is to find balance in your life, benefiting from others while still making choices that reflect who you are.

Tyler Wilson was a good old country boy. He was a smart young man, but, nevertheless, the word "redneck" frequently popped into peoples' minds when they heard him speak. He had been raised on a small farm in southern Alabama, lettered in four sports in high school, and recently graduated with honors from Georgia Tech. He had accepted a job offer from Coleman Development Corporation, one of Chicago's oldest and most prestigious commercial architectural firms, with more than 2,000 employees.

He was now sitting in his newly-rented Chicago apartment talking to Jim Ebbits, who joined Coleman just over a year ago after his graduation from New York University. He'd been appointed Tyler's corporate orientation guide. Jim, who met Tyler about an hour earlier, was having a hard time believing what he was seeing and hearing.

"I'm really excited about starting my new job at Coleman tomorrow." *Tyler said slowly, his southern drawl causing Jim's eyebrows to rise slightly.*

"I'm sure you are," *Jim responded.* "But you aren't planning to go dressed in blue jeans and that old sport coat, are you? You know most of the men at Coleman wear suits and ties."

"That's what I heard," *Tyler responded.* "But, where I come from, this is considered being dressed up. And besides, John Coleman said in my interview that he would take me to the new Hyatt construction site my first day on the job. This is just the outfit for that!"

Jim couldn't believe that someone could be so naïve as to think that John Coleman would remember his offer to take Tyler to an important job site, much less actually do it.

"Tyler, you ought to take some voice and speech lessons," Jim said. "Most of the Coleman employees won't think you're very bright when they hear the way you talk. I probably shouldn't tell you that, but my responsibility as your orientation guide is to tell you everything you need to know to become successful at Coleman," Jim stated with an air of authority in his voice as he stood to leave the apartment. "Think about it. I'll see you bright and early tomorrow morning."

Tyler sat there, feeling like a misfit before he even put his foot in the door at Coleman. Should he go to the store and buy a suit so he would "look the part" tomorrow? Should he buy some new shoes to replace the work boots he loved wearing to every construction site he'd been on the past year? Should he be very careful of what he said tomorrow to help prevent giving other employees the wrong impression about him? Should he start making changes to himself so he could be successful like the others? What should he do? He certainly didn't want to get off to a bad start.

As things worked out, Tyler Wilson walked in the front door at Coleman Development the next morning wearing his standard "jeans and jacket," his favorite work boots, and carrying the rather worn architectural briefcase that served him well for four *years at Georgia Tech. After John Coleman gave the customary "Welcome to Coleman Development" pep talk to the new-hire group that morning, he approached Tyler, shook his hand aggressively, and said, "Tyler, I see you remembered my offer to take you to the Hyatt construction site today. Be up in my office at 11:00, I'll get my boots on, and we'll head out." They spent more than two hours touring the site that day, and Tyler asked so many insightful questions that John Coleman never once thought anything about the clothes he had on. He did think, as they got back into the SUV, "This boy is going to build a lot of great buildings during his career at Coleman."*

In his advice to Tyler, Jim Ebbits had made the age-old mistake of placing a higher value on appearance than on skills and abilities...more importance on looks than on knowledge and intelligence. Fortunately, Tyler was smart, and, therefore, not easily misled. As he sat and thought about what to do that afternoon after Jim left, he'd decided that his clothes served him well in college, that Coleman hired him even though he dressed casually in his interviews, and that...well, he just felt better when he dressed like that. He had rationalized that he was joining Coleman to build special buildings, not to become a fashion plate. So, he went to work that first day dressed as he always had.

It was now eight years later. Jim Ebbits was no longer with the company. Tyler was sitting in the front row at the company's monthly management meeting, reflecting on "the clothing choice" he made many years ago, when he heard John Coleman say to the management group: "It's my distinct pleasure to announce the youngest-ever vice president of Coleman Development, Mr. Tyler Wilson." As Tyler gave his brief thank you, his slow drawl still intact, no one was thinking "country boy" anymore. All his fellow managers could think about was what a gifted architect this young man turned out to be.

Life is never any fun if you aren't willing to take some risks, make some choices for yourself, and accept the responsibility for the way things turn out. You'll never be yourself if you leave all of the important decisions to someone else.

Understanding Your Basic Needs

Anyone who's studied psychology has heard about Maslow's Hierarchy of Needs. Abraham Maslow was a humanistic psychologist, a field of study that focuses upon human potential. In his theory, Dr. Maslow noted that people are motivated by unsatisfied needs and that our lower-level needs must be met before we can attend to a higher-level need. Maslow defined five basic levels of need, labeling them as <u>*physiological*</u> needs, <u>*safety*</u> needs, <u>*love/belonging*</u> needs, <u>*esteem/recognition*</u> needs, and <u>*self-actualization*</u> needs.

Level One: Physiological Needs
(air, water, nourishment and sleep)

These are our strongest needs and always come first in a person's search for satisfaction. For most of us, these first-level physiological needs are adequately satisfied. In cases where they are not, it's nearly impossible for someone to think beyond this point.

Level Two: Safety Needs
(living in a safe place, medical support, job security and financial resources)

When our physiological needs have been met, we're able to focus on the next level of need – safety – which has to do with creating stability, predictability and consistency in a seemingly chaotic world. Again, most of us have adequate housing, don't live in fear and have a reasonable sense of security in our lives.

Level Three: Love/Belonging Needs
(friends, belonging, giving and receiving love)

When our physiological and safety needs are met, we can focus on the third-level of need identified by Maslow – the need for love and belonging. Humans need to be connected to other people, to be loved and accepted. This need provides the impetus for us to join clubs, religious groups, work groups and even gangs.

Level Four: Esteem/Recognition Needs
(self-respect, achievement, attention, recognition and reputation)

When the first three levels of need are satisfied, the needs for esteem become dominant. This level of need refers to both the sense of accomplishment we derive from mastering a task, as well as obtaining recognition, praise, or attention from others. When these needs are met, the person feels self-confident and valuable as a person in the world.

Level Five: Self-Actualization Needs
(truth, justice, wisdom and meaning)

Finally, self-actualization, the highest level of need, is "the desire to become more and more what one is, to become everything that one is capable of becoming." Maslow described self-actualization as a person's need to be and do that which the person was "born to do." As he stated, "a musician must make music, an artist must paint and a poet must write."

Few people actually make it to the highest level of trying to satisfy their self-actualization needs. Too many of us, it seems, get stuck in a never-ending search to satisfy our esteem/recognition needs. Unlike the need for air, we don't have a way of knowing when we've adequately satisfied our need for recognition. In looking for recognition and the power that accompanies it, we want to acquire the expensive cars, the designer clothes, or the new home to show others what we can afford, thus "earning" their admiration and respect.

But the problem is that there will always be a more expensive car, more fashionable clothes, and a bigger house. No one is likely to tell us when enough is enough. Therefore, you must recognize for yourself when you've adequately satisfied your need for attention from others, and that additional attention isn't necessary. If you can break from the materialistic treadmill and seriously reflect on your life's development, you may realize that you adequately met your needs for belonging and esteem some time ago, and that your attempts to better satisfy these needs are keeping you from attending to your highest-level need, to maximize your own potential as a human being.

I invite you to take the time to assess where you currently fit into Maslow's Hierarchy of Needs. If Maslow was right in his belief that we must satisfy one level of need before we become capable of moving on to the next, it is likely that many of us, without a special effort to do otherwise, will live our entire life somewhere in the middle of these needs, never getting to the all-important level of self-actualization.

Distractions from Becoming "Who You Are"

Although most of us consider ourselves to be in control of our lives, there are, in fact, many things that influence how we live as well as many of the choices we make. It is important, as we work to become more independent in our thinking, to recognize what some of these stronger influences can be.

The Expectations of Others

Our parents expect us to be successful: to graduate from school, have a family, and live happily ever after. Our friends expect us to join in the fun and be a socially acceptable member of the group. Our spouse expects us to work hard and to perform well within the relationship. Our employers expect us to "go the extra mile" and do our jobs in an exceptional manner. Everywhere we turn, in one form or another, we encounter expectations that influence our behavior, including the way we think, the way we act, and the way we live. Pfc. Lynndie England, who was charged along with several other soldiers for sexual abuses of Iraqi prisoners at Abu Ghraib Prison, offered this explanation at her court martial: "I chose to do what my friends wanted me to do."

An important aspect of being who you are is to understand that you've been inundated with these expectations from other people from the day you were born. While the sources of these expectations may change over time, you'll continue to encounter them throughout your life. Employers, families, friends, and even strangers will continue to expect certain things of you. The key is to recognize that these influences are all around you, to learn to think independently, and to select those influences that you want to affect the way you live your life.

> *"There is often as much independence in not being led,*
> *as in not being driven."*
>
> TYRON EDWARDS
> Author

Our Need to Be Accepted

Because of our desire to "be okay" in the eyes of other people, we tend to conduct ourselves in ways we deem acceptable to others. We have this inner yearning to be accepted by various groups – by our friends, fellow employees, and our family members. As a result, consciously or otherwise, we become willing to modify our conduct in order to win the acceptance of others.

Some of us decide where to go and what to do based on what our friends are doing. Some of us make our clothing selections not solely on what we like, but in consideration of what others will think about our appearance. Some of us drop names of successful or noteworthy friends not really to inform but because it makes us seem more important in the eyes of others. While these actions aren't dreadfully wrong, they hinder the development of becoming the person we really are.

When we compromise our conduct to impress others, it's a signal that we don't understand or don't value the opportunity that our lives represent. We can become anything we want to be. However, if you're more concerned about what other people think of you than becoming the individual you were intended to be, you hinder your ability to develop in your own special way. With such a view, you'll tend to spend your time doing things that are acceptable to others instead of doing things that allow you to grow, to learn, and to develop your own individuality and capabilities.

> *Patricia Jenkins, "Patty Girl" as her friends called her, was 18 years old and would be graduating from high school in a few months. She was sitting in front of her mirror getting ready to apply her lipstick, a new gloss that many of her friends were already using. It was a reddish-orange color with shiny sparkles that flashed when the sun hit them. She knew she had to try it when she saw a couple of her favorite young movie stars on TV sporting the latest thing in cosmetics...Flash Lips.*
> *As she looked down at her package of lipstick, for some reason she started thinking about all of*

the fads she'd experienced during her high school years. There was the bright hair phase during her freshman year when her friends dyed their hair in purple and orange stripes. She was featured on a local TV newscast with her rendition of that one. The hair was followed by stack-pierced ears...one of her friend's wore seven earrings in each ear, and she herself had three on one side and two on the other. Next came the tattoos. She wasn't so sure about the barbed-wire look around necks and arms, but she had gone for a small rose on her left rear cheek.

As she reflected on the past years, a thought suddenly popped into her mind. These fads had seemed so important at the time, but now, out of nowhere came the realization that all of this was sort of stupid. Her participation in these fads had made her feel special at the time, but, for some reason, Patty's mind was now creating a different perspective. She recalled a girl shouting to a friend in the hallway the day before, "I just got my college acceptance letter!" It did not register with her at the time but now Patty thought, "I've been focused on being one of the gang, on being accepted, while other kids focused on grades and getting into college." In an instant, she had a strange feeling that she was about to miss the boat.

Patty looked in the mirror again and then down at the lipstick in her hand. She looked at her colorfully dyed hair. She looked at her exposed midriff. She thought about her tattoo. Where was she going with all of these things? All of a sudden, she thought of the answer...nowhere!

As things turned out, Patty never put on the new lipstick that day. Instead, she experienced a moment of truth, and it changed her life. She suddenly realized that she was conducting her life with the wrong set of priorities and, right then and there, she made the choice to change them.

Following through with her decision proved to be a difficult task. Her close friends saw the changes... no makeup, conservative clothes, and more interest in college... and stopped including her in their weekend parties. The "regular kids" thought she was acting strange and whispered about her as she walked down the hall. Even Patty, as she started to explore the requirements for going to college, got discouraged and had second thoughts on several occasions. But, she hung in there, determined to "get to the other side."

Now 15 years later, Patty is married to a wonderful man, Gabe. They met while attending Florida State, graduated together and now have two very active daughters, Ashley 11 and Amy 9. Gabe was their small town's only vet, and Patty occasionally filled in as a substitute teacher at the high school. They had lots of friends and a great family life.

Now and then Patty still wondered, "Where would I be today if I had not come to my senses in front of that mirror years ago?" She didn't really want to know the answer to that question. As she sat in her kitchen and experienced one of those reflective moments, Ashley walked in and said, "Mom, all of my friends are getting their navels pierced. It's really cool, and the rings look really neat. Can I have mine done, too?"

Deja vu, Patty thought. "Ashley, I know this is very important to you," Patty replied. "However, if you always copy what other people do, you'll have difficulty identifying what is important to you as an individual. It's much better to be yourself and to make your decisions independent of those around you."

"Oh, Mom, you don't know what it's like!" Ashley retorted.

"Ashley, I understand more than you think," Patty said. "Let me tell you about this girl at my school when I was growing up. Her nickname was Patty Girl and she..." Patty took Ashley through the whole bit...the hair, the clothes, and even the lipstick. More importantly, she explained the feeling she experienced in front of the mirror that day, why she decided to change what she was doing and how she lost several of her friends in the process. She then stood, pulled down the top of her shorts and showed Ashley the rose tattoo, something Ashley had never seen before. She went on to explain the difficulties she encountered getting into college and how thankful she was to have met Gabe and now have such a wonderful family. "But, honey, concerning that navel ring, that's a choice you'll have to make for yourself."

> *Ashley now realized that this was a bigger deal than she thought. She was not exactly sure what she was going to do. But, as she walked slowly out of the kitchen, she sensed that her mother was teaching her something about life that was very important.*

<u>Our Desire for Greatness</u>

We all want to be great, to feel special, but we often misunderstand greatness. When we talk or think about greatness, we often confuse <u>what we do</u> with <u>who we are</u>. For example, a man may be a great politician, but is he really a great person? A woman may be a great actress, but is she really great in the way she treats other people? While each of these may be great at what they do or how they look, whether they are also great people requires digging further into their personal lives and their actions toward others. The same is true for you. You may see yourself as a great lawyer or a great homemaker, but that achievement alone doesn't determine whether you're a great person.

When we say "John is a great guy!" what do we mean by this? Typically, such an exclamation is recognition of a good feeling we have about another person. For example, John may have done something worthwhile in his community, gone out of his way to help someone in need, or just been especially nice to the people around him. Whatever he said or did, a byproduct of his actions or concerns is this special feeling we now have about him. John didn't decide he was a great guy... we made that decision about him.

If we achieve greatness, as I am defining it here, it will be because <u>someone else</u> bestows this qualification on us. No one achieves such status on his own, or by saying, "I want to be great in the eyes of others." Greatness is not available to be a part of the opinion we have of ourselves. It is only through the feelings of someone else that our potential greatness materializes. Greatness is not a gift we can give ourselves – it is a gift that can only be given to us by someone else.

It is interesting to note how the public reacted to President Ronald Reagan's death on June 7, 2004. More than 250,000 people stood in line to pay their respects at the Reagan Library, some for as many as eight hours, to walk by his closed coffin for just a few seconds. More than 500,000 did the same at the Capital Rotunda in Washington, D.C., and millions more visited funeral homes around the country to sign books of condolence. His funeral was attended by dignitaries from throughout the world as well as many of his former political foes.

Why did people react to Reagan this way? Was it because he was a great president? Or, was it because he was a great man? I contend that it was the latter. Reagan was not the most popular president. The two presidents who followed Reagan, George H.W. Bush and Bill Clinton, each had higher average approval ratings than Reagan, as did three earlier presidents -- Lyndon Johnson, John F. Kennedy, and Dwight Eisenhower. Nevertheless, Reagan has appeared in the top 10 in Gallup's annual Most Admired Man poll more than 30 times, more often than any other person except evangelist Billy Graham.

Not only did Ronald Reagan treat everyone with the greatest of respect, Nancy Reagan commented on several occasions that he never talked about himself or what he had accomplished. He was known by his staff for being respectful of all people – even his adversaries. He was an openly religious man who explained that everything got easier when he decided to "look up" for guidance and not back at those who were nipping at his heels. He maintained a keen sense of humor; after being shot, he famously commented, "I guess I forgot to duck." Consistent with his natural concern for others, he responded to thousands of letters with personal notes, some rather lengthy, penned in his own hand. Reagan believed in people, and, as a result, they believed in him, too. The undertone of his entire life is reflected in the inscription on his burial tomb in California:

> "I know in my heart that man is good.
> That what is right will always eventually triumph.
> And there's purpose and worth
> in each and every life."
>
> RONALD REAGAN

You can't just decide to go out and become a great person in the minds of other people. Their opinion of you, and hopefully the respect they have for you, is, in effect, a gift they give based on how they feel about the way you conduct your life. It isn't something you can earn as it comes voluntarily from the giver, frequently without that person fully realizing when or how that determination was made. It isn't your position, your appearance, or even your intelligence that creates this respect. It has almost nothing to do with these things, and everything to do with the type of person you choose to be.

> *Zachary Wilburn had been a custodian at The First Presbyterian Church for more than 47 years. He dropped out of high school in the ninth grade and still had some difficulty reading. In spite of his routine job, Zach was a very positive fellow. He was always happy, always smiling, and always had a good word for everyone. He could even explain his beliefs in such a way that anyone could easily understand them. The church staff loved Zach, and church members always enjoyed their chance encounters with him.*
>
> *He started work at the church when he was 20 after several years as a construction worker. He had enjoyed seeing the church grow and had been very grateful for his promotion to senior custodian several years ago. Zach frequently thought to himself, "I'm a very lucky man!"*
>
> *When Zach passed away, the sanctuary at the church was filled with family, friends, and church members. As the pastor rose from his seat to begin the service, a church member near the back of the church leaned over to his wife and said, "You know, Zach was a really great guy!"*

How Do I Become Myself?

This may sound like a silly question, but many people go through life simply accepting their circumstances and never try to determine if they should be doing otherwise. Most of these are good people, "doing their best" as the saying goes, but, nevertheless, living without giving any serious thought as to who they are or what they should be doing with their lives. Some may even feel trapped by family or financial circumstances...or by a poor choice they made many years ago. Granted, it's easy for me to say this here, but most people in such situations are not trapped by their circumstances, but rather by their own way of thinking. Therefore, if you are ever to break out and become who you are, <u>you must first be willing to think critically about how you have been living your life</u>.

> *"Most people I meet are still playing the right, safe and certain game. The rules are: project a positive image; don't be too different from the norm; deny or cover up any doubts about yourself; don't rock the boat; and act like you know even when you don't."*
>
> SUSAN CAMPBELL, PH.D.
> Getting Real

Most of us have the freedom to make almost any choice we want to make. Some take advantage of this freedom and try to minimize the work and maximize the fun in their lives. Granted, having fun is an important part of life. However, becoming who you are is not always fun. It requires careful thought, insightful planning, hard work, and sometimes great sacrifice. Most of the fun comes from knowing that you are living according to your own plan and, ultimately, from accomplishing something important with your life. To be successful in these efforts, <u>you must be able to put freedom in perspective and use it to your full advantage</u>.

Good Choices Good Life

> *"There are two freedoms, the false where one is free*
> *to do what he likes,*
> *and the true where he is free to do what he ought."*
>
> CHARLES KINGSLEY
> Parson, Novelist and Christian Socialist

Many people believe they are the product of their circumstances, not the result of the choices they have made. To me, this way of thinking dooms one to live a life heavily influenced by others and void of "cooking the creative juices" that every life contains. To create a special life and feel good about what you've done, one has to feel personally accountable for the result. There is no satisfaction from just letting things happen. Therefore, if you are ever to live in your own unique and special way, <u>you must be willing to acknowledge that you have had the primary role in creating the life you have today. And that you will play the same role in creating the life you will have in the future</u>.

> *"People often say that this or that person has not yet*
> *found himself.*
> *But the self is not something one finds,*
> *it is something one creates."*
>
> THOMAS SZASZ,
> "Personal Conduct," The Second Sin

The last point I would like to make in this regard, concerns my underlying "thesis" for this book – that there is an intended life for each of us. I'm not saying that every second has been preplanned for you, or that your spouse, family, and profession have been pre-picked for you, or that your exact role was predetermined for you at birth. These things could be true – I don't know – but that's not what I'm saying here. I'm saying a couple of things – one, that it is intended for you to live your life for the benefit of others and that if you live only for yourself, you have missed at least half of your calling. In addition, there is an individual inside of you – with interests, abilities, insights, knowledge, and feelings that are unique – and _you are expected to take these ingredients and turn them into someone special_.

> *When Akiba was on his death bed, he bemoaned to his rabbi that he felt he was a failure. His rabbi moved closer and asked why. Akiba confessed that he had not lived a life like Moses. He began to cry, admitting that he feared God's judgment. At this, the rabbi leaned into his ear and whispered gently, "God will not judge Akiba for not being Moses. God will judge Akiba for not being Akiba."*
>
> FROM THE TALMUD
> A collection of Jewish laws and traditions.

So, what should you be thinking about if you want to position yourself for realizing your individual potential? The list of considerations will vary for each of us and you will have to do some careful thinking just to identify what should be included on yours. However, there are three areas common to all of us – _values and habits_, _interests and motivations_, and _goals and objectives_ – that you should include on your list and think carefully about. As you do, try to make a determination of how and to what extent these three areas are currently influencing the conduct and direction of your life.

Think About Your Personal Values (and Bad Habits)

Before you start to think about "being an engineer" or "fulfilling my role as a parent," you should reflect on the values – as well as the bad habits – that influence your life today. Your values, when actively at work in your life, influence your thinking and determine, to a great extent, how you react to problems and opportunities when they appear. Being honest, having an interest in the well-being of others, and keeping yourself in good physical condition are just some of the values that influence your life in good and positive ways. Good values help you make better choices and therefore you should devote some careful thought to the identification of the values that are <u>actually</u> <u>active</u> in your life today.

Although we think of values as being the good influences in our lives, there can be other things we "value" that are influencing our lives in detrimental ways. These bad habits could include a lack of respect for others, allowing alcohol, drugs or cigarettes to impair our well being, or the practice of putting "fun and games" before work and responsibilities. If there is one thing I am certain of, it's the fact that bad habits have no role in the life we were intended to live. We must, not only come clean with ourselves about the bad habits that we have, but also do everything we can to minimize or eliminate their influence in our lives.

The point here is that the potential your life represents can be enhanced by the good values you practice or virtually eliminated by a bad habit that is controlling your life. It matters little what you are interested in doing or becoming if you are not the kind of person that can pull it off. So, getting your "value house" in order should be a priority in the process of becoming who you are.

Think About Your Personal Interests and Motivations

I think I could write another book on this one because our interests and motivations seem to point us to the very essence of our lives. If you are ever to discover your intended life, you must be able to surface the things that "make you tick" and ensure that they are actively pursued through the choices you make each day.

As you do so, think carefully about your personal interests. What things do you really enjoy doing? What do you feel motivated to do or to pursue? If you could do anything you wanted, what would that be? Based on what you've done in your life and what you know today, what subjects, projects, or activities really get your attention? What really gets you excited? Where are the loves in your life, and what are they saying to you?

As you identify these signs and signals, take note to what extent you are actually pursuing them in your life. Some of your strongest interests may be present in your thinking, but not reflected in the choices you are making. The objective of this effort should not only be to identify these interests, but, once identified, to begin to make the choices that will allow you to deploy them in your life.

Think About Your Personal Goals

I've devoted an entire chapter of this book to the topic of goal setting, but I would like to share one additional point here. Our lives have been given to us, without cost or obligation. Most of us take that for granted, but just stop and think for a few moments how special "a life" really is. It's almost unbelievable how the live body works – it can walk, it can run, it can see, it can hear, it can touch, and it can feel. It can love, it can hate, it can reason, and it can multiply. It can talk, it can sing, it can shout, and it can make noises of great enjoyment. It can draw, it can plan, it can work, and it can build. It can heal, it can grow, it can change, and it can develop. It can do so many things. So, there you are...in full control of this absolutely awesome "machine." It's raring to go and wanting to run a great race with every bit of its being. All it needs is a great driver. Will that be you?

> *"Regardless of the circumstances, each man lives in a world of his own making."*
>
> JOSEPHA MURRY EMMS
> Playright

To Be (Yourself), or Not to Be

Getting in touch with your inner self and finding your own personal sense of direction is difficult in today's world. Most of us have many possibilities concerning our friends, our activities, and our livelihood. To identify and select the ones that are right for you requires thoughtful evaluation and effective choices, frequently resulting in some degree of anguish and uncomfortable moments. Being yourself isn't something you just go out and do. You're the only person "inside your head" but somehow other influences find their way in and can misdirect your life. Therefore, it takes careful thought, good choices, and hard work to become the person you are intended to be.

Sometimes we think we have it all figured out, only to find that life seems to be taking us in a totally different direction. Becoming who you are is an ongoing process that will have its starts and stops along the way. You may have to change some habits that are distracting you from the person you really are. You may have to associate with a different group of people, change jobs, or even move to a new town or city. You may have to take some risks or address doubtful questions from friends and associates as you follow your feelings and beliefs. The point is that this is important and difficult work, almost always requiring that you make some hard choices to fully uncover the unique potential that you possess.

Is all of this work worth it? If it's important to you to know that you've fashioned a life of your own making and not simply become a copy of those around you, the answer is…<u>yes</u>. If it's important to you to know that you have enhanced your life and the lives of others with the skills and interests that God has given you, the answer is…<u>most definitely</u>. If it's important to you to establish specific goals and objectives for your life and follow them through to fruition, the answer is…<u>without a doubt</u>. Please remember that you were given your life for free. It's what you choose to do to with that life that determines its value and meaning to yourself and to others.

*"The important thing is this: to be able at any
moment to sacrifice
what we are for what we can become."*

CHARLES DU BOS
French and English Literature Critic

CHAPTER 6

ACTING ON FAITH

"Faith is to believe what we do not see; and the reward of this faith is to see what we believe."

ST. AUGUSTINE
Philosopher and Theologian

The Role of Faith

You may be asking...what is a chapter on faith doing in a book about choices? The answer is this. Many times we make choices, even important ones, "in the moment" without considering what we expect to achieve or to become at some future date. Faith helps us bridge the gap between "now" and "then" and to get a better view of what that future may be. It is through faith that we are able to factor in a potential outcome and determine more accurately whether the choice we're about to make will move us closer to that eventuality...or not.

Faith facilitates living beyond this very moment. Faith allows us to live our lives in consideration of the future and to consider more than what seems to be important right now. With the longer term perspective that faith provides, we're better equipped to react to current circumstances. By utilizing faith in our lives, we allow a future objective to participate in our current choice making processes. Faith helps us live our lives "today" in concert with the life that we want to have "tomorrow" and to maintain an awareness of something we want to accomplish in the future.

In making this connection with our future, faith provides us with a view of how we expect things to work out and fuels our motivation for turning that expectation into reality. Through faith we can visualize a time yet to come and see ourselves accomplishing an important goal or developing into the type of person we want to be. It's faith that allows us to reach out and bring that future into our lives today. By doing so, we can make choices that, in turn, point our lives in that direction.

We all live with a degree of uncertainty about ourselves and others. Faith allows us to attach a level conviction to that uncertainty as we work to make our lives more meaningful and more productive. For example, a young man may have great uncertainty about how he'll pay for college and law school, but yet have great faith that he'll be a successful attorney someday. It's his faith in this outcome that will help him make the proper choices as he looks for ways to overcome the uncertainties and difficulties involved.

It's through faith that we "journey on" to a view of successful children or an enjoyable retirement. It's through faith that we see our hard work or dedication to an important project turn into reality. It's through faith that we can live consistent with our beliefs in honesty and fairness, content that such practices will improve our lives and make us a more valuable friend to those around us. It's faith that gives us insights into times and circumstances yet to come and, in effect, helps to guide our choices as we move toward those future points in our lives.

> *"Faith is like radar that sees through the fog –*
> *the reality*
> *of things at a distance that the*
> *human eye cannot see."*
>
> CORRIE TEN BOOM
> Nazi Concentration Camp Survivor

What is Faith?

Defining faith and explaining how it works in our lives is a difficult subject – one that's open to many viewpoints and interpretations. In spite of this difficulty, faith can play a major role in many of the choices we make. Recognizing that there's much that we don't understand, I've nevertheless decided to address the subject in this book, "keeping the faith" that you'll read between the lines to develop your own view of how faith might help you make choices that will lead to a more meaningful life.

First of all, faith does not confine itself to religious quarters. In fact, faith can be at work in many different areas of your life. While you can have faith in God, you can also have faith in yourself, your spouse, your children, your country, your employer, or in some action you're about to take. As a result, faith can influence what you think, what you say, what you do, and how you feel about many different things. When you start to view faith as being a relevant influence in many areas of your life, you can more easily consider the role that faith could play in the choices you make.

> *"I want to encourage delight in the word, to help reclaim faith as fresh, vibrant, intelligent and liberating. This is a faith that emphasizes a foundation of love and respect for ourselves. It is a faith that uncovers our connection to others, rather than designating anyone as separate and apart. This faith is not a commodity we either have or don't have – it is an inner quality that unfolds as we learn to trust our own deepest experience."*
>
> SHARON SALZBERG
> Faith

Faith is More Than Wishing...

Faith is more than wishful thinking. While our lives may be filled with many wishful thoughts, these tend to be passing moments associated with short-term wants or circumstances. I wish we had been invited to the party...I wish I had a new car...I wish I had gotten the promotion...I wish I were smarter...all of these are examples of wishful thoughts that might pass our way, most of the time quickly disappearing as our attention moves on to other matters. Wishing is a "mental moment" about something we'd like to have or like to do, but without much additional thought or action to attain it. Wishing is simply a way of expressing our desires to ourselves and occasionally to others.

> *"I wish I knew the good of wishing."*
>
> HENRY S. LEIGH
> Wishing

...and More Than Hoping

Faith is more than hoping, even if it's a strong sense of hope. While hope is typically associated with more important events in our lives – I hope I graduate next year...I hope I'll get a good job...I hope I get married – it often lacks conviction. Hope is the vehicle we ride when we want something good to happen, but don't really know how to get there. We all want to enjoy life, and hope is the way we express our desires for favorable outcomes to ourselves and to others.

> *"Hope is the boy; faith the experienced, smiling man.*
> *Hope lives on ignorance; faith is built upon a knowledge of our life."*
>
> ROBERT LOUIS STEVENSON
> Author and Observer of Humankind

Faith Provides Conviction in the Face of Uncertainty

Faith guides our lives when we believe we're headed in the right direction, although neither the comfort of the trip nor the final destination can be guaranteed. Faith involves trust... trusting that our thoughts, words, and actions will lead us to an outcome we may feel in our hearts or see in our minds, but yet have no guarantee that it will happen. Faith promotes and supports our actions even when we cannot be totally certain that such actions will produce the envisioned result. In spite of such uncertainty, we're able to "step out on faith" trusting that what we are doing will work out in a favorable way.

Jonathan loved his brother, in spite of Justin's recent conviction on drug charges. It was Justin's first offense, but the judge sentenced him to three years in prison due to the amount of drugs involved. While Justin was incarcerated, Jonathan visited him every week, made sure his wife and children had what they needed, and even arranged for Justin to be enrolled in a prison-sponsored drug rehabilitation program. From their weekly discussions, Jonathan became convinced that Justin would remain "clean" when he was released and would become a law-abiding citizen once again. As Justin's release date neared, Jonathan contacted almost every friend in their small town until he found one who was willing to give Justin a job.

Obviously, Jonathan did these things because he loved and cared for his brother and his brother's family. But even though love was a motivating factor, it was really Jonathan's faith that guided him in this effort. He had no way of being sure that his brother would be free of his drug habits, but he did these things because he could see Justin leading a normal and productive life after his release from prison. In addition, he had developed a conviction about his brother's future from his weekly visits with him. It was a combination of his perspective about Justin's future life and his conviction that Justin could live drug free again that gave him the will to act as he sought to find employment for his brother. It was Jonathan's faith in his brother that spurred him on and guided him in his efforts.

This story is an example of how we act on faith even when the future is not definitely known. Although the long-term outcome of Justin's rehabilitation was uncertain, Jonathan had "a personal perspective" about Justin's future that helped Jonathan see his brother living a responsible life. In spite of the circumstances, Jonathan continued to believe in his brother and envisioned Justin living a normal life someday. Jonathan's faith in his brother, while severely shaken, remained intact, and he was constantly thinking about how to help Justin return to a normal life.

> *"Faith doesn't wait until it understands;*
> *in that case it wouldn't be faith."*
>
> VANCE HAVNER
> Author of 40 Books

Faith Moves Us Beyond Just Believing

Believing, especially in good things, is a very important quality in our lives. I believe you should be polite to other people...I believe you should study hard when you are in school...I believe you should be honest in your business dealings...I believe you should eat a healthy diet are all examples of believing worthwhile things. However, simply possessing a belief will do little for you. You must somehow activate that belief if it is to affect your life in a special way.

When you say you believe in something, you're really saying that you agree with the thought or principle. Sometimes you may simply sit on your belief, letting it affect little more than your own thoughts. In other instances, you may act as a result of your belief, allowing it to impact your life, and possibly the lives of others, in some way. The difference between an inactive belief and an active one rests on whether that belief is accompanied by faith – a "sighting" or feeling about what will happen if you act on your belief. Your belief defines a framework for your thoughts, but your faith defines a framework for your actions and helps you visualize what the outcome of those actions might be.

For example, you may be quick to say, "I believe in being honest." However, if you never let that belief influence your daily actions and the choices you make, at best, it is an inactive belief, and, at worst, not really a belief at all. On the other hand, if you have faith that honesty will improve the communications and increase the level of trust you have with others, you can more easily make choices that favorably affect the way you treat other people, the way you conduct your school or business activities, or even what you do with the wallet you find lying on the street. Faith helps you translate what you believe into actions by allowing you to "see" the potential result of a choice you're about to make.

> *Nathan loved animals all his life. He fed the birds in his backyard every day, enthusiastically volunteered to look after the neighbor's dog during vacations, and would have performed his after-school duties at the local animal shelter for free. Following his high school graduation, he packed some of his clothes, told his hard-working mother "don't worry, Mom, I'll be okay," and caught the bus to Auburn, Alabama. He had no idea how or where he would find work when he got there, much*

> *less how he'd get into Auburn's nationally-recognized veterinary program. But Nathan believed that he was meant to be a veterinarian – a very special one – and he was acting on his faith that somehow, someday, he would accomplish this goal.*

Just believing in something isn't enough; we must act on our beliefs if they are going to impact our lives. As another example, just believing in a healthy diet will do little for you. However, if you have faith that healthy eating will improve your well being, you may look ahead and "see" yourself with a trimmer appearance, an increased level of energy, and better health in general. As a result, you are in a much better position to make choices to eat the right foods as you guide yourself toward these envisioned outcomes. While your basic belief is important, it is your faith in the future that will prompt you to make choices that result in a healthier lifestyle. This is definitely one step – a big step – beyond just believing that a healthy diet is a good thing.

The Components of Faith

If you think carefully about some aspect of your future, you can develop certain perspectives or envisioned outcomes. If you consider and evaluate your feelings about one of those future outcomes and allow it to become clearer in your mind, you may discover a conviction that makes you want to achieve it. As you think more about it and your conviction grows, you may develop the will to make the choices that allow your perspective to become a reality. Somewhere in this mental process, faith emerges, signifying your commitment and guiding your choices from that point on.

Therefore, faith seems to have three components...a <u>perspective</u> about a future condition or circumstance, a <u>conviction</u> in the face of uncertainty that this perspective will become reality, and the <u>will</u> to make choices that align our lives with that perspective. Some of our perspectives about the future trigger convictions inside of us and others don't. Some of these convictions are strong enough to support our will to make choices, and others aren't. Therefore, for faith to actually be "at work" in our lives, all three of these components must be present.

<u>Perspective</u>

Can faith work in our lives if we have no outcome in mind? No, I don't believe it can. For faith to work in our lives, we must have a perspective about the future. Without a perspective of what the future might be in some area of your life, it is very difficult for faith to work within you. If you want to engage faith, you must be willing to work hard enough to clarify your perspective about a future development. Such visions, understandings, or faith outcomes, if you will, may require a great deal of thought, research, discussion, and even prayer to define. If you're not willing to work to define your perspective about something in your future, it will be difficult, if not impossible, for you to activate your faith to achieve it. Granted, that perspective may not always be crisp and clear. At times it may be made up more of feelings than an actual vision of the perceived outcome. As you live and make choices under the influence of faith, you are continually making adjustments to gain a clearer view and better understanding of that future.

Nevertheless, you must have some idea of where you're going for faith to begin to work in your life and influence some of the choices you are making.

> *"Columbus found a world,*
> *but had no chart save one that faith*
> *deciphered in the skies."*
>
> GEORGE SANTAYANA
> Spanish Philosopher

Conviction

How convinced do we have to be that we will achieve the outcome we have in mind for faith to influence the choices we make? The answer depends on the relative importance of what we're trying to accomplish. For instance, it's not that winning the ball game or the weekend golf match aren't important, but other feelings such as wishing or hoping seem to guide us at these levels. It's when we want to accomplish something more important in our lives that conviction becomes a factor in how faith influences the choices we make. Becoming an influential teacher, building a successful company, or finding the right marriage partner are examples of these more important events. If faith is to guide us in our choices as we work toward these ends, we will need to have conviction about what we expect to accomplish. For example, a young lady who has a strong feeling that she will have a husband with high moral character will be able to use her faith to help her find a man with that quality. A perspective of your future – the first component of faith – is not enough. You must also have a high level of conviction about this perspective for faith to guide you.

> *"Send the harmony of a great desire vibrating through every fiber of your being.
> Pray for a task that will call forth your faith, your courage, your perseverance and your spirit of sacrifice. Keep your hands and your soul clean, and the conquering current will flow freely."*
>
> THOMAS DRIER

Will

Why is will so important if you have a perspective of the future and a high level of conviction that you can achieve the intended outcome?" Because little happens without the will to work in support of a perspective we may have. For example, at some point in our lives almost all of us have wanted to accomplish something important or meaningful. We talked about it with our friends, and may have stated our intentions with great conviction…"I'm going to own my own business some day." However, because we lacked the will to act – to make the associated choices – nothing ever happened. Therefore, in spite of the presence of a clear perspective and a strong conviction, our faith will fall short of its target if we don't have the will to work, to sacrifice, to study, or do whatever we have to do to accomplish the envisioned outcome.

> *"Lack of will power has caused more failure than lack of intelligence or ability."*
>
> FLOWER A. NEWHOUSE
> Founder of Questhaven Retreat

Anytime you want to test to see if faith is at work in a given circumstance within your life, you can ask yourself these three questions. Do I have a perspective or vision of what I want to accomplish? Do I have the conviction that this outcome is right for me? Do I have the will to make the choices that will allow this to become a reality in my life? When all three answers are "yes," you can be assured that faith will guide the choices you make.

Developing Faith

Developing faith requires careful thought. Unlike love, which typically enters our lives unexpectedly, the onus is on you to discover and confirm where your faith can work in your life. Whether that faith be in a member of your family, in a special project or business activity, or in the practice of your religious beliefs, you must take the initiative to activate faith in your life. There are many opportunities for faith to guide your choices, but you have to clarify them in your own mind (develop a perspective), test your personal feelings about this eventuality (level of conviction), and be willing to make the sometimes difficult choices that lead you to that outcome (showing the will) if faith is to become a motivating factor in your life.

To position yourself for faith development, you should recognize that faith is a personal experience not a group effort. You may attend church every Sunday with hundreds of people, but it's not their faith that will guide your life – it's only your faith that will do that. You may go to school with hundreds or even thousands of other students, but it's not their faith that will help you make important choices – it's only your faith that can do that. You may live in a neighborhood with dozens of friends, but it's not their faith that will determine how you will raise your family – it's only your faith that can do that. Granted, other people can set examples for you to follow, but when it comes to being led by faith and moving your life toward the future you were intended to have, only <u>your</u> faith can provide you with the insight as to what your choices should be.

> "The relation of faith between subject and object is unique in every case.
> Hundreds may believe, but each must believe by himself."
>
> W. H. AUDEN
> English Author and Poet

We have observed that faith contains both conviction and uncertainty – conviction that what we are setting out to do is the right thing, but uncertainty about the expected result and whether it will indeed be achieved. Therefore, faith is accompanied by both motivation and doubt – motivation to accomplish something that may be very important in our lives, but doubt as to whether the outcome will be as we anticipate. Many times our doubts turn into fears and we don't really allow faith to guide our lives.

> *Terri had always wanted to own a flower shop. She loved everything about flowers – growing them, arranging them and sharing them with her family and friends. Three years ago her brother-in-law, a successful businessman, helped Terri put together a*

> business plan that showed she needed $25,000 in cash to start the business. Terri was so anxious to get her flower business started that she saved, cut corners, and worked overtime to build her start-up fund, which she did in record time.
>
> While she was doing this, the economy slowed and many business owners were expressing concerns about the future. In addition, Terri fell in love with William and they expected to marry within year. Her doubts about the economy turned into a fear of losing her money, especially when she realized she might need it to help with wedding expenses. As a result, her money was still sitting in her account, and her vision of Terri's Flower Shop was growing dimmer each day.

Developing and maintaining your faith is seldom without difficulty. You are likely to encounter disappointments and even setbacks along the way. You may receive advice from those around you that shakes your faith or, in some instances, misdirects you so much that your faith journey is curtailed or never even taken. Faith may be leading you to make certain choices, but outside pressures may be sending you a different message – one that could hamper or even kill the will you were in the process of developing.

I have no pearls of wisdom to offer that would prevent this from happening, but I suggest that faith – especially faith about very important or life-defining choices – is not likely to develop if you don't take the initiative. "I'll just wait until something strikes my fancy" is not an attitude that is likely to produce the life-changing choices that are most often based on faith. Wishful thoughts may be abundant and may appear without any work on our part, but activating faith requires a specific effort. Gregg Levoy, in his book titled Callings, explains the way our lives react to us this way:

"Your life mirrors what you put into it or withhold from it. When you are lazy, it is lazy. When you hold back, it holds back. When you hesitate, it stands there staring, hands in its pockets. But when you commit, it comes on like blazes."

Developing Faith in Yourself

One of the most important things in life is to have faith in yourself. When you have faith in yourself – in what you are doing and trying to accomplish with your life – you are not only more content but, in general, you are a much happier person. In addition, you have a sense of purpose about your life and are in a much better position to make choices concerning your future.

If you don't currently have faith in yourself, you can develop it. By saying this, I don't want to imply that there is a simple "process" you can use to create faith in yourself. This is serious and important work and I don't want to infer that it is easy or that there is a special way of doing this effectively. However, I do believe, and strongly so, that the ingredients and clues to your intended life are resident within you. If you are willing to devote the time and effort required to "investigate yourself" you can come to a very logical conclusion about what you are supposed to do with your life. The wonderful byproduct of this effort is faith in yourself – the result of knowing that you are using your life to do what was intended for you.

> *"Faith is the great motive power, and no man*
> *realizes his full potential*
> *unless he has the deep conviction that his life is*
> *eternally important and*
> *that his work well done is a part*
> *of an unending plan."*
>
> CALVIN COOLIDGE

Developing faith in yourself starts by accepting the fact that you are here for a purpose. You have been given certain interests, abilities, and motivations which, when identified and utilized, direct you to the role or life you were intended to have. Think about this for a few minutes. You have come into this world pre-equipped to do something special with your life. Doesn't just the thought of that make you want to look inside yourself and think carefully about what you will do with the special qualities you already possess? Someone once said, "Trust life, and it will teach you all you need to know." We echo that thought here...trust in your individuality, trust that you are here for a reason, and aim your efforts toward its discovery. Here are a few suggestions that may help you in this regard.

Start by Thinking About Yourself

When you stop and think carefully about your interests, your abilities, and what motivates you, you have, in effect, started this faith building process. This thoughtful time is not something that you do one afternoon, but is a series of thinking sessions, most likely extending over a period of months or even years, in which you reflect on what "makes you tick," what you feel you want to do, and, more specifically, what you want to accomplish with your life. Quietly consider the fact that there is no one in the world like you, no one who can say or do something the way you can. You are, in fact, unique. Use this time to wonder and reason why this is true.

Work to Gain a Perspective About Your Future

This thinking time provides opportunities for you to focus on certain feelings you have about your life – how you are living it right now and, to a greater extent, how you want to live it in the future. Some of these feelings about your future may be externally triggered, having developed as the result of something you learned, or something you experienced in some way. Other feelings appear out of nowhere and take the form of an idea or desire to create, build or develop something. Whatever their source, the objective is to use these feelings to develop a perspective about how you will utilize the personal qualities and interests you have, and, as a result, "give texture" to the faith you are building in yourself.

Use Your Convictions to Sort Out the Alternatives

The most likely result of this thoughtful work is that you will develop several perspectives about what you may ultimately want to do with your life. It may even be that you have been doing something with your life and have been working at it for many years when a new perspective about your future appeared and now tugs at your heart, creating new conflict in your life. At this point you have to read your level of conviction – the intensity of your feeling that an opportunity or personal plan you have developed is right or "a fit" for you. By definition, conviction infers the presence of strong feelings. If, after careful and extended thought, your conviction about a possibility you are considering continues or increases, you can know that you are on track. As you clarify and reconfirm your conviction about something you want to do, you, in effect, further strengthen your faith in yourself and what you can accomplish.

Do You Have the Will to Act?

Up to this point, your faith development work has taken place primarily in your head. If you have been sincere and diligent in these efforts, I'm sure your heart has played an important role as well. You now have a well-thought-out and "heart checked" understanding of what you want to do. At this point, you may even be feeling good about your future. However, the ultimate test of faith in yourself is your will to act. In order to turn your thoughts, perspectives, and convictions into reality, you must have the will to make choices that allow you to live the vision that you have developed. When you exhibit the will to act and make choices supported by your convictions, you are confirming this faith in yourself, and, from that first step in this new direction, you can rely on this faith to guide you. As you continue to take steps and make choices concerning your envisioned future, that faith will become stronger and, at some point, you will know that you are developing and living the life that was intended for you.

Good Choices Good Life

> *"Our only legitimate end in life is to finish God's work – to bring to full growth the capacities and talents implanted in us."*
>
> ERIC HOFFER
> The Ordeal of Change

The other consideration in building faith in yourself is how you treat other people. We all need to frequently remind ourselves that we are here for each other. As a result, our happiness, although influenced greatly by living up to our potential, is also determined by how we treat other people. When we are nice to others, when we check to make sure the other guy is okay, when we go out of our way to help someone in need, we experience what being happy is all about. When you start to develop the perspective that your underlying role is to be here for others, when you start to develop a conviction that focusing on other people will produce more happiness in your life, when you have the will to make choices that put others' interests ahead of yours, you are, in effect, developing faith in yourself and what your life can produce.

Is Developing Your Faith Worth It?

In spite of a well-developed faith, things don't always turn out the way we had expected. There are times when faith motivates us to devote a major portion of our lives to certain people, projects, or plans, only to encounter disappointment, or outright failure, somewhere along the way. It's this reality of faith, and of life in general, that makes some people hesitant to live based on their faith, secretly concerned that difficulties or even heartbreak could be just around the corner.

Therefore, one has to wonder…is developing faith in yourself and acting on it worth the effort? What if things don't work out as you expect? Do you receive any benefit from your faith-driven activities when your dreams don't develop the way you thought?

In trying to answer these questions, it is helpful to reflect on how our faith comes to be. Unlike love, which finds us, or some of our personal attributes with which we are born, faith in ourselves is something that we develop. This effort is subject to personal interpretations. Sometimes we get it right and sometimes we don't. We may have to make several attempts over an extended period before we successfully complete this thoughtful work. Therefore, if you want faith to play an important role in your life, you must be willing to make some mistakes and to devote the time it takes to fully develop the faith and understanding you seek.

So, if giving some careful thought to your life and how you will live it is important to you, certainly the process of developing your faith is, as well. If confirming a plan or way to live that gives meaning and purpose to your life is important, certainly the time and effort to establish your faith is worthwhile. If having the satisfaction that you responded to the feelings you have about the future and subsequently lived your life in concert with them is important, then developing your faith is well worth the struggle to do so.

Granted, faith comes with risks. As a result, some of us may not be open to having faith of any kind in our life. Some prefer to live one day at a time with little thought about the future. These individuals want to be free to experience whatever each day may bring their way. They prefer not to be encumbered with the responsibility of having to live up to some expectation although it may be their very own. Well, faith is indeed optional, but those who elect to minimize it or eliminate it from their lives are ignoring the fundamental guidance system that can help them realize the true potential that their lives possess.

> *"You can think too much, which is something Dante and his guide, Virgil, discovered on their outing to the Inferno. They were not permitted to pass through one particular threshold until they left all reason and intellect behind. These faculties are useful, in other words, but only up to a point. Beyond that, the door will be barred to us if we attempt to cross by way of reason. No amount of intellectual authority, arrogant confidence, name dropping or ambition will allow us passage. Beyond a certain point, faith is the magic lamp and humility the abracadabra."*
>
> GREGG LEVOY
> Callings

It's safe to say that a life sprinkled with faith will accomplish more than a life lived according to the practice of "only the facts, please!" The development of faith helps you visualize outcomes that are based on what you feel and have inside of you. As such, by developing your faith in many areas of your life and then making choices based on that faith, you are much more likely to accomplish the things that you were intended to do.

CHAPTER 7

GIVING TO OTHERS

"They who give have all things; they who withhold have nothing."

Hindu Proverb

"Getting It"

We tend to be the focus of our own lives, and, as such, most of our choices are all about us. However, the truth is we benefit more from helping others than from helping ourselves. This chapter is intended to help us see the benefits of giving and to understand that the choices we make that improve the lives of others, in turn, improve our lives, as well.

Most of us spend the majority of our waking hours thinking about ourselves. We think about our jobs, our schoolwork, or other responsibilities that we may have. We think about things we want – cars, clothes, houses, or the latest electronic thing. We think about bills, personal problems, and whether we will be "a success" or not. Many of us spend so much time focused on ourselves that other people and their needs become secondary or of no concern at all. Granted, looking out for our own well-being is important. However, if our choices always reflect an attitude of <u>getting</u> <u>for</u> <u>ourselves</u>

and almost never one of <u>giving</u> <u>to</u> <u>others</u>, we'll miss out on some of the greatest feelings that life has to offer.

> *Todd was dreaming. He was at his own funeral and, after a lifetime of getting just about everything he wanted, he couldn't believe his time had come. Nevertheless, he was there. As his spirit rose from the casket and looked out over the sparse crowd, he couldn't believe what he was seeing.*
>
> *He looked for Josh, the guy he'd "negotiated" out of thousands of dollars in several real estate deals, but he wasn't there. He looked for Bill, the friend he'd described to some as "not having a lick of common sense," but he wasn't there. He looked for Grace, the woman at his office with whom he'd flirted for years, but she wasn't there. He looked for Chris, the parking attendant he'd always short-changed on tips, but he wasn't there. And then he looked down at the front row expecting to see his wife and family, but lo and behold...they weren't there either.*
>
> *"Why didn't more people come to my funeral?" he thought. "They were all part of my life, so why aren't they here?" As Todd thought about the circumstances surrounding each person missing today, he suddenly knew the answer. In one way or another, he had taken something from each of these people...from some it was money, from others it was self-respect, and from others it was time that they could have spent together.*

> *None of these people ever said anything to Todd about what he had taken from them, but now, at his funeral, their absence was speaking to him loud and clear. Todd had never felt this bad in his entire life, and now he was dead. He was starting to wish he had treated these people differently. Then, the alarm clock sounded...and Todd woke up.*

Intuitively, we know that it is "more blessed to give than to receive." Most of us have even experienced how much better we feel when we give than when we take. Nevertheless, for some reason, human nature pushes us in the wrong direction, toward a mindset of <u>getting</u> rather than <u>giving</u>. Over time, we become convinced that getting is the way to go. We see ads on television about a new car and we want one. We see friends buying a bigger house and we want to do the same. We see the professional athlete landing a huge signing bonus and we suddenly want to get our fair share. It's not that any of these things is wrong, but if we are not careful in our thinking they can lead us to believe that life is more about what we get than about what we give to others.

I'm not sure why we let this happen to us; greed, I guess. We can be so mistaken about the benefits of getting for ourselves versus giving to others that we actually go out and live our lives in the wrong way. We have opportunities every day to improve how others feel, but instead we use many of these moments to try to make ourselves feel better. Instead of asking our friends about their lives, we frequently use these encounters as opportunities to tell them something about ours. When we approach life in this self-focused way, things just don't work out as well. However, when we place our focus on others, we experience important benefits in our own lives. Life often works opposite of the way we think. In this case, the best way to help ourselves is to go out and help others.

> *K.J. was only 16, but he had already robbed at least a dozen elderly women, snatching their purses and running as fast as he could until he was many blocks away. By the time the police started canvassing the neighborhood, K.J. had taken out the cash and the credit cards, dropped the purse in the nearest dumpster, and was back at home congratulating himself as he counted the loot. After a week or so passed and he started getting low on funds, he'd start planning his next heist.*
>
> *Like most crooks, K.J.'s luck eventually ran out. As he dashed full speed around a corner, his latest snatch tucked tightly under his arm, he tripped over an abandoned tricycle and crashed head first onto the sidewalk. Before K.J. could extract himself from the wreckage, two men, who had witnessed the robbery and joined in the chase, jumped on top of him and held him down until the police arrived.*
>
> *Given that he'd been caught red-handed and that the police were able to connect him to other robberies of elderly women, K.J. was easily convicted and sentenced to three years in prison. Needless to say, K.J. had plenty of time to think about what he had done. But it wasn't this extended time of reflection or even one of the special prison programs that turned K.J.'s life around. It was someone totally unexpected.*

One day, the guard came to his cell and said, "K.J., you have a visitor."

"Who in the world could that be?" K.J. wondered. "I haven't had a visitor in weeks, and I certainly wasn't expecting anybody today."

"I don't know who the lady is," the guard replied, "but she's got gray hair, looks to be about 80 years old, and, as I understand it, she was very emphatic about seeing you today." K.J. had a very puzzled look on his face as he left his cell.

As he sat down on the other side of the visitor's glass, K.J. looked over at the little old woman who was already sitting there. "I'm Estelle Bennett, one of your robbery victims!" she told him.

"Wow," K.J. responded, "why in the world would you come to see me?"

"Because I don't want to see you throw your life away, and that is exactly what you are doing." K.J. – Mr. Independent, know-it-all, robber boy – had never had anyone express concern like that about him. He really didn't know what to say. So he just sat there staring at the woman through the glass.

Estelle continued, "K.J., you will never get anywhere in this world, either in prison or out of it, by taking things from other people. You can only get ahead in life by giving to other people."

K.J. wasn't sure what she was saying to him, but he responded with his street-based logic, "How can I give anything away? I don't have any money, much less anything else that anyone would want from me."

Estelle sat up on the edge of her chair, "That's where you are wrong, K.J. You've got a lot to give to other people! And you can start by giving me your undivided attention for the next few minutes." K.J. still didn't understand what was happening to him but he could see that "Miss Estelle" was dead serious about what she was saying.

Gaining momentum from her convictions, Estelle continued. "K.J., the first thing you need to understand is that the things you take from others – money, possessions, credit cards – never last. Look at you. You've robbed dozens of people and what have you got to show for it? Absolutely nothing except three years in jail!"

"Yes ma'am, you're right about that." K.J. replied starting to think about what Estelle was saying.

She did not let up. "More importantly, K.J., some of the things you can give away last a lifetime," she explained.

K.J. was wondering to himself, "What could I possibly give away that would last a lifetime?"

Before he could ponder the thought very long, Estelle continued to challenge him, "K.J., you have so much to give. But before you can see the importance of those gifts you have to see that there is a better way to live, from being self-centered doing things for yourself to being a people-centered person doing things for others. You have a 14-year old brother who's now home alone. What do you think he could turn out to be if you gave him some of your *friendship, your advice, your time, your interest, your help, your love? Don't you see it, K.J.? You can impact your brother's life – most likely prevent him from following in your footsteps – by what you start doing for him this very day. Even from your prison cell you can make a difference in your brother's life."*

K.J. looked across at this frail woman who obviously believed strongly in what she was saying. "Honestly, Mrs. Bennett, I've never thought about being able to influence someone else's life...that's pretty heavy stuff," K.J. said thoughtfully.

"It's called respect, K.J., and you show your respect by sharing your gifts with other people – your concern, your help, your assistance, and even your love – not by taking things from them. Everybody's life is important, K.J. – yours, mine, and your little brother's. By sharing your gifts with other people you can make a difference. And yes, you might even change their life in some way. It's not by taking, K.J.; it's by giving that you get ahead in this world."

K.J. sat there quietly for a few moments and then he said, "And, that's what you've done for me here today, isn't it, Mrs. Bennett?"

The two of them – the little old woman and the purse snatcher – just sat there looking down and then up at each other. "I'm sorry about your purse, Mrs. Bennett. If I had known what a nice person you were, I would have never done that to you."

"Thanks K.J., but that's the least of my concerns at the moment," Estelle commented. "And, by the way, there are a lot of nice people out there if you take the time to get to know them." The guard, who had been listening to the entire conversation, let the time allotment slip by as he waited to see what the outcome of this conversation would be.

Finally, K.J. summarized his new understanding in his own terms, "You know, Mrs. Bennett, I've never been concerned...as you say, respectful...about anybody but myself. I never listened to my mother when she was alive, and I thought my teachers just didn't understand what it took to live on the streets. But, you coming here today, especially considering the fact that I'm the guy who robbed you, has made a big impression on me. If you can still respect me enough to take your time to come out here and talk to me like this, I can certainly respect my own little brother enough to start trying to help him lead a better life."

"K.J., I know you can make a difference," Estelle said as she slowly rose from her chair. "And, just to make sure that you do, I'll be back next Monday. We'll talk about respect some more, and you can tell me what you've done for your little brother."

K.J. looked at the gray-haired woman, quietly happy that she had come to see him. "Yes, ma'am, I'll look forward to that," K.J. said as he smiled and gave a quick salute to the little old woman who had given him something very important today.

If we want to feel great about ourselves, if we want to have a true sense of accomplishment, if we *want to experience a feeling of importance, we'll only achieve these feelings by giving to others. An encouraging word, a warm smile, a visit to a friend, volunteering in the work of a local charity...the list of things we can give to others is endless. One thing is for certain – if you can find your way to becoming a <u>giver</u> instead of a <u>getter</u>, your happiness will extend far beyond your expectations.*

> "It is one of the most beautiful compensations
> of this life
> that no man can sincerely try to help another
> without helping himself."
>
> RALPH WALDO EMERSON
> Influential Thinker and Writer

Our Self-Centered World

When we wake up each morning, we immediately start to think about our own little world. We think about our problems and wonder how we'll ever resolve them. We think about our bills and wonder if we'll ever get them paid. We think about our jobs or our schoolwork and wonder if our efforts will produce success. For seemingly valid reasons, we think, wonder and worry – first and foremost – about our own surroundings and our own circumstances. If we're not careful, we can live our entire lives inwardly focused, always thinking about ourselves and never having much real concern for those around us.

In addition to our tendency to be self-centered, we also become accustomed to "living at a distance" from many of those around us. The morning paper reports a major accident in our city, but we don't know any of the people involved. We pass many cars on our drives to work, but we don't know the people in them. We work in companies or go to schools where we don't know everyone we walk past each day. We even live in neighborhoods where we don't know the person who lives right down the street. We get used to living our lives with strangers all around us, and, as a result, may become conditioned to having little concern for them.

Closer to home, we frequently take family members for granted, failing to fully recognize that we could be a positive influence in how they'll feel or act today. We notice our business associates or our schoolmates, but don't understand the importance of making them feel better or in helping them in some way. We tend to focus on ourselves, and just don't spend much time thinking about the role we might play in these "moments of connection" with other people. Many of us fail to give any serious thought to the opportunities we have to make a positive impact on another person's life.

> *James, a company vice president, had only 10 minutes before the sales meeting started. As he moved quickly down the hall, shuffling through his sales file, he ran into Ben Daniels who was walking with another man. "James, I'd like for you to meet my cousin, Ted," Ben said. "I brought him down to see our office this morning."*
> *"Nice to meet you," James responded, as he quickly shook the cousin's hand and hurried off down the hall, placing the importance of his sales meeting far ahead of his encounter with Ben's cousin.*

GIVING TO OTHERS

A few moments later, Ben and his cousin ran into Scott Mullins, the President of the company, also on his way to the morning sales meeting. "Scott, this is my cousin, Ted Newel. I brought him in today to see our operation."

"Good morning, Ted, it's nice to have you with us. Where are you from?"

After a quick discussion about who they both knew in Richmond, Scott said: "I need to get to the morning sales meeting, but after you guys make the rounds, why don't you stop by my office and I'll be happy to answer any questions Ted might have about our business. And I can show him that eight-pound bass I just hung on my wall."

"That would be great, Scott, we'll definitely see you later," Ben replied enthusiastically.

Two different introductions...two vastly different impressions. It's doubtful that cousin Ted will even remember meeting the "all-important" vice president, James, but his encounter with Scott the President was very special. He'd actually felt Scott's interest in him.

As he was leaving that day, Ted commented: "Your president is a super guy, Ben. It's no wonder the company is doing so well."

"Thanks Ted, I agree. It's great to have a guy like Scott leading our company."

How many times have you and I said "nice to meet you" and let it go at that? Clearly, showing a sincere interest in other people – as Scott the President did in this example – is the exception rather than the rule. However, treating people as Scott did doesn't require a "gift of gab" or even an outgoing personality. You simply have to have a genuine respect for the other person…and for the potential their life represents. I don't know what Scott's company was selling, but I'll tell you one thing – from now on, Ted's buying it.

The Foundation of Giving is Respect

The choice to be respectful of others is a very important one. Every encounter that you have with someone gives you the opportunity to be an influence on that person's life. It doesn't require a unique skill to make these moments count for everyone involved. It just takes a genuine respect for the other person…not for what he can do for you, or for his position or achievements, but because he's another person whose life and potential accomplishments are just as important as your own.

Many of us are misguided when it comes to extending respect. For example, we tend to allocate our respect to individuals who have accomplished something special – great athletes, successful business people, or TV/movie celebrities. We don't know any of these "special people" personally but, nevertheless, we have a tendency to hold them in high regard. On the other hand, we tend to show less respect for the people right around us, sometimes being indifferent toward family members, fellow students, business associates or even close friends. However, the choice to show respect for those around us will not only enhance their lives, but, in turn, will improve our lives, as well.

> *"This is the final test of a person;*
> *their respect for those who can be of*
> *no possible service to them."*
>
> WILLIAM LYON PHELPS
> American Educator

Respect – Feeling It vs. Showing It

Just thinking respectfully isn't enough. You must act on that respect for it to make a difference in your life and in the lives of others. It's one thing to feel respect for someone else, but it's so much more when you allow that respect to be a call to action. Out of your respect for someone and what they are trying to accomplish with their life, you can take advantage of opportunities to say or do things that will help or influence that person in some positive way. The key is not to just feel this respect for others, but to show it in your interactions with them.

> *Noah had always been a quiet guy and never had much to say. Some of his fellow students said he was "a little slow" and frequently snickered about him behind his back. He felt their stares and sometimes could even hear their whispers. For fear of further ridicule, Noah never took the chance to answer questions in class or participate in any group activities. He was turning into a real loner, and spent most of his time between classes by himself.*
> *Things had always been difficult for him at school, but the eighth grade seemed particularly*

difficult. One afternoon as he walked home, he looked up and saw Drew Roberts just a few yards up the sidewalk. Drew was "Mr. Everything" – president of the eighth grade class, a straight-A student, and the most promising new member of the school golf team. Drew lived a few houses down from him, but, in Noah's view, they actually lived worlds apart.

Noah stopped and pretended to look through his backpack, hoping Drew would move along and the encounter would be avoided, but it was too late. He heard Drew's voice: "Hey, Noah! Mind if I walk home with you today? My mom couldn't pick me up."

There was nothing Noah could do. "Sure, no problem," he replied. Noah was already thinking to himself: "What a twosome…Drew the super star and me the nobody."

As they walked along, Drew did most of the talking, chatting about his dog, the new girl at school, and, of course, his golf game. Drew was aware of Noah's "condition," but this was the first time he'd experienced it firsthand. Noah's limited responses made Drew feel even more concerned about him, and, right then and there, he decided to do something about it.

"Hey, Noah, why don't you play golf with me this afternoon? I've got an extra set of clubs and, if we hustle, we can get in 18 before sundown."

"No way, Drew. You're practically a scratch golfer, and I've never played in my life."

Giving to Others

"That doesn't make any difference, Noah, I'll show you some things that I've learned and we'll just play for fun. We won't even keep score," Drew urged.

After further assurances and some verbal pushing by Drew, Noah gave in. "Okay, Drew, but you've got to promise you won't laugh at me."

"Laugh at you? Let me tell you about the first time I played golf," Drew responded as they rounded the last corner and headed down their street.

That one round of golf was the start of a big change in Noah's life. He found that Drew was more "good guy" than superstar as he carefully showed Noah how to hit the golf ball...short, but straight. Noah discovered that he liked golf, and when they completed the last hole, Noah felt as if he might be able to play this game someday. As they walked off, Drew said, "Noah, you could be a good golfer...you have a natural swing...you just have to work at it." That comment along with the friendship Drew displayed that afternoon sparked a motivation that Noah had never felt before.

As a result, work at it is exactly what Noah did. He played golf every chance he got over the next year, including many rounds with Drew. "Hey, Pro," as Drew now called him, "you'll soon be hitting it longer than I do." Noah's parents gave him a new set of clubs for his birthday, and he really enjoyed showing them to his new golfing buddies. Gradually, Noah's grades improved and the kids at school seemed to be nicer to him. He couldn't *believe it when Coach Brinker asked him if he'd like to join the high school golf team. "That would be great," Noah responded, knowing full well that Drew had planted this idea with the coach.*

As things worked out, Noah was eventually offered a half golfing scholarship at the university. Although he never tried to get on the pro tour as his friend Drew had done, golf became an important part of Noah's life. He played almost every weekend, and, over the past 20 years, he facilitated many a business deal on the golf course. He'd done well in his company, had a great wife and had been blessed with two wonderful boys, who were starting to be pretty good golfers on their own.

As he sat at his desk one rainy afternoon and reflected how great his life had turned out to be, Noah couldn't help but wonder what things would have been like if he hadn't bumped into Drew Roberts that day. "I wonder what would have happened to my life if Drew hadn't taken a special interest in me. Without him and his invitation to play that first round of golf, there's no telling where I'd be today."

Every life is important. When you fully recognize this fact, you almost automatically begin to show respect to those around you. Every life goes through a development process that includes difficult times, as well as rewarding moments. By actively practicing your respect for others, regardless of where they are in this "life process," you create opportunities where you can contribute in small, but often important, ways to the lives of other men and women.

> *"If you have respect for people as they are, you can be more effective in helping them become better than they are."*
>
> JOHN W. GARDNER
> Former Secretary of Health, Education and Welfare

Respect – The Chicken or the Egg

We often read that in order to respect others, we must first respect ourselves. While I'm sure there's some truth in this statement, this approach or way of thinking seems backward. It seems to me that it's through the practice of showing respect for others that you, in fact, gain respect for yourself. You can certainly have respect for the opportunity that your life represents. However, it's difficult to have respect for yourself if you use that opportunity without consideration for how you treat other people. If you want to develop self-respect, you must start by showing more respect for those around you.

Each time you choose to be respectful of someone, even in the smallest of ways, you're choosing to make a positive contribution to your own life and to further define the person you are. Each time you show respect for someone else, you're showing yourself the kind of person you can be. Each time you go out of your way to perform a special act of respect for someone experiencing difficulty, you prove to yourself that you're capable of making a choice that improves your life, as well as the lives of others. Collectively, these acts of respect further define the person you are and the life you have chosen to lead.

The actual practice of respect involves placing another person's feelings or needs ahead of your own. Since we all have a natural tendency to think of ourselves first, this can be a challenging prospect. It's not easy to make choices that favor other people's feelings over yours. The secret, so to speak, is to understand that it is through making other people feel better that you, in turn, feel better yourself. It's through your acts of respect and caring for others that you deliver happiness and well-being to yourself.

> *"The human being who lives only for himself finally reaps nothing but unhappiness.*
> *Selfishness corrodes while unselfishness ennobles and satisfies.*
> *Don't put off the joy derived from doing helpful, kindly things for others."*
>
> B. C. FORBES
> Founder, Forbes magazine

Level I Giving – The Little Things

Maybe someday you'll be in a position to donate millions of dollars to an important charity, your favorite university, or some worthy cause. If you are and if you do, may God bless you for it. However, we don't have to donate a fortune to accomplish something very important with our lives. Instead, just doing the little things can make a big difference not only in how you feel about yourself, but in how you make other people feel as a result of your life touching theirs.

> *My friend, Ed, was one super guy. He was always positive, always interested in what you had to say and always greeted you with a big smile on his face. Ed had an upbeat spirit that you could feel when you were with him. He possessed that wonderful ability to make everyone who knew him feel like they were his very best friend. Every time I was around Ed, I just felt better.*
> *Unfortunately, cancer took Ed's life several years ago. Nevertheless, seldom does a week go by that I don't think about him and wish that he were back here making us feel great again. Ed gave us something very special – a good feeling about ourselves – and I value his friendship to this very day.*

The fundamental question is this: How do you make others feel when they come in contact with you? Are they a little happier, feel a little better, a little more important as a result of how you treated them? If they do, you've developed the ability – recognized or not – to give your respect to others. If not, maybe this is an area of your life that needs your attention. You don't need exceptional skill or intelligence to focus your attention and actions on the well-being of others. You simply need to understand that looking and living outwardly instead of inwardly can change your life dramatically, while making a significant impact on the lives of those around you.

Freddy the Frog was a neat little guy. He was always polite and helpful to others around the pond. He was the first to jump off his lily pad when an older frog was looking for a place to sit. He smiled at all the minnows, laughed at all the turtle jokes, and spoke admiringly to the beavers as they hauled more limbs inside their dams. Freddy always kept an eye out for the little tadpoles and was quick to escort them to safety when Billy the Bass came looking for dinner. Almost everyone in the pond liked Freddy…and they enjoyed their time with him whenever he stopped by.

Tommy the Toad was one smart toad but, unlike Freddy, he was aggressive, competitive, and always looking out for himself. Tommy was quick to grab a potential snack before the other toads could get to it. He would "nudge" others out of his favorite spot on the sunning log, believing he was entitled to his special place. He greeted others, but you could always tell that he was happier that they got the chance to meet him than he was to meet them. Tommy had one primary objective – looking out for Tommy – and he did an excellent job of that.

Over the years, Freddy worked faithfully at his job in pond maintenance and was always quick to respond to the needs of others who lived in the pond. Tommy, on the other hand, worked relentlessly in his business of renting sunning spots on the big log. Freddy enjoyed helping others around the pond. Tommy enjoyed counting his money and looking for the next big log to add to his business. In short, Freddy gave and Tommy took.

When Barney the Beaver announced that his fifth term as mayor of the pond would be his last, Tommy the Toad seized the moment and quickly announced his plan to run for mayor. He had the money, the business experience, and the motivation, but the thought of someone like Tommy being mayor of their nice little pond didn't appeal to those who lived there. After some discussion, a small group approached Freddy and asked him to run for mayor. Freddy was so honored by their request that without much thought about campaign funds or qualifications, he quickly agreed to do so.

It was a spirited campaign, but a lopsided election. In spite of outspending Freddy 10 to 1, Tommy the Toad garnered less than 20 percent of the votes and most of those came from customers who had "the better spots" on the big log. For the first time in pond elections, fish didn't vote for fish and turtles didn't vote for turtles. Because he had been so nice to them, almost everyone "crossed party lines" to vote for Freddy. Freddy couldn't believe the outpouring of support, and he was overjoyed by the thought of how, in his new position, he would be able to help even more citizens with life around the pond.

The point of this little story is that, regardless of what we look like, we are all "in this pond" together. Whether you are a "fish," a "frog" or a "beaver," you can make an important contribution to those around you and help others even though they may look different and be different from you. When our respect for others transcends how they look, we are approaching the truest sense of giving as we make choices to help others without being influenced by how they look or the circumstances they are facing.

This basic level of giving – what I have called "Level I" giving – includes those things that we all have and can pass along to others if we want to. A warm smile, a caring comment, a friendly greeting are all things we can do for someone whether they are our dearest friend, a new acquaintance, or even a total stranger.

> *Getters don't get happiness; givers do. You simply give others a bit of yourself – a thoughtful act, a helpful idea, a word of appreciation, a lift over a rough spot, a sense of understanding, a timely suggestion. You take something out of your mind, garnished in kindness from your heart, and put it into the other fellow's mind and heart.*
>
> CHARLES H. BURR
> Thoughts on Giving

If you want to experiment with this, try passing along a smile to people you encounter and see what you get in return. When you meet a friend or new acquaintance, try showing some real interest, listening to what he has to say, asking a few sincere questions and see what you get in return. When you know of someone who is hurting or has a special need, try going to them and simply saying: "I've been thinking about you, and I certainly hope that things get better" and see what you get in return. We don't have to go out and conquer the world to be important to other people. A little Level I giving works just fine.

I would like for you to consider one more perspective about this type of giving…

> "For I was hungry and you gave me food, I was thirsty and you gave me drink, I was a stranger and you welcomed me, I was naked and you clothed me, I was sick and you visited me, I was in prison and you came to me.' Then the righteous will answer him, saying, 'Lord, when did we see you hungry and feed you, or thirsty and give you drink? And when did we see you a stranger and welcome you, or naked and clothe you? And when did we see you sick or in prison and visit you?' And He answered them, 'Truly, I say to you, as you did it unto one of the least of these my brothers, you did it unto me.'"
>
> THE BIBLE
> Matthew 25: 35-40

Most of us have searched for a better understanding of how God works in the world today. All of us would like to have more clarity as to where God is, and more knowledge of what God is doing. As I've stated, I believe that God lives in each and every one of us and that the spirit we sometimes feel is God "at work" within us and through us as individuals. The verses above seem to support this belief. Therefore, depending on how we choose to treat others, we're either helping or hindering God who I believe is trying to be "at work" in every life. As a result, we could view this basic level of giving, as simple and unimportant as it may appear to be, as a partnership with God – one in which both are trying to enhance the life of another person.

> "We learn that God is; that he is in me; and that all things are shadows of him."
>
> RALPH WALDO EMERSON

Level II Giving – Your Time and Your Money

Obviously, any gift of time or money that you give to someone in need or to some worthwhile institution will be of some benefit. However, common sense tells us that larger donations will help get more done than smaller ones. As a result, institutions and causes that solicit our support tend to focus on the amount of the gift, typically urging us to "do more" or "give more" in order for them to "achieve more." There's nothing wrong with that. But if you want to fully understand the role that giving can play in your life, you need to distinguish between the institution (which is focused primarily on the <u>amount</u> of the gift) and the giver – where it's your <u>attitude</u> toward giving, not the amount, that makes it an important factor in your life.

> "It is the heart of the giver that makes the gift dear and precious."
>
> MARTIN LUTHER
> Started the Protestant Reformation

So, what makes our gifts significant? The significance of our gifts comes not from writing the checks, but from our level of concern and commitment to the people or causes we're supporting. It's not from the amount of time we devote to coaching the kids, but our love and interest is helping them delight in the game. It's not the amount we give to the local shelter, but our concern about helping people return to a normal life. It's not that we give to our church, but our devotion to see that the church is capable of carrying out its work in the community. In other words, it's not the amount, but in feeling the potential impact that our giving may have on others that allows it to be a significant influence in our lives. It's not the gifts, but the love that accompanies those gifts that makes them significant.

Like so many things, developing a more giving life starts with a choice – a decision we make to improve the lives of others by doing whatever we can to help them. That choice may require that we make some adjustments in our life in order to implement it. Few of us have all of the time and money we need, so some reallocations may be required in order to devote more of our resources to a project that is important to us. Our choice must be followed by specific acts of giving – not just our thoughts about giving – if we want to experience the feeling of knowing we did our part.

> *It was 1929 and the Depression was taking its toll, not only on personal lives and established businesses, but on churches and non-profits, as well. As people lost their jobs, they were no longer able to give to their church or meet other financial pledges they had*

made. As a result, churches and other organizations encountered great difficulties paying their staff; many couldn't make their mortgage payments and were subject to foreclosure.

One church, located in a small town in Mississippi, faced this situation and was a matter of days away from being repossessed by its mortgage company. In a last minute meeting to discuss the situation, the church board members were almost unanimous in their feeling that there was nothing they could do.

However, Matthew Keefe, who had been on the board for many years and loved the church, could not bear the thought of it being repossessed. "We gave our word when we made that loan...we have to do whatever is necessary to make sure it gets paid."

Matthew pondered before making a choice few men would make. He went down to the local bank, put his personal residence up for collateral, and borrowed enough money to make the payments on the church building to prevent its foreclosure. Matthew loved his church and wanted to make sure it continued to function. His gift was a reflection of that love.

Almost all of us would agree that giving to a worthy cause is the right thing to do, but, according to recent IRS statistics, less than 30 percent of us record charitable giving on our returns – and those who do donate less than 2 percent of their income to such causes. When we reflect on how much giving to others can enhance our own lives and feeling of self worth, one would have to agree that the greatest self-improvement program available to mankind today is the practice of giving our time and money to help others. Imagine what this country would be like if 100 percent of us gave some portion of our resources to others.

> *"I have been a selfish being all of my life in practice, though not in principle."*
>
> JANE AUSTEN
> English Novelist

This last point is a bit tricky, because I've just said that it's not the amount of our gifts but our attitude toward giving that determines their significance. While this is certainly true, it's also important to take a look at the level of collective giving within your life to determine to what degree you are utilizing your abilities and resources to help other people. Obviously, if on a collective basis you're choosing to give very little of your time or money to others, it will be hard for you to justify that you're living anything other than a self-centered life. I don't have a giving scale that you can use to determine if you're contributing enough or not. However, an honest self-assessment of your giving followed by a few good choices can significantly improve how you feel about yourself and the life that you are living.

There are so many institutions, activities, causes, projects, and people who need your help. Your options are limitless. A special project within your community, a neighbor down your street, a local youth sports team, a growing church, or an important charity…the list goes on and on. Finding a

GOOD CHOICES GOOD LIFE

potential target for your giving is the easy part; making the choice to actually do so is the challenge. The statement that "one person can make a difference" is so true. If you just make the choice and then follow it with action, you may very well change the life of someone who would have otherwise experienced great difficulties without your help or assistance.

> *Oseola McCarty was born in Wayne County, Mississippi, on March 7, 1908. She had to quit school in the sixth grade to help the family make ends meet and to care for her aunt and grandmother. She took in laundry and ironing, charging a going rate of $1.50 a bundle.*
>
> *She ran her laundry business for 75 years and served multiple generations of clients. She put what money she didn't need in the bank. Over the years, her laundry service charge increased to $10.00 a bundle and she was able to save more money. "I would put most of it in savings. Never would take any of it out. It just accumulated," she explained.*
>
> *In 1967, McCarty was left alone after the deaths of her grandmother, mother, and aunt. She kept washing and living frugally in the home she had inherited. She didn't own a car and walked everywhere she needed to go, including to the local supermarket which was more than a mile away.*
>
> *In 1995, at the age of 87 and after taking care of her family and other people's laundry for most of her life, McCarty had no one to take care of her. With the help of her banker, she worked out a plan to provide funds for her care and to provide*

an inheritance for a few members of her extended family. What was left – $150,000 of her $250,000 life savings – she gave to the University of Southern Mississippi and designated it for a special scholarship fund. Having very little formal education, she hoped her money would help talented African-Americans achieve a degree.

Word spread quickly. The fund grew via additional endowments from other USM supporters and Americans inspired by her gift. In addition, Oseola was recognized in many ways for what she had done.

She received the Presidential Citizen's Medal from President Clinton, received an Honorary Doctorate of Humane Letters from Harvard, and was one of Barbara Walters' "Ten Most Exciting People of 1995." In October of 1996, her book <u>Simple Wisdom for Rich Living</u> was released. A review of the book in Newsweek said that McCarty "reminds us that even the humblest among us can leave the world a better place for having walked on it."

At the age of 91, Oseola McCarty died in 1991 of liver cancer in Hattiesburg, MS. Her legacy lives on through the nine students who have to date attended USM on the Oseola McCarty Scholarship and by the countless individuals who have been touched by her generosity.

In an interview with USM, she had been asked why she didn't spend the money on herself. Her reply was, "Oh, but I did."

Level III Giving – Yourself and Your Life

Level III giving starts with believing that your life has an underlying purpose and that your primary role, whatever you choose it to be, is to help improve the lives of other people. It is based on the premise that we are here for each other and, as such, the fundamental objective of our lives should be to do helpful things for other people. It involves seeing your life as an opportunity to make the lives of others better and more enjoyable. Level III giving requires that you consider the purpose of your work or your daily activities to see how the role you're playing is working for the good of others and not simply for yourself.

To clarify, let's look at the basic difference between a "regular banker" and a "Level III giving" banker. The former is likely to see his responsibilities as effectively managing the bank's resources, making good quality loans and working cooperatively with other associates in the bank. All of these are good things, but all are job oriented. The Level III banker recognizes the same responsibilities, but views his job function differently. His primary focus is on the bank's customers…individuals who have needs and are trying to accomplish certain things in their lives. The regular banker sees himself as helping the bank, while the Level III banker views himself as helping the customer. The regular banker sees himself as working for the bank, but the Level III banker sees his role as working for the customer within the guidelines the bank has established for doing business.

Some of you may say I am "splitting hairs" here and that it's just a matter of selecting a viewpoint. That may be true, but, in this case, the viewpoint you have can make a major difference in how you approach your daily activities and how you feel about what you are doing. If you see yourself as only a banker, you're not as likely to feel the importance of what you do. If, on the other hand, you view yourself as a Level III banker, you are much more likely to feel satisfaction from your work and, over time, make more progress in your career. And, while I have used banking in this example, the same would be true for a Level III salesman, a Level III homemaker, or a Level III engineer.

There are many examples of Level III givers including people like Mother Teresa and Martin Luther King, who gave their lives to a cause they believed in. These individuals devoted their lives to helping other people. While we readily recognize their names, there are thousands of other Level III givers, many in your town or neighborhood, who devote their lives to helping others. In thinking about your primary role and the extent to which you are living in Level III mode, here are a few additional points to consider.

Satisfaction in life comes from doing for others, not doing for yourself.

No matter what our ultimate career or life role might be, if we evaluate our options in terms of what we can do for others, not for ourselves, we will come closer to making choices that will bring us great satisfaction from our living. So many times, we make career or role choices based on what we will get – the money, the benefits and the amount of vacation time are some of the typical considerations. While these may be factors in your final choice, you would be better served to think in terms of how your work or primary role in life will help others. How will you make someone's life better? How will you make this world a better place for those who follow? It's what you do for others – not what you get for yourself – that creates the real rewards in life.

More heart-based than head-based.

Whether you are thinking about being a banker or boat builder, a dentist or a doctor, a minister or mother, good career choices depend as much on what you feel in your heart as on what you know in your head. When you make a choice to devote your life to a specific vocation or endeavor, your inner feelings are just as important as your well-thought-out logic. To make a choice that fits your life and its intended direction, you must be sure that you're listening to what your heart is saying to you. If your heart doesn't play a significant role in such a choice, the odds will be against your success as you pursue it.

Your life choice should have some connection to your gifts.

In Chapter 11, I make the point that every individual possesses certain gifts with which to accomplish his or her purpose in the world. To confirm this is true, simply look at the diversity of interests and skills within your own family or group of friends. The people around you are all different, and they're good at different things. So, you should reflect on your own gifts and hopefully achieve a reasonable level of understanding of what these gifts are before making a choice to devote your life to a particular type of work or special cause. In fact, the best way to find a rewarding vocation is to follow your gifts and let them lead you there.

And then there are callings.

Callings evoke the highest form of Level III giving; one in which you have very strong feelings about your commitment to something you want to do. Callings typically require a high level of devotion, much personal sacrifice, and a clear faith that your efforts will help others in very special ways. Devoting your life to a special cause is the giving of a gift like no other. To devote your life to something worthwhile without the expectation of personal gain has to be the highest form of giving. In effect, making your life count for something very special by "losing it" for others.

I don't know the precise difference between making an important choice that you feel is right for you and reacting to a calling that is touching your life in some special way. "There is no checklist against which we can test our callings...no list of ingredients for a true call," writes Gregg Levoy, author of Callings: Finding and Following an Authentic Life. Maybe any feeling that we have to go and serve others is a calling. Clearly, a call is something we feel deep inside and tends to be "a direction" revealed more by our heart than by our head. However we ultimately define them, it seems to me that callings to help others, with their emotional pulls at our heartstrings, are yet more examples of God "at work" in us.

> *"I have ceased to question stars and books;*
> *I have begun to listen to the teachings*
> *my blood whispers to me."*
>
> HERMAN HESSE
> Prolog to Demain

What Will You Give?

What will you give to others that will make a difference in their lives? When will your smile brighten someone's day? When will you take the time to do something special for a friend, a relative, or for someone unknown to you, but in great need? When will you give in a significant way to a special cause or project in your community? The answers to these questions will come from the choices you make in the days and months ahead. Clearly, the choice to live "a giving life" is one that we all can make and the rewards of such a life are many. As John Bunyan reminded us, "A man there was, and they called him mad; the more he gave, the more he had."

CHAPTER 8

Developing Friendships

"There is no wilderness like a life without friends; friendship multiplies blessings and minimizes misfortune; it is a unique remedy against adversity, and it soothes the soul."

BALTASAR GRACIAN
The Art of Worldly Wisdom

The Importance of Friendships

It is important to be aware of the potential influence your friends can have on the choices you make. When such influence is good and proper, you should embrace it. However, you should also understand that close friends can sometimes influence you in bad or improper ways. In your efforts to become who you are – the person you were intended to be – you must use your own good judgment and make your own choices independent of what your friends may say or do.

There are many things we might consider fundamentally important in living a happy and fulfilled life. Experiencing true love, having a wonderful family, watching our children grow up, enjoying a worthwhile career, and helping others would likely be among them. I'm not sure exactly where developing friendships fits into these, but when you stop and think about the things that make life really special, friendships would be near the top of the list. Our friendships not only bring joy in the good times, but they support us in the difficult moments, as well. It is through our interactions with our close friends that we make our lives more enjoyable and create experiences that we cherish and remember for a lifetime.

> *"I keep my friends as misers do their treasure, because, of all things granted to us by wisdom, none is greater or better than friendship."*
>
> PIETRO ARETINO
> Italian Author and Playwright

Our friendships provide us with our own little world inside the larger world in which we live. Friendships establish a framework for many of our activities, provide the audience for many of our conversations, and convey a feeling of belonging and being special. Friendships create a comfort zone in which we can be ourselves, say what is on our minds, or seek advice we know will be offered with true concern. Friendships function as emergency support centers when we have an unexpected problem or trouble within our family life. Friends are, in effect, our "connections" to the world around us and much of our living is experienced with and through the friends we have.

A Few Points About Friendship

There are millions of people living within a few hundred miles of most of us. However, our personal world of friendship includes a very small portion of these. According to Lewis Smith in *Whatever Happened to What's-His-Name?* we have approximately 400 "pals, mates, chums or buddies" during our lifetimes, but only about 30 at any one time. Smith points out that, on average, only six of these would be described as "close friends in whom we can confide and trust." Other studies by federal and state mental health organizations report that our close friends number only about "a dozen or so." Although the exact number is difficult for most of us to pin down, the important point is this – <u>the benefits of friendship are delivered to us by a very limited number of people</u>. Therefore, we should put some careful thought into who our friends will be.

> *"One friend in a lifetime is much;*
> *two are many; three hardly possible."*
>
> HENRY ADAMS
> American Writer and Grandson of President John Quincy Adams

The second point concerning the importance of friendships is this – <u>the level of influence that friendships have in our lives and the way we live is very significant</u>. Your friends can influence you in many ways. What your friend is planning to wear to the party can determine the clothing choices that you make, as well. The opinion that your friends have about politics or something within your community can, with little awareness, become your view. In deciding how you'll spend your time, where your friends want to go and what they want to do can quickly become your plans, too. Even your friends' little sayings or mannerisms can frequently become a part of your conduct. If you fail to manage these influences, you can adopt many things from your friends without feeling that you made a conscious choice to do so.

> *"We've all heard the saying...if your friends jump off a bridge, would you? The answer is probably no, but it is a testament to how powerful friends can be, especially to our kids," explains Curtis Gilbertson, a seventh grade teacher in South Bend, IN. "Friends are everything to these kids, because what their friends do, they do."*
>
> WWW.WNDU.COM / FEBRUARY 15, 2005

Another important point – <u>friends influence your health and the things you do in regard to it</u>. According to research conducted at the University of Iowa, "College students' drinking behaviors are influenced more by their friends' drinking behaviors than by social norms." A New York Times essay by Daniel Goleman reported, "Research on the link between relationships and physical health has established that people with rich personal networks – who are married, have close families and friends and are active in social and religious groups – recover more quickly and live longer."

> *Older adults with a strong network of friends were significantly less likely to die over a 10-year period than older adults with a smaller network of friends according to a 10-year study of the association between friends and longevity published in the July, 2005 <u>Journal of Epidemiology and Community</u>*

> <u>Health</u>. *The study was based on extensive information about each of the 1,477 participants, including age, gender, income, education, physical and mental health status, disabilities, cognitive function, smoking status and activity level. Interestingly, strong social ties with children or other relatives did not positively affect survival.*
>
> URMILA R. PARKER
> Here's to Good Friends and Long Life

When you consider the influence your friends can have, it becomes apparent that your friends can make a very big impact on your life. Friends influence your daily activities and even help you live a longer life. So, as you work to make better choices, choosing your friends seems to be a very important subject.

The Development of Friendships

Although our friends may have a major influence on us and how we live our lives, I'm not sure we stop and think about "friendship development" very much. For most of us, it's a condition that just happens. We don't plan friendships, we don't control them; they just happen, somewhat unexpectedly. One day, we suddenly become aware of a special connection that we have with a neighbor, an associate, or a new acquaintance. We enjoy being around them, and they seem to feel the same way about us. We share special times and look forward to more opportunities to be together. Most of us can't say exactly how a great friendship came to be, but we know what it feels like when it happens.

So, if friendships just happen, maybe we don't need to spend much time thinking about them. If we can't see them coming ahead of time, maybe we should just go about our business and wait for them to come along. If we can't make them happen, maybe we shouldn't ponder the subject in any great detail. Why worry about something we can't control?

While it's true we can't predict specific friendships, the choices we make can determine the groups from which many of our friendships will emerge. You may not consciously select the individuals who become your closest friends, but, through some of the choices you make, you'll determine, to a great extent, from whence they come. Like shopping, although you may not know exactly what you're going to buy when you leave home, you determine the type and quality of the merchandise when you select the stores you will visit.

> *Sydney had just turned 21, and for many years she'd thought this would be the best birthday in her whole life. Instead, she was feeling depressed and wondering what had happened to her. It was a rainy afternoon as she sat and talked with her grandmother, who had tried to take care of her after Sydney's mother died.*
>
> *"Gran, I don't know why things aren't working out for me. I'm trying, I promise, but I can't find a decent job. I don't ever have any money and most of my high school friends don't want to hang out with me anymore. I thought I was going to be so happy when I finally turned 21, but things haven't worked out that way."*

Her grandmother looked at her lovingly as she thought about all of the wild things Sydney had been involved with over the years. "Sydney, you know I love you more than anything in this world, but I must tell you I'm disappointed, too. I could see this coming from the time you were 15 years old. Sydney, I wish I could tell you something different, but you have no one to blame for your unhappiness but yourself."

Sydney knew where her grandmother was headed. She'd been working so hard to be accepted by her friends – getting the requisite tattoos, moving in with her boyfriend, skipping college so she would have more time to play, and wearing outfits like her friends wore. She'd even learned how to drink those special martinis her friends enjoyed so much.

"Sydney, you have made the age-old mistake of thinking that doing what your friends do will make you happy. But that's poor thinking. If you want to be happy and have a nice group of friends, Sydney, you have to start making choices that are good for you, not the choices that make your friends happy."

Sydney sat there for a few minutes before she spoke. "Gran, I know you're right. I've known what you're telling me for some time. I just didn't want to admit that I was being so foolish, or to upset the friends I have. But I'm not sure I can turn my life around by myself. Will you help me?"

Gran looked directly into Sydney's eyes. "Sydney, if you'll commit yourself to making better choices, I will help you. But, if you want to go back out there and just do what your friends do…well, I'm getting too old to worry about you anymore."

Sydney paused for a few moments, then looked directly at her grandmother and said, "Gran, I know I've made this mess and that I've let my so-called friends influence me in the wrong ways. I promise you I'll do better if you'll help me make the right choices this time."

As she and her grandmother had agreed that afternoon, Sydney moved out of her boyfriend's apartment and into one of her own. Over the next eight months, Sydney had frequent "working sessions" at her grandmother's house. First, they changed her look. Sydney removed all of her earrings except one pair, lost the hip-huggers and low-cut blouses, and, covered her tattoos with the new clothes her grandmother had purchased for her. Sydney gave up the martinis and going to the bars with her buddies. Instead, she enrolled in a pre-nursing program at the local college, and spent a lot of time at the library. At her grandmother's urging, she took an after-school job at the local hospital, and the money she earned, along with what her grandmother gave her for college expenses, greatly improved her financial situation.

Eight months later as Sydney sat on a bench outside of the science building, she reflected on her new life. She'd accomplished a lot, and her grandmother had been exactly right about the friendship thing. By making much better choices, she was starting to make much better friends. Abbey, a store clerk who had helped her create a more conservative look, had also turned out to be a great person and was quickly becoming Sydney's best friend. Sydney was particularly enjoying doing things with Jennifer and Samantha, two of the girls who worked at the hospital after school. And although it was way too early to be sure, she was elated when Spencer, a nice-looking guy also working his way through college, asked her to go to the movies with him. She wasn't sure where all of this would lead, but she knew that by taking her grandmother's advice and making better choices, she was developing a new life and a new set of friends as well.

Positioning Ourselves for Friendship

Friendships develop for a variety of reasons. In part, due to proximity, you're much more likely to become friends with someone close by than someone who is far away. In part, due to common interests; the seeds of a life-long friendship are often sown as people work together or involve themselves in shared pursuits. In part, friendships are due to chemistry; how you make each other feel when you're together. Over time, your friendships align themselves with these three factors – where you go physically (proximity), the activities you choose to pursue (interests), and the ways you make other people feel (chemistry).

If we want to improve the quality of our friendships, we must improve the quality of our choices in these three areas. For example, the friends you make at a bar aren't likely to be the same type of friends you make at the gym. The friends you make when you're trying to become a member of a gang aren't the same as the friends you'll make if you're trying to become a member of the basketball team. The friends you make if you're a boisterous know-it-all aren't the same type of friends you'll make if you're courteous and truly interested in other people. Maybe friendships do "just happen," and maybe you can never be certain when they'll occur. That doesn't mean, however, that you can't position yourself for friendships that will have a positive influence on your life.

> "A man is judged by his friends, for the wise
> and the foolish have never agreed."
>
> BALTASAR GRACIAN
> The Art of Worldly Wisdom

What are some choices you can make to position yourself for good friendship development? What can you do to properly influence the type of friends you will have? Although I'm sure there are others, here are some fundamental choices that I feel are important in positioning yourself for the development of good and proper friendships.

Go where the right friends are

If we want to develop new friends, especially the right kind of friends, we have to pick the spots where such friendships can occur. You can select a number of places or activities where the kind of people you seek may be. By selecting the right places and activities, it is possible to pre-qualify potential friendships. There are a number of good "locations" for friendship development including church functions, school activities, community development projects, work with non-profit organizations, travel with selected special interest groups, after-school tutoring programs, and serving meals to shut-ins. Where the activity or mission is to serve a good purpose, you are likely to find good and interesting people.

Show your interest in other people

We've all been in those one-way conversations where the other person, for some strange reason, believes that we're really interested in every last detail about her hip operation: what the doctor said, what the X-rays showed, what the surgery was like and every detail of her six-week recovery period. Although usually an innocent mistake, boring the other person to death is no way to start a life-long friendship. Instead, you should learn to use the power of asking questions to show your interest in the other person. In doing so, you may not only learn something, but you'll increase your chances of developing a new and interesting friendship.

> *"You can make more friends in two months by becoming really interested in other people, than you can in two years by trying to get other people interested in you."*
>
> DALE CARNEGIE
> Be yourself

People are almost always attracted to those who are genuine. Other qualities seem to be secondary to the importance of "being real" and honest in our conversations. Many of us, especially in situations that involve meeting new people, feel that we must prove that we are a worthy choice for a friendship. As a result, we feel the pressure to tell our best stories to make a favorable impression. There's no real problem in doing this, but you should remain mindful that you are not there to impress anyone. You are there to be polite and to be yourself remembering that you never know when a new friendship might develop. You should simply be yourself, and work to develop a true interest in the other person through your questions and inquiries about them. This is a much more effective approach to friendship development than one in which you make an effort to impress someone with how special you really are.

A Friend is a Friend is a Friend... or Maybe Not

If someone asked us to make a list of our good friends, some careful thought would likely produce a list of 20 to 30 people. This list might include friends from high school or college, friends from work, friends who live in our neighborhood, and friends from church, sports, or other activities. If we categorized each of these friends as 1) acquaintances, 2) good friends, or 3) very close friendships, we would likely have friends in each of these groups.

The point is this: there are different types of friends or, more precisely, different levels of friendship. Not everyone whom we consider "a friend" would also be considered "a <u>close</u> friend." Therefore, you should be mindful of these different levels of friendship, especially when you feel that a choice you're about to make is being influenced by "a friend" of yours. You may make the mistake of allowing an acquaintance – someone you really don't know that well – to influence an important choice you are about to make. Unless you know someone well, you should be careful how you accept their advice or allow them to influence your choices.

In addition, you should expect that your mix of friends will change over time. Over the years, you can lose track of your best friend from high school or that special person you worked with when you took your first job. A person who is exerting influence over your life today may not even be around or even considered to be a friend months or years from now. Your group of friends will change over time. Therefore, you must work to make choices that are right for you over the long term, not necessarily right for the friends you have <u>today</u>.

Close Friends vs. Good Friends

This is an important distinction, especially considering that the influence of our friends can be a significant factor in many of the choices we make. All <u>close</u> friends are not necessarily <u>good</u> friends, and the opposite is true, as well. We frequently make the mistake of thinking that close friends and good friends are one and the same.

Good friends want what's best for you, in spite of what the circumstances might be at the moment. Good friends influence you in positive, do-the-right-thing ways. Good friends don't cause you to make rash decisions or lead you to do the wrong things. If you're going to trust someone, it should be someone who is not only a good friend but is, in fact, striving to make good choices in his or her life, as well.

Close friends, on the other hand, may or may not be good friends. Many of us have close friends who, for a variety of reasons, have made serious mistakes in their lives or lived in a questionable way. If we follow their lead or allow them to influence us, we might do the same. Such friendships are the result of a unique chemistry. We like these people in spite of the choices they made. That is as it should be. However, you must understand that some of your close friends may not be a good friend when it comes to the influence they have on your life.

> *It was a very special week for Brianna. On Saturday she was going to be 18. As part of her birthday celebration, she went out to dinner the night before with her two dearest friends, Jessica and Emma. She had known both of them since the first grade and, in addition to spending most of their free time together, they knew everything about each other: their crushes, the problems they had at home, their favorite movie stars, fashion preferences, and even the type of guy they wanted to marry. It had been a tight little group for many years.*
>
> *Over dinner, the conversation turned to sex as the girls had become increasingly interested in the subject in recent months. "I'm going to give Brady the surprise of his life this weekend," Jessica said. "He's been trying, but I think it's time for me to see what it is like. In fact, it's time for all of us to experience this for ourselves." Jessica had always been aggressive in her thinking, but these "green light" comments surprised even Brianna and Emma.*

Developing Friendships

The next day as they were walking to their cars after school, Brianna asked Emma what she thought about the suggestions Jessica had made the night before.

"Well," Emma slowly replied, "it's a choice we'll each have to make for ourselves. But from what my big sister says, boys will take advantage of you and then move on. I don't think that's something I'm ready for, and I'm not sure you're ready, either."

Jessica and Emma were two of Brianna's best friends, but they were influencing her in such different ways. Jessica was yelling "yes" to her, but Emma was quietly saying "no."

Over the next few days, Brianna thought a lot about what Jessica and Emma had said. It was turning into a real learning experience for her – how two close friends, people she'd known for most of her life, could try to influence her in such different ways. But Brianna was smart – she knew that the final choice was hers to make.

"God gives us our relatives; thank God we can choose our friends."

ETHEL MUMFORD

It is only natural to want as many friends as possible. Therefore, we don't tend to be very critical or restrictive when the opportunity for a new friendship presents itself. However, we should be careful to consider the qualities that our friends have and choose which of those qualities will influence our lives. In other words, we want to welcome friends into our lives, but remain on guard as to how we will let our friends influence our behavior and what we choose to do. Our focus should remain on our own personal growth and development, and we should be wary of individuals who, through their choices, detract from our goal of becoming the person we were intended to be.

CHAPTER 9

Letting Love into Your Life

"And think not you can guide the course of love. For love, if it finds you worthy, shall guide your course."

Kahlil Gibran

"On Love"/The Prophet

Bingo!

Suddenly, you just feel it. You don't know where it came from or exactly what created it, but all of a sudden you detect this special feeling about someone in your life, or about something you are doing or wanting to do. You didn't find this special feeling; it found you. It's not a feeling you created, or made happen, but rather it was an unexpected development that resulted from your interactions with other people, your involvement with something that you enjoy doing, or, in some cases, simply your thoughts about something you hope will happen in the future.

We don't choose love like we would choose to buy a car or go on a trip. Instead, love chooses us and can appear in our lives in unexpected ways and at unexpected times. Love is one of life's most important signals as we work to discover what we should do with our lives and what choices we should make to get there. We must be mindful of how love works so that we recognize its influence when it tries to enter our lives. Equally as important, we must be willing to follow that recognition with choices that allow this love to develop and play its very important role in the person we ultimately turn out to be.

At times, love can be the most important influence in your life and, as such, it can play a major role in how your life develops. Its presence can control your thoughts, "floating you away" into a world of hopes, dreams, and wonder. Love creates a special drive within you and can lead you to make great sacrifices to accomplish something you deem to be important. The motivation that love provides can be the difference between an average performance and an extraordinary achievement – the difference between an average and an extraordinary life. Love is indeed a wonder drug, and its presence can energize you in very special ways.

The challenge is to be able to recognize love when it appears and to have respect for what this special feeling can do in our lives. Hopefully, most of our choices are very logical ones as we "think our way through" the life we are living. However, love is not always logical. It is a feeling that can stimulate us to head off in a direction that only we understand, to devote our lives to an important work, or to care for an individual whose friendship we value greatly. If we want to develop a life that has excitement, energy, and accomplishment, we must be willing to look beyond our logical moments, and, when love is "at work" in our lives, to rely on the feelings that it provides.

> "Whoso loves, believes the impossible."
> ELIZABETH BARRET BROWNING

Many of us would describe our lives as "about average." While there's certainly nothing wrong with this label, there seems to be a need inside each of us to experience more than average conditions. We have this life and, whether we openly acknowledge it or not, we want it to be a special one. The difficulty, however, lies in making it so. One the best ways to accomplish this objective – to create a special life – is to be open to love and willing to follow where it leads.

> *Graham was in the ninth grade and lived in a poor part of town in an old house that needed repainting. His mom worked hard to keep food on the table and to provide suitable clothes for Graham and his younger sister. Although they had few material things, his mother's work ethic and almost constant urging to do his homework every night gave him some early insights into what was required to be successful in life.*
>
> *Since the mayor announced the plans to build NASCAR's largest and most active raceway just outside the city, all Graham and his buddies could talk about was racing...who was the best driver, which type of car was better, and who would win at Talladega this year. The more Graham learned about the sport, the greater his desire became to be a part of it some day.*

By the beginning of his junior year, the new track and grandstands were nearing completion. Graham followed the progress closely. He'd even go out to the track several times a week to stand behind the fence and watch the construction. As the structure took shape, Graham could easily visualize more than 100,000 people in the stands and the cars racing around the track. As the checkered flag came out, it was his favorite driver who won yet again.

One afternoon when he was turning to leave the construction site, Graham was approached by an older gentleman in a racing jacket. "Hello, young man," he said. "I bet I've seen you out here at least 10 or 15 times. Do you like NASCAR?" Before he could respond, the gentleman continued, "By the way, I'm Red Gibbons. I own the Gibbons Racing Team, and we're moving our operation here next week."

Young Graham, almost blown away by the sudden appearance of the well-known Red Gibbons, somehow managed to say, "Yes sir, Mr. Gibbons, I love NASCAR and I want to be a part of it some day."

Red studied the young man for a few more moments and then in his customary, quick-decision style, said to Graham, "Well, if it's okay with your folks, you can join our team and work for us every day after school." Graham couldn't believe that this was happening to him.

That night, he told the whole story to his mother and, being as insightful as she was, she could easily see that Graham's excitement – and his love – were for real. "Graham, we could certainly use the extra money. As long as you keep your grades up, it's okay with me."

Graham was ecstatic. "Oh, thank you, Mother!" he shouted. He couldn't wait to tell Mr. Gibbons what she had said.

Graham loved being on the Gibbons Racing Team. He worked every afternoon after school and volunteered to work all day on Saturdays, as well. Graham was given all the grunt work…cleaning up oil spills, going to get lunch for everyone, and replenishing the parts bin. In spite of these assignments, Graham did them enthusiastically and quickly won the admiration of long-time members of the team. And, he was learning so much from these guys – about cars, about hard work, about competition, and about people.

From time to time, Corey, the lead mechanic who had worked for Gibbons for many years, would let him use some of the tools. At first, it was just to disassemble something so the more experienced mechanics could work on it. But Corey noticed Graham's care and precision, and realized that Graham's love for the sport was turning into a special talent. It wasn't long until Corey gave him the task of helping one of the guys redo the brakes on the team's No. 2 car. Graham loved every second of it.

The next two years flew by, and Graham couldn't believe that his senior year was coming to a close. Several of the team members came to watch Graham graduate second in his high school class. Although Graham enjoyed the moment, he was also worrying about finding a full-time job to help his mother. His alcoholic father, who lived in another city, had recently stopped sending his mother any money due to Graham's graduation. "Tell that boy to find a real job," he had said.

Graham's mother worked on the production line at Lowell's Dairy Products for almost 25 years, and her boss had agreed to hire Graham full-time. When Graham's mother told him about the job offer that night, Graham thought it was just about the worst news he'd ever heard.

The next afternoon, Graham explained everything to Corey about his mother's financial situation and the job offer from Lowell's Dairy. "I love working with you and the guys more than anything in this world, Corey, but I won't be able to help my mother like I need to if I'm only working part time," Graham said quietly. Corey could see how disappointed Graham was, but he also knew that Graham was the type of young man who would do whatever he had to do to help his mom. It was the same dedication Graham had shown in his work on the team. It was this dedication and his love of the sport that had led Corey to believe that Graham would be a great member of their racing team.

"Graham, I've already talked to Mr. Gibbons, and we'd like for you to continue with us as a full-time junior mechanic. "The starting pay is probably less than your offer from the dairy, but with the potential victory bonuses you should do just fine. And, Graham, you were made for this business. I don't know what brought you to the fence where Red found you that day, but he was just as lucky to find you as you were to find him."

When Graham talked to his mother, she told him something that he never forgot: "Graham, some people do things for love, and some for money. If you take the route you love, you'll be a very successful man. And, don't worry about the difference in the money Graham, we'll be okay."

Four years later, Graham was standing in the pits at Talladega with his headset on. He loved every minute he spent on the Gibbons Racing Team. Working full-time, his skills developed quickly, and his teammates respected him for his dedication and hard work. Corey had promoted him several times, most recently to senior mechanic, the youngest in NASCAR. As Graham watched the Gibbons car pass first under the checkered flag, he relished the thought that this victory bonus would be the down payment on that new house he was going to buy for his mom.

Love will guide us if we just let it. Love will bring special people and stimulating activities into our lives if we recognize when love is "at work" within us. The truth is, it's impossible to live a happy life without love in it. You need love's connections to other people and to activities that stimulate your skills and interests. But, for it to do so, you must be respectful of love and willing to let it "work its magic" when it comes knocking at your door.

> *"Love is a sport in which the hunter must contrive to have the quarry in pursuit."*
>
> ALPHONSE KERR

Responding to Love When It Appears

We can be so busy with our family, work, or school activities that we don't even notice when love is trying to play a role in our lives. We all have things that must get done, and, therefore, we can become so focused on them that we fail to recognize love when it tries to signal us in some special way. It's always helpful to take some time away from your daily routine to think about the feelings you may be experiencing. Is love trying to tell you something? Is love trying to provide a sense of direction about something in your life? If you feel that love may be trying to direct some aspect of your life, find the time to think carefully about what love's message might be saying to you.

We may feel love pulling on our lives but not be willing to make the choices or pay the price required to follow its path. For example, a person may love to be around animals and take a special interest in their well being, but still not be willing to devote the years of work and study required to become a successful veterinarian. When you are unwilling to accept the responsibilities that love places upon you, in effect, you turn love away. Love is looking for everyone, but there's no guarantee we will recognize it or respond appropriately when it appears.

Here is one more thing to think about. You may have clearly defined goals and be working hard to accomplish them when love comes along and attempts to send you off in a different direction. You may be marching down a well-defined path when love comes along and presents a new one. If you feel this happening in your life, you should not make the mistake of thinking that a personal goal, well-developed though it may be, is more important than the goal that love may now be trying to set for you. Without the presence of love in establishing our goals, we can live totally logical lives, but yet be void of the special feelings that love provides and which are so fundamental to our success.

Love isn't going to handcuff you and haul you off in some new direction. Instead love makes its effort to enter your life and does its best to direct you in very special ways. However, you make the choice of how you will respond to love…whether you will follow where it leads or simply head off in another direction.

> *Carl was a good student, and with a little extra work, he graduated in the top 10% of his high school class. He thought he wanted to be an engineer and headed off to college with that in mind. In his freshman English class, he particularly enjoyed writing essays and his teacher frequently wrote glowing comments on his papers.*

Love was tapping on Carl's shoulder, but he didn't feel a thing.

Carl soon switched from engineering to business. Although not an exceptional student by any means, he was quickly acknowledged by his advertising professor for his knack for writing motivating messages in his advertising campaigns. *Love was waving another flag at Carl, but he still didn't see it.*

Carl graduated from college and embarked on a successful business career. His forte was planning and, more specifically, putting those plans in writing so that others could clearly understand the goals and direction of the business. The chairman of the company pulled Carl aside one day, "Carl, the plans that you have written really motivated and united our management team. You did a great job of pulling all of our thoughts together." *Love was sending another signal to Carl, but it went flying by him with little notice.*

Carl had a successful business career and retired comfortably, but there was something missing in his life. He wanted to do something else, but he wasn't sure what it was. As he reflected on his life one day, he thought about some of the comments that people had made to him over the years. His freshman English teacher: "I really enjoyed reading your paper." His advertising professor: "I feel something when I read your copy." His old boss: "Your plan has motivated our management team." Suddenly, it became clear to him – he loved to write. *Love had*

> been trying to reach him all of this time, but only
> now had it finally gotten his attention.
>
> Carl is working on his first book. It may never
> be published, but that isn't the important thing.
> What <u>is</u> important is that Carl found his love and
> the time and effort that he's putting into his writing
> are rewarding and satisfying to him. This love
> had been there all along; it just took Carl almost a
> lifetime to recognize it. So it is with each of us. It's
> not what we do, but in finding the love of what we
> do that really counts.

While Carl in the example above would agree that it is never too late for love to find you, his life might have been different if he had recognized love tapping on his shoulder many years before. Recognizing love when it comes along is not always easy. How do you know it's love? How do you know when love is trying to get your attention? Is this the real thing or some other motivation? Only when you listen with your heart can you recognize love when it appears. If you are not careful, love will come to you, but, as a result of your choice to head in another direction, you turn love away.

> The old Christian gentleman was stranded in
> his home by a flash flood. As he thought about
> his many years of faithful service to God, he was
> confident that God would take care of him in these
> circumstances. As the waters rose, the old man
> climbed up on his roof to escape the flood. As he
> was sitting on the roof, two men came by in a boat
> and offered him a ride, but the old man, responded,

> "No thanks, God will rescue me!" Later, after the water continued to rise, he climbed to the top of the chimney. A helicopter appeared, but he waved it away and shouted, "No problem, God will save me!"
>
> Well, as things turned out the waters rose even more and the old man drowned. When he got to the pearly gates, he was really miffed about the whole thing and told St. Peter, "Look, I've been a good and faithful servant all of my life and you guys let me drown."
>
> St. Peter looked at him, somewhat amazed, and replied, "We sent a boat and a helicopter...what more could we do?"

Like the old gentleman who turned down his rescuers, we sometimes fail to let love help us even though it is trying to do so. How do you prevent this from happening to you? How can you make sure you don't "miss the signal" when it appears? First, you must remember that love finds you, not the other way around. Love can come and redirect your life at any time. Love can touch you at any moment, lighting up your life with a new mission or objective. Therefore, if you want love to guide your life, you start the process by simply being open to love, even though you don't know when and where it might appear.

Next, you must remember that love is a feeling, not necessarily a logical thought. As Shakespeare described it, love "sees with the heart and not the mind." Therefore, for love to guide you, you must be aware of your feelings and be able to distinguish when love is signaling you in some way. Such feelings may not be clearly understood at first, but if you're willing to acknowledge the love you are feeling and work to clarify your understanding of its message, love will at some point clarify a course for you to follow.

Once a love becomes known to you, it requires the support of good choices. You may have this wonderful feeling about something you want to do in your life, but if you can't make the choices to follow it, nurture it and go where it leads, that love will do little for you. You may already have plans or a vision for your life when love steps in and attempts to send you in a different direction. It may be that you were expecting to "marry Taylor" or "be an architect" or "live in California" when love comes along and speaks to you about doing things a totally different way. For love to work in your life, you have to be both ready for it to arrive and willing to follow where love leads.

> *"Perhaps love is the process of life leading you back to yourself."*
>
> ANTOINE DE SAINT-EXUPERY
> French Novelist

Letting Love Lead You

Whether we recognize it or not, we can achieve important things with the lives we have been given. We may have obstacles, but they can be overcome. We may have handicaps, but they can be offset. We may lack skills, but they can be developed. We may not know the way, but it can be found. You have the opportunity to do something special with your life. If you believe that you possess this potential and open the door to let love enter and help you live in a very special way, you can accomplish much in the time you have left on this earth.

If, at the moment, you aren't satisfied with your life, you shouldn't simply accept your circumstances. Don't let yourself off the hook by saying: "Well, I'm doing the best I can!" Few of us are doing our very best, and everyone has room for improvement. No matter how unhappy you may be right now, you can go on to live a special and rewarding life if you will allow love to be "at work" in you. You can start a change in your life by opening yourself to love, listening carefully to what love is saying to you, and then making the choices that allow love to lead your life.

> *Ava's life was really coming together as she neared the end of her freshman year in college. She loved college life and everything about it. Ava had pledged her favorite sorority and been elected president of her pledge class. She had decided to be a nutritionist and was off to a flying start toward that objective. She'd achieved a 3.5 average over the first two quarters and was confident she would have a 4.0 in the current term. She had dozens of friends and was clearly a favorite with her sorority sisters. She had even met a wonderful boy, Jeff, who was a leader on campus and, as the other girls put it, he was "easy on the eyes."*
>
> *Ava enjoyed her classes, her professors, and going to the sorority house for her meals and meetings with her fellow sisters. She also valued her*

time with Jeff. She even liked walking through the campus and frequently sat under the trees to do her studying. Ava often thought to herself: "Life just doesn't get any better than this."

But things suddenly changed. She could not believe it when the doctor told her, "No question about it Ava, you are pregnant." What in the world was she going to do? She'd never disappointed her parents in her entire life, and now what would they think? Her sorority sisters had come to count on her for leadership, but how would they feel about her if she couldn't carry on her work with them? How could she ever get through the rigors of college if she had a baby to look after? The good life seemed to be coming to a screeching halt as she sat there reflecting on her situation.

When she told Jeff, he quickly offered the solution, "Ava, I have a trust fund…we'll use it to pay for an abortion." She could not believe that Ava Ann McDougal, who less than a year ago was the valedictorian of her high school class, was now in this predicament.

Ava slept very little, studied even less, and was constantly worrying over her options of having the baby or having an abortion. Clearly, the abortion would be the easy way to go. No one would ever know and she could get back to the life she was enjoying when this unexpected news came along. On the other hand, she wondered about the life that was now inside her. What would this child look like and what kind of a person would he or she grow up to be? Could she ever overcome the void she would feel if she never saw or never heard the baby that was now growing inside of her?

Jeff, who had now realized that this would change his life as well, was pushing Ava hard. "I've found the doctor," he said as he urged her to take the abortion route. Although she wanted to follow Jeff's plan, she still wondered what this child might become some day should she decide to be its mother.

Ava finally confided in her friend, Mary Ellen, and explained the choice she was facing. "No one can make this decision for you" she told Ava. "It's your choice to make because you will be the one who will live with that choice, whatever it may be. Ava, there is no greater love than a mother's love for her child, and it's that love that you should consider in making the choice that you have to make. Although unexpected, a special love is trying to enter your life. You can let it in or you can turn it away."

They sat there for several seconds, then Mary Ellen continued, "I don't know what you should do, but this much I do know. When we have the right kind of love in our lives, everything else seems to work out okay."

As Ava walked back across campus, the potential repercussions of her situation were passing through her mind...her parents' reactions, how her wonderful sorority life would end, how she might never become a nutritionist, and the many other college experiences she might now miss. Clearly, an abortion would keep all of those things on track.

That seemed to be the best answer. Then, Ava thought about what Mary Ellen had said "when we have the right kind of love in our life, everything else seems to work out okay." Somehow, love seemed to be the key factor in this decision. She would have to think about that before she gave Jeff her decision that night.

Over 20 years later, Ava and Jeff were sitting in the large crowd at their alma mater. With their 15-year old daughter, Jenn, they were attending the school's graduation ceremonies. As the commencement speaker charged the seniors with their responsibilities to make their contributions to this world, she began to think about the contribution she had made: Jeff Jr. He had been a challenge at times, but today he was graduating in the top 10% of the class. He had proven to be a leader throughout his high school and college years, winning many honors, and serving as president of his college fraternity. And, yes, like his dad, he was easy on the eyes.

Mary Ellen was right..."when we have the right kind of love in our life, everything else seems to work out okay." She and Jeff had been married for 21 years, and their love had seemed to increase as the years went by.

As Ava sat there, floating in her thoughts, she knew that she had made the right choice that day. She knew that she would have achieved most of these other things in her life...getting married, becoming a nutritionist, having a family...but without "JJ" as they called him and the love they

> *shared, it just would not have been the same. She remembered Mary Ellen's words... "Although unexpected, a special love is trying to enter your life. You can let it in or you can turn it away." Ava sat there being thankful...thankful that she had listened to Mary Ellen, thankful that "JJ" had entered her life, and thankful that she now understood the importance of making love a priority in every choice she makes.*

Letting love lead us doesn't mean that life will always be easy, but it will definitely be more enjoyable. Love increases our commitment to do more with our lives and to work harder at making our lives count for ourselves and those around us. So, take a longer view of your life and believe that you can accomplish special things. Although you may not know what these special things are at this moment, discovering and following the love in your life will most certainly get you where you need to go.

Where Does Love Come From?

We all would like to have a better understanding of how this happens – how love comes to play such an important role in our lives. It becomes a little clearer to me when I reflect on my belief concerning the relationship between love "at work" and God "at work" in our lives. I believe that God works in and through people and not through lightning bolts or modern day miracles. Therefore, it seems logical to me that love is the way God works "in us" to reach and help other people. For example, the cure for some disease may come via an individual whose love of medicine was so great that she devoted her life to such a discovery. Or another is the fact that the assistance a young widow and her children need may be delivered by a "love touched" couple who live right down the street.

In order to accomplish these things, I believe that God has given each of us certain feelings, interests, and motivations along with the opportunity to use them in some special way. Therefore, one could logically say that love is God speaking to us and confirming what we should do with our lives. I believe your willingness to let love guide your life is not only the way you find your intended way in this world, but, in doing so, you come to an understanding of the purpose God has for your life.

If you carry this thinking one step further, you may start to wonder why certain loves develop within one person, while different loves develop within another. To explain this by simply saying that each of us is different doesn't seem adequate. Again, I see this as God "at work," but with a broader objective. Whatever God's plan is for this world, it will be accomplished through people like you and me. Because this world has lots of problems God needs each of us to be "at work" if we are ever to have a world where peace and caring are the order of the day. As a result, we've been given different skills and abilities so that we will be equipped – as a community – to help each other "have life and have it more abundantly."

If this is true, why is there so much strife in the world? If God is "at work" in this way, why do we seem to be getting further from a state of universal caring in this world, not closer to it? The reason is because collectively we're not listening to the love in our lives – we're not letting love guide us. We're trying to guide ourselves with logic, misguided though it may be. Many of us have turned a deaf ear to the love that God is trying to awaken in our lives. Instead of working to feel and spread that love, many of us are making choices without consideration of the role that love may be playing in the lives of people throughout the world. One has to wonder if the countries in this world fought their wars with doctors, farmers, nurses, and engineers who had love in their hearts for a problem country instead of soldiers equipped with guns and ammunition, just how long any war would last.

If you start to identify with what I'm trying to say about God "at work" in this world, you will agree with my last point…<u>every</u> <u>single</u> <u>life</u> <u>is</u> <u>important</u>! If you believe as I do that every person comes equipped with certain interests and abilities, that God has inspired these qualities within them, and that through love these qualities are confirmed and brought to life, you understand why <u>every</u> life has a role to play. As I see it, every person, regardless of their age or circumstances, is a part of God "at work" in this world. Therefore, to interfere with any life is to interfere with God's work. Therefore, it seems to me that if we are ever to achieve a state of universal caring, we must come to value <u>every</u> life as each one – born and unborn – has an intended role to play in the plan God has for this world and for the people in it.

> *"When I speak of love, I am speaking of that force*
> *which all great religions*
> *have seen as the supreme unifying force of life.*
> *Love is the key that unlocks the*
> *door to ultimate reality."*
>
> MARTIN LUTHER KING, JR.
> Where Do We Go From Here?

Maybe understanding God is not as complicated as we have tried to make it. Maybe your connection with God is not dependent on an impressive church building or on large choirs singing lovely anthems. Maybe your relationship with God is not dependent upon your knowledge of things that transpired hundreds of years ago or your ability to interpret the stories of miracles that have been passed down through the ages. Maybe it's not a matter of just doing the things that will "get you to Heaven" someday. Maybe it doesn't matter which religious denomination you belong to, but simply on your willingness to connect – on a personal level – with the love in your life.

Maybe it's just a matter of being more aware of love and bringing love into a greater focus within you. Maybe an understanding of God is developed by looking and listening for love in your life and being willing to follow the path that love provides. Maybe it's really a matter of letting love lead you and show you the way as you do your part to help those around you. Maybe God is love and, if you ever want to understand God and feel God's presence, you must honor the role that love plays in your life, allowing love to guide almost every choice you make. Just maybe.

> *"Fear of God builds churches, but love of God builds men."*
>
> LOUIS O. WILLIAMS
> American Botanist

Being able to identify and distinguish love in our hearts from the many other emotions that we feel is an important ability. While love does indeed find us, so do many other feelings.

Because love is so important and fundamental to developing the life we were intended to have, clarifying love and the signals it provides is well worth your time and effort. The all-important question…is this real love leading me or is it something else? The right answer is often the difference in making a good choice and making a poor one.

CHAPTER 10

Discovering Your Gifts

"Now, go and be the person you were born to be."
Anonymous

Our Gifts

Have you ever wondered why each of us is so different? One person loves the outdoors, while another prefers to be inside reading a book. One person excels in math, yet the student next to him is a history buff. One of us wants to fly airplanes, but another prefers to walk in the woods. One wants to paint, another to sing, and another to have a business of her very own. One wants to move to the city, and another to the countryside. One is motivated to be a doctor, another to be an engineer. We may be similar on the outside, but inside, where it really counts, we are very, very different.

Each of us has certain qualities, or "gifts" as they are referred to here, that when discovered and properly utilized, allow us to make a special contribution to the people and the world around us. These gifts are personal "ingredients" that, over time, give our lives uniqueness and the ability to develop and accomplish intended things. These qualities may reside in our minds, our hearts, our bodies, or even in our souls. They may be reflected in our abilities to speak, to think, to teach, or to lead. They may help us become an influential parent, or even a long-remembered friend. These gifts push us in certain directions, create our special interests, and, in some instances, motivate us to dedicate our lives to an important cause. If we let them, our gifts will fuel our very existence and help us achieve great satisfaction from our living.

During your infant years, your gifts are hidden although they may already be developing within you. As you move into your childhood and teenage years, these gifts start to surface and become noticeable as long as you don't hinder their development or extinguish them outright by the choices you make. As you enter adulthood, you have many opportunities to confirm and activate your gifts provided you don't let "the ways of the world" distract you from this work. No question about it...discovering, confirming, and utilizing your personal gifts are three of the most important projects you will ever undertake.

> *"Every individual has a place to fill in the world and is important,
> whether he chooses to be so or not."*
>
> NATHANIEL HAWTHORNE
> The Scarlet Letter

Whether you believe so at this moment or not, you are very special. You have interests, feelings, and abilities that not only make you unique, but also position you for making important contributions to the people and the world around you. I personally take these circumstances one step further in that I believe that these personal qualities, or gifts, define much of our purpose for being here, and, potentially, the life we were intended to live. The challenge for us is twofold. First, is to discover our gifts and clarify our understanding of them. Second, is to make choices that allow these gifts to grow and develop for the benefit of ourselves and for others.

The Gift Discovery Process

Gift discovery is a personal process, a voyage of undetermined duration that you choose to undertake for yourself. While other people may influence or help you along the way, the ultimate identification of your gifts depends on you and choices you make based on feelings that you have. The process requires a careful evaluation of what your interests are telling you and a totally truthful self-examination of what is "driving you" or starting to do so. The outcome is dependent on your ability to decode certain inclinations that you have and a determination of what your feelings are telling you. Although it may take time to develop the understanding you seek, you can be assured that your life is trying to speak to you and tell you what it wants to do – you have to find a way to interpret what it is saying.

It is one thing to determine what you <u>want to do</u> with your life. It is something altogether different to determine what you were <u>meant to do</u>. The former is simply a matter of searching the marketplace, identifying the alternatives, and selecting the one you like best. The latter, on the other hand, requires that you look inside yourself to determine "what you are made of" and to decide how you will utilize the life you've been given. The former is low risk as we often tell ourselves that if our selection doesn't work out, we can always do something else.

The latter is high risk because if we choose to pursue the wrong gifts or not pursue our gifts at all, we can spend our entire life doing things we were never intended to do.

> *"A man's true greatness lies in the consciousness of an honest purpose in life, founded on a just estimate of himself and everything else, on frequent self-examinations, and a steady obedience to the rule which he knows to be right, without troubling himself about what others may think or say, or whether they do or do not that which he thinks and says and does."*
>
> MARCUS AURELIUS ANTONINUS

As a result of the busy lives we lead and the difficulty of the task, most of us will have to focus carefully on the discovery of our gifts. In order to do this successfully, we have to make the identification and confirmation of our gifts a high priority in our lives. And, the identification of those gifts will be just the starting point, as you must then be willing to make the choices that support their development. Gift discovery and development is like many things in life – you have to devote time and effort to it if you want to achieve something important.

This is a personal process, and each of us will pursue it, work on it, and hopefully reach a state of understanding in our own way. Therefore, there are no step-by-step directions I can offer that will get you there. It does begin with a specific choice: the choice you make to do the work required to identify the gifts that are yours. In other words, the ultimate discovery of your gifts depends on your choice to do so. By making this choice, you are committing yourself to finding a higher purpose for your life, one that is far beyond the objective of successfully reaching retirement someday. It may take you months, years, or almost a lifetime, but you're not likely to discover and confirm your gifts if you don't commit yourself to doing so. Your personal gifts exist, but only you can make the choices required to discover them.

> *"If a man has a talent and does not use it, he has failed.*
> *If he has a talent and uses only half of it, he has partly failed.*
> *If he has a talent and somehow learns to use the whole of it,*
> *he has gloriously succeeded*
> *and won a satisfaction and triumph*
> *few men will ever know."*
>
> THOMAS WOLFE
> American Novelist

Where Do Our Gifts Come From?

This is an important question and, as we know, there is no clear-cut answer. My personal belief is that our gifts are God-given, although I have no idea of how they are "inserted" into our lives. Although I believe that God provides these gifts – or places us in circumstances in which we will receive them – I also believe that it's left to us to identify, develop, and use them in our daily lives. Therefore, I see our gifts as a partnership with God, one in which we are given the beginnings of our lives, but the endings are left to us.

Granted, it's easy enough for me to say that our gifts are God-given, but why do I believe this? There are three reasons. The first is because our gifts emanate from deep inside of us. Although our gifts may play out in external or physical ways, it's the love in our hearts that "bears them up" and presents them to us. Individual gifts are as varied as anything in the universe, but they share one common characteristic – they grow out of love. Our gifts are related to something we love to think about, love to work on, or love to experience. Since many of us believe that love is God "at work" in us and have felt that presence in our lives, it seems logical to believe that because our gifts are love-inspired, they are, therefore, God-inspired.

The second reason emerges as we try to understand how God works in this world. Because God does not have a physical presence, it seems totally logical to believe that God works through people. In order to accomplish his purposes, he provides us with gifts which we, in turn, can use to touch the lives of others. As we develop our gifts, we're helping to carry out God's will and purpose here on earth. This seems to be supported by the fact that individual gifts, while limitless in type and number, are given to us for one common reason: to help us help other people.

Third, we've all wondered about our purpose in life – why are we here and what are we supposed to do? It's not possible for one person to answer these questions for another since these involve personal feelings and beliefs. However, one thing seems to be apparent: our purpose appears to be connected to our gifts. In other words, whatever the purpose of our life may be, we seem to be "pre-equipped" to fulfill it. Therefore, if our gifts are God-given and they point us to our purpose for being here, it seems logical that the purpose for our lives – whatever it might be – is based on God's intentions for us.

If the reasons I have presented here are true, you are given the awesome opportunity to connect your life with the purpose God has for it. You accomplish this through the choices you make. Your choices will either move you closer to that purpose through the utilization of your gifts, or they will move you further from it. It is through your choices – day in and day out – that you either utilize your gifts or throw away your opportunity to become the person you were intended to be. This is no casual exercise; it's your life and you'd better get serious about the choices you are making if you want to live it to its fullest.

> *"From the beginning I had a sense of destiny, as though my life was assigned to me by fate and had to be fulfilled. This gave me an inner security, and though I could never prove it to myself, it proved itself to me. I did not have this certainty, it had me. Nobody could rob me of the conviction that it was enjoined upon me to do what God wanted and not what I wanted. That gave me the strength to go my own way. Often I had the feeling that in all decisive matters I was no longer among men, but was alone with God."*
>
> CARL G. JUNG
> Memories, Dreams and Reflections

How Many Gifts Do We Have?

Obviously, some people have more gifts than others. I don't know why this is true. Either some are given more than others or many of us simply fail to identify and develop all of the gifts that we have. In either event, each of us has gifts, but the exact number is not the important thing. The important thing is whether you identify your gifts and fully utilize them in your life.

> *Most of us are familiar with The Parable of the Talents in the Bible, in which the three servants were given talents by their master before he left on a long journey. To the first servant he gave five talents, to the second three talents, and to the last, one talent. Upon his return, the master found that the first two servants had invested their talents, doubling their value, and he expressed the same sentiments to both of them: "Well done thy good and faithful servant, you have been faithful over few things...I will set you over many."*
>
> *But when the last servant with the one talent explained to the master that "I was afraid and went and hid the talent in the earth to protect it...here you have what is yours," the master became very angry, took the talent away from him, and cast the servant from his sight.*
>
> PARAPHRASED FROM THE BIBLE
> Matthew 25: 14-30

I believe that the story above, originally told thousands of years ago, applies to us today in our efforts to find our "talents" and leverage them in our lives. As the story points out, the number of talents isn't the important thing. What's important is what you do with the gifts you've been given. If you hide them and don't try to use them in your daily living, you are likely to be "cast out" from this wonderful experience we call life. If, on the other hand, you develop, expand, and multiply your gifts, you're likely to "hear" those very same words…"well done thy good and faithful servant." The goal, therefore, is not to attain a certain number of gifts, but rather to make sure you fully utilize the gifts you have.

Never Assume It's Not a Gift

One of the characteristics of a gift is that it comes naturally to the person who possesses it. The woman whose friends always come to her for decorating ideas and advice may never see her skills as a gift because it's so easy for her to do. The man who is known throughout his neighborhood for being very helpful may not recognize his gift to make life more enjoyable for others because it just comes naturally to him. The young girl who sang the solo so beautifully with the church choir may not believe her music is truly a gift because it is something she has always been able to do. Because something seems so easy for us, we sometimes don't acknowledge or validate it as a gift we already possess.

> *James was an ordinary guy. He had never done anything especially noteworthy. He'd been a C student in high school and had struggled to get*

through college. After lots of interviews, he'd landed a job as a sales rep with a small food supply company. A few years later, he married Alexis who was a quiet and steady person much like himself. They now had two teenage sons, a decent house, and, by any measure, an ordinary life. In fact, James often thought of himself as just "an ordinary guy."

James never said very much. He seemed to blend in with almost any situation, but inside he was as honest a guy as you'd ever want to meet. He always told the truth to his customers, to his children, and to his wife. He always did the basic, but important things...worked hard, attended church every Sunday, went to his boys' games every weekend, and enjoyed a night out with his wife every week. James was a "Steady Eddie" if there ever was one.

As James pulled into his driveway one afternoon, he noticed his recently-widowed neighbor, Elaine, walking toward him. "James, I wanted to come over and tell you and Alexis what fine young men your two boys are turning out to be. They are so polite, so helpful, and have gone out of their way to do things for me since Ralph died. My daughter told me they were the two most respected boys in the entire school. You should really be proud. All the work you have done on them has really paid off. You're really gifted when it comes to raising children."

James looked at her for a few seconds thinking about what she just said – "you're really gifted when it comes to raising children." Then he quietly responded, "Thanks very much, Elaine."

In fact, he and Alexis hadn't "worked on" the boys at all. James had just gone about his life, working to pay the bills, and doing the things he thought were important to his family. Many times he'd wished that he had won that sales contest or gotten one of the promotions that always had seemed to pass him by. But, all of a sudden, Estelle's comments made those things much less important. In a matter of seconds, he had come to realize that his day-to-day actions and conduct over these past years had had a big impact on his boys. Now, as Estelle had just told him, they were "the two most respected boys in the entire school."

At that moment, James realized that the example he had been for his boys was indeed very special. The sudden clarity about what had actually taken place over these many years was almost overwhelming. "Wow," he thought, "this is no ordinary feeling." And just like that, James realized that he was no ordinary guy.

Your Gifts Evolve with Your Choices

You may discover a gift and feel that it is one of yours. However, the development of that gift depends on the choices you make if it is to become a reality in your life. When we first gain insight into a gift, we are seldom certain of exactly what the gift means to us. For example, you may feel that you are mechanically inclined and should work with cars...but does that gift mean you should own an automobile dealership or be a racecar driver? Further thought and study, and possibly a few mistakes along the way, are almost always needed to fully interpret your gifts and incorporate them into your life. As a result, we depend on our choices in support of a gift to gain a clearer understanding of how that gift will affect our lives.

Kristopher had shown remarkable compassion for others from a very early age. When he was just a youngster, he fed a bird with a broken wing for weeks until it was strong enough to fly again. When his 80-year old neighbor had been ill, he stopped to check on her every afternoon after school. When someone in his class was sent to the nurse, it seemed the teacher almost always selected Kristopher to go along. He often recalled what the school nurse said to him, "Kristopher, I bet you would make a good doctor someday!"

However, Kristopher's early thoughts were more about survival. He was raised in a crime-ridden section of Detroit, and from an early age his mother taught him to watch out for the drug dealers on their street. Kristopher's brother had been gunned down on the outskirts of the city.

In spite of this environment, Kristopher was an outstanding student who whizzed through his chemistry, physics, and botany classes with straight A's. All through his high school years, Kristopher dreamed of attending medical school but always doubted he'd ever get the chance.

With his father nowhere to be found, Kristopher would occasionally walk next door to talk to Mr. Davis who sat out on his porch every afternoon. Kristopher was thinking more and more about wanting to be a doctor, but he wasn't sure if he should even try. Mr. Davis, now 86, had helped Kristopher think through things several times in his life so Kristopher decided to see what Mr. Davis thought about his situation.

The two talked for over an hour that afternoon about Kristopher's school work, his mother, and Kristopher's desire to be a doctor. It turned out to be the most important conversation in Kristopher's life.

"Kris, your mom told me how well you were doing and that you had a good chance to finish near the top of your graduating class," Mr. Davis said. "Your momma is really proud of you, son."

"I want to help her as soon as I can, Mr. Davis," Kristopher said. "Although I would love to go to medical school, I could help my mother sooner by taking a job at the tire plant after graduation."

"Kris, you can help your mom the most by being all that you can be, and by using the gifts you have been given," Mr. Davis said. "You may not see exactly how you're going to do it, but God made you a smart boy and has planted this idea of you becoming a doctor one day. Now it's up to you. You can let these gift's guide your life, or you can do your *own thing. It's a choice, Kristopher, that only you can make."*

After a few more "coaching sessions" with Mr. Davis, Kristopher committed himself to becoming a doctor. His high school counselor was so excited when Kris told him about his decision, and his mother cried she was so happy at the thought of her boy being a doctor. He would never forget Mr. Davis' reaction when he confirmed his plans to him, "Kris, you will be one of the best doctors this city has ever seen."

The past 15 years hadn't been easy, and Kristopher's gifts had been tested thoroughly. But Kristopher had relied on his interests, his motivations, and the advice that Mr. Davis had provided. He was now one of the most respected heart surgeons in the city of Detroit. He was proud of what he'd accomplished, and his mother was definitely proud of "my boy, the doctor." And, if he were still living, Kristopher knew that Mr. Davis would be proud of him as well.

And so it is with us. We may feel that we have certain gifts, but yet not fully understand how they will work out in our lives. We are, therefore, dependent on the choices we make to support that gift and help it become more defined. For example, you may have a strong feeling about a potential gift and decide that you want to pursue its development. In order to do so, you must be willing to make additional choices to confirm the specifics of that gift. If you work through this process, supporting your initial feelings about a potential gift with the choices that help you further understand and develop it, at some point your true gift will become clear to you. If you are not willing to do so, your gift will likely fade, over time, from your thoughts and have little or no impact on your life.

> *"If we choose to be no more than clods of clay,
> then we shall be used as clods of clay
> for braver feet to tread on."*
>
> MARIE CORELLI
> English Author

As You Think About Your Gifts

I have made no attempt to precisely define what gifts are, believing that each great surgeon will hold the scalpel differently. Every great friend won't accomplish the gift of friendship in the same way, nor will every great musician play the same music. Our gifts become personalized and shaped as we apply our own skills, feelings, and way of doing things. However, it does seem that all of our gifts reflect the same objective – to help us help other people. If we want to fully utilize our gifts we must not only answer the question – how can I help other people? – but we must also go out and actually do it.

Many of the books written about gifts address the idea that you'll be more successful if you do what you like to do. Certainly, I agree that your gifts are fundamentally important in this regard. But, I also believe that the benefit of using your gifts reaches far beyond the work place. Your gifts can affect your life with your spouse, children, and friends. Your gifts influence your hobbies, volunteer work, and recreational activities. It's important to see the need to discover and use your gifts in all facets of your life. For example, someone who is a great salesperson isn't likely to have a meaningful life if he's unable to discover other gifts that help him be a good father, a good husband, and a good friend. So as you work to discover and develop your gifts, you need to look beyond your life at work...to the life you share with the people around you.

The Seeds Are Already in the Ground

The discovery of our gifts is not like inventing something from scratch. We're born with the seeds of these gifts; our job is to discover them and then set about doing the things that allow them to fully develop within our lives. In other words, the answers that we seek are somewhere inside of us. They already exist in one form or another. It's a matter of discovery and development, of taking the clues as they reveal themselves and putting them together in such a way that we come to an understanding of what our gifts are and how we will use them in our lives.

> *"There is a calling with your name on it. And, you're already answering it. You have a unique personality, combined with a one-of-a-kind set of skills, talents, passions and experiences. All of these have combined to and conspired to put you on the road to your true life's work – work that you can do like no one else on this planet."*
>
> MARTHA FINNEY AND DEBORAH DASCH
> Find Your Calling, Love Your Life

The Importance of the Project

What project could be more important than becoming the person you were meant to be? What could be more individually exciting than knowing that you reached your potential? What could possibly bring you more satisfaction than knowing that you used your true capabilities for the betterment of people and the world around you? The most rewarding thing about using your gifts is your opportunity to make a difference...to your friends and family, to those who live and work around you, and even to people whose names you will never know. A great life is inside each one of us. The way you "let it out" is by discovering and using the gifts that you possess.

> *"The question for each man to settle is not what he would do if he had means, time, influence, and educational advantages, but what he will do with what he has."*
>
> HAMILTON WRIGHT MABIE
> American Essayist, Critic and Lecturer

Your Gifts Lead You to Your Purpose

Almost all of us want our life to have meaning and to count for something. We really don't want to waste the life that we have. We want to have a purpose and to be remembered for what we did and how we lived our life. As important as this is, few of us understand how to achieve it. We find true meaning in our lives and maximize our impact on others by the way we use the gifts we have been given. If you want to live a life that will satisfy you, as well as those around you, you must follow your gifts as they lead you to an understanding of your purpose in life.

> "The greatest tragedy is not death,
> but life without purpose."
>
> RICK WARREN
> The Purpose-Driven Life

The Realities of Gift Discovery

We're here living our lives, but there are many uncertainties that are part of our life experience. Because life is filled with uncertainties, many of us elect to simply live day by day and never devote much thought to the possibility that our life might have a mission, or that our unique design and thinking were provided so that we could accomplish specific things with our life. For those who are willing to stop here and simply live with the uncertainties of life, I have no facts to make you think and act otherwise. However, if you'll venture on with me, there are some realities that I believe more than offset the uncertainties as you work to identify your gifts and find a true sense of direction for your life.

The Reality of the Spirit

We all seem to have an "inner voice" that, when we are open to it, speaks to us and attempts to guide us in some special way.

This is a spiritual feeling and, when it wells up in us, it seems to want to take us in some direction. It's interesting to note that this spirit calls us to do good and worthwhile things, never bad or improper things.

This spirit may speak to you as you're driving your car, while you're in church, during a business meeting, or as you sit and look at your children one afternoon. It may come to you at a totally unexpected moment. Clearly, there is a spirit inside of us that awakens at various times to touch our lives with perspectives about certain actions we're about to take or concerning our long-term future. To ignore the reality of the spirit is to live without an influence that can ignite your life in very special ways.

A USA Today poll revealed that if we could ask God one question, for most of us it would be, "What is the purpose of my life?" Most of us are seeking insights into what is intended for us and to have a personal plan for achieving it. I can't tell you a simple way to find this out, but I will make this suggestion to you. You can start the process by recognizing that there is a spiritual presence in your life. If you will give it the opportunity to do so, that spirit will provide you with many of the "clues" that you seek about your life and how it should be lived.

The Reality of Personal Interests

Another reality is the fact that very specific interests and motivations appear in our lives. As our lives evolve and we gain knowledge, we develop special interests in something we are doing as well as insights concerning what we might enjoy doing in the future. These interests, which evolve over time, are indications of what you are meant – or are being led – to do. They may feel like an easy tap on the shoulder causing you to look in a new direction to find a more specific heading for your life. In other instances, these motivations "pull at your heart" as they call you to some special work or effort. The reality is that your interests guide you in special ways, and motivate you to do specific things with your life.

The Reality of Love

The reality of love – the caring and concern we have for others or for an effort of our choosing – is one of the strongest and clearest indications that we have certain gifts that should be utilized in our lives. An entire chapter of this book has been devoted to its potential role in our lives and the choices we make. Love not only directs our interests, but it also intensifies our motivations. Love gives you the energy and courage to "press on" when others don't really understand why you are doing so. Love causes you to commit for all of the right reasons. As Goethe said, "we are shaped and fashioned by what we love." Love is a reality that not only helps us identify our gifts, but also provides us with the motivation to pursue them.

The Reality of Choices

There is one more reality that we need to consider – our choices reside inside of us, as well. Until you make your choices, the spiritual influences in your life, the interests you may have, and the love you may possess are in a state of limbo. They may be trying to direct you in a special way, but until you make your choices, they have no chance to affect the outcome of your life. Through the implementation of your choices you either enhance or extinguish these influences. This is why your choices are so important. They not only support you in the discovery of your gifts, but they also determine to what extent your gifts will ever be used.

In summary, these four realities reside inside each of us – the _spirit_ that speaks to us in special ways, the _interests_ we develop as we live our lives, the _love_ we feel for others or for something we want to do, and the ability to make _choices_ as to what we will do with our lives. If we pay attention to these influences – these realities – as they work in our lives, we not only gain knowledge of our gifts, but will have the opportunity to live the life intended for us. We have to focus and work on it, but everything we need to gain these insights is within us. As Moses pointed out to the people of Israel 2,000 years ago, no "long trips" are required to obtain the understanding we need:

> "This command I am giving you today is not too difficult for you to understand or perform. It is not up in heaven, so distant that you must ask, 'Who will go to heaven and bring it down so we can hear and obey it?' It is not beyond the sea, so far away that you must ask, 'Who will cross the sea to bring it to us so we can hear and obey it?' The message is very close at hand; it is on your lips and in your heart...."
>
> THE BIBLE
> Deuteronomy 30: 11-14

Some Closing Thoughts About Gifts

In wrapping up this chapter, there are two thoughts that I would like to leave with you. The first is that underlying this whole experience we call life, there is something <u>very important</u> that we all need to acknowledge. Simply stated, it is the fact that <u>we</u> <u>are</u> <u>here</u> <u>for</u> <u>each</u> <u>other</u>. It's not about discovering your gifts so that you can use them for yourself, but so that you can make other people's lives better. Whether we ever fully understand "how this works" or not, we can greatly broaden our own life experience if we accept this universal purpose of living and try to make our lives count first for others, and then for ourselves.

> *"No man has come to true greatness who has not felt in some degree that his life belongs to his race, and that what God gives him He gives him for mankind."*
>
> PHILLIPS BROOKS
> Episcopal Bishop

The second thought is simply a reminder of what I've tried to say in this chapter. The insights into living a full and meaningful life are not in some faraway place, not in the wise mind of someone else, but rather right there inside of you. You were born with certain ingredients, you have the opportunity to fully discover what they are, and through your choices you can bring them to full throttle in your life. The secret to living a meaningful life, it seems to me, is to listen carefully – to your inner voice, to the interests you have, and to the loves that enter your life – so that you can determine what your life is telling you to do.

CHAPTER 11

TENDING TO YOUR BODY

*"The human body was designed to walk, run
or stop; it wasn't built for coasting."*

CULLEN HIGHTOWER
American Salesman and Sales Trainer

The Unhealthy Truth

You may be wondering why a book about choices contains a chapter about our bodies. Well, I chose to address the subject of personal healthcare in this book for two basic reasons. First, many of us – in fact, you could easily argue <u>most</u> of us – are making some very poor choices when it comes to taking proper care of our bodies. The medical statistics overwhelmingly support this fact. Second, if you are one who chooses to "let yourself go" and not do what you should concerning exercise, eating habits, and general healthcare, it is likely that you will encounter a medical condition that, at some point, will limit the choices you can make.

It's a fact that many of us make little or no effort to manage the condition of our bodies…whatever happens, happens. The types of food we eat combined with our lack of exercise are testimony to the fact that many of us are lackadaisical when it comes to taking care of our bodies. Most of us don't work at improving our health, either because we're lazy or we just don't comprehend the importance of the health-related choices we are making. For some reason, we think we'll be okay no matter what we eat or what we do. However, the evidence is overwhelming that healthy choices make us feel better, look better, and live better. It would seem that all of us would want to take good care of our bodies, but, in fact, most of us aren't doing so.

> *"By any measure, America's health is failing. We spend far more, per capita, on health care than any other society in the world, and yet two-thirds of Americans are overweight, and more than 15 million Americans have diabetes. We fall prey to heart disease as often as we did 30 years ago. Half of all Americans have a health problem that requires taking a prescription drug every week, and more than 100 million Americans have high cholesterol.*
>
> *To make matters worse, we are leading our youth down a path of disease earlier and earlier in their lives. One-third of the children in this country are overweight. Our kids are increasingly falling prey to a form of diabetes that used to be seen only in adults, and children now take more prescription drugs than ever before."*
>
> T. COLIN CAMPBELL AND THOMAS M. CAMPBELL II
> The China Study

It's amazing that so many Americans ignore the need to tend to the physical side of their lives. We could eat healthier foods, but most of us don't. We could exercise more, but most of us fail to do so. We could give up some of our bad habits, but most of us won't. We're not stupid, so why do we continue to live this way? Because we don't think anything bad will ever happen to us. It's true that we can't predict exactly who will have a heart attack, develop high blood pressure, or have a diabetic condition. Because we can't predict these occurrences on an individual basis, we tend to go about our lives thinking that such problems will never happen to us. Most people continue to make poor health choices until something bad actually happens…and, then, it's often too late.

> *"Although the United States is the most powerful nation on earth, the one area in which this country does not excel is health. And the future is not bright. Almost a third of our young children are obese, and many do not exercise. No matter how much information becomes available about the dangers of a sedentary lifestyle and a diet heavily dependent on processed foods, we don't change our ways. In the United States the majority of adults are overweight and undernourished."*
>
> MEHMET C. OZ, M.D.
> Foreword / Eat to Live

My, That Was Big of You

If you want to develop a better understanding of the general health of Americans today, you can start by looking at how many of us are overweight. According to the National Center for Health Statistics, more than 64 percent of Americans are overweight and 30 percent of us are obese. Joint studies by the Endocrine Society and the Hormone Foundation produced the following overweight profiles for various age groups:

Age (Years)	% Men Overweight	% Women Overweight
20 to 34	57.4%	52.8%
35 to 44	70.5%	60.6%
45 to 54	75.7%	65.1%
55 to 64	75.4%	72.2%
65 to 74	76.2%	70.9%
75 and older	67.4%	59.9%

What's the big deal about being overweight?

Overweight people are more likely to have heart disease and strokes. High blood pressure and high cholesterol levels, both risk factors for heart disease, are more common in people who are overweight. A three-decade study of 17,643 patients by Northwestern University found that being overweight in mid-life substantially increases the risk of dying of heart disease. The study found that obese or grossly overweight participants were 43 percent more likely to die and four times more likely to be hospitalized for heart disease than participants with acceptable weight levels.

Overweight people are twice as likely to develop Type 2 diabetes. Excessive weight is a major cause of early death, heart disease, kidney disease, stroke, and blindness. The Diabetes Prevention Program, *a federally-funded study of 3,234 people at high risk for diabetes, showed that exercising 30 minutes a day five days each week, and lowering intake of fat and calories reduced the risk of getting Type 2 diabetes by 58 percent.*

<u>*Overweight and obese people are at higher risk of dying from cancer.*</u> *In a study published in the New England Journal of Medicine researchers determined that excess weight and obesity may account for 20 percent of all cancer deaths in U.S. women and 14 percent in U.S. men, which means 90,000 cancer deaths could be prevented each year if Americans could only maintain a normal, healthy body weight.*

<u>*Overweight people have less energy than others.*</u> *In a National Weight Control Registry database of people who had reported weight loss of 30 pounds or more that they had kept off for at least one year, 85 percent reported improvements in physical health, energy level, general mood and self-confidence.*

<u>*Overweight people have less desire and more problems with their sex life.*</u> *According to a study performed at Duke University's Diet and Fitness Center, up to 30 percent of obese people seeking help in controlling their weight indicate problems with sex drive, desire, performance, or all three.*

As the studies referenced above show, the problems associated with excess weight are numerous and, in many instances, severe. In spite of these facts, Americans continue to rely on fast food as their primary food source. Couple these eating habits with little or no exercise and we have a simple, but often ignored formula for creating health problems in our lives. It's not something that is beyond our control – we are choosing this high risk lifestyle.

So, how did so many of us get this way?

If the increased risk of heart disease, diabetes, and cancer, not to mention a lower energy level and a less satisfying sex life, doesn't motivate us to do better, what will? According to a study by Shape Up America, a nonprofit group founded by former Surgeon General C. Everett Koop, almost 7 out of 10 seriously overweight Americans believe that their health is not at risk because of excess weight. For some reason, we aren't willing to make choices based on reality. Instead, we manage our health and make our eating and exercise choices under the basic belief that being overweight will have no repercussions as far as our enjoyment of life is concerned. The facts tell us one thing, yet we do another.

> *During his high school years, Joseph played football and stayed in top physical condition. However, when he went off to college, things began to change. With no parents to tell him what to do, no coaches to remind him of what not to eat, and no teammates to urge him to run a few more laps, he realized he had the freedom to do whatever he wanted.*
>
> *The clean living of his high school days was soon replaced with weekend beer parties, lots of snacking, and the habit of going to bed at one or two in the morning. One weekend, someone offered Joseph*

a cigarette and without much thought about it, he took the first "smoke" of his young life. Although he felt a bit dizzy at first, he went on to smoke a dozen cigarettes that evening. The next day he bought his first pack of cigarettes.

Joseph smoked throughout his college years and never thought too much about diet or exercise. When he graduated, he was over 30 pounds heavier than when he entered the university. He soon accepted a job in a nearby city and continued to make poor choices concerning his eating and exercise habits.

Although he never thought much about his ever increasing weight, Joseph made good choices at work and moved right along in his career. At the age of 32, he was promoted to vice president and enjoyed a great reputation in the firm. But he continued to smoke. Some days almost two packs. He continued to drink cocktails after work and even more on the weekends. He continued to eat lots of fast food and never bothered to exercise.

Then one day it happened. He hadn't been feeling well for several days. His pulse rate was rapid and he'd been sweating for no apparent reason. When he felt the tightness in his chest, the only thing he could see was the cigarette in his hand. As the pain suddenly increased, he couldn't put that cigarette out quick enough. His associates got him to the nearby hospital, and a few hours later, Joseph was looking up at the emergency room physician who had just saved his life.

"Wow, I never thought this would happen to me," he said.
"Nobody ever does," the doctor replied.

At what point does being overweight actually create a health problem?

No one knows the precise moment excess weight affects your health, but to simply turn away and believe that you will never have any of these problems – no matter what you weigh – seems to be a very foolish choice. Obviously, the best thing to do is to make sure you get regular medical checkups; if you're overweight, you should consult with your physician about potential problems as well as what you should be doing to get back in shape.

There are several tests you can use to determine if you are overweight. One of the first and easiest tests is to simply look in the mirror. An honest person can quickly see if there is a weight problem in that mirror. If there are activities you can't do without breathing problems – for example, playing with your children or walking up a flight of stairs – you can be assured that you need to get in better shape. Or, if every time you buy clothes you seem to be looking for a larger size, you should know you need to do something about your weight. If you are not capable of making these assessments yourself, you should ask someone who will give you an honest answer. Your health is just too important not to "fess up" to a weight problem.

> *"Health is so necessary to all duties, as well as*
> *pleasures of life,*
> *that the crime of squandering it is equal to the folly."*
>
> SAMUEL JOHNSON
> Author of A Dictionary of the English Language

We Diet…Really?

A quick search of Amazon.com for "diet books" produced 30,593 individual responses, meaning that we can order far more books than we could read in a lifetime about the latest diet and how we can drop a few pounds by going on it. Needless to say, the term "fad diet" was coined because of the popularity, not necessarily the effectiveness, of a new diet. Calories, carbohydrates, proteins, fat, starches, white foods – there are so many focus points of diets today that it becomes very difficult for an individual to decide which is the most effective way to control weight. When it comes to diet choices, you have thousands of them, but the real question is…is a diet the best thing for you?

> *"Almost all diets are ineffective. They don't work,*
> *because no matter how much weight you lose when*
> *you are on the diet, you put it right back on when*
> *you go off. Measuring portions and trying to eat*
> *fewer calories, typically called dieting, almost*
> *never results in permanent weight loss and actually*
> *worsens the problem over time. Such dieting*

> *temporarily slows down your metabolic rate, so often more weight comes back than what you lost."*
>
> DR. JOEL FUHRMAN, M.D.
> Eat to Live

The point is we don't need a diet book. We simply need to become better educated about the foods that are good for us and those that aren't. To accomplish this, you should read well-researched books that have nutritional information and study them so that you develop an informed basis for making your food choices. Once you have an understanding about which foods are good for you, you don't have to resort to short-term diets. Instead, you can make choices which, not only reduce your weight, but also promote a healthy lifestyle.

> *"Burton Baskin was my father's brother-in-law. Together they founded, owned, and ran Baskin-Robbins Ice Cream Company. A talented man with a great sense of style, my Uncle Butch, as we called him, touched countless lives with his expansive spirit. His fatal heart attack struck when he was still in his early fifties, with a loving wife, two incredible kids, a wildly successful business and everything in the world to look forward to.*
>
> *Tact was never my strong suit, and maybe I should never have mentioned it, but a few years later, I asked my father whether he thought there could be any connection between the amount of ice cream my uncle had eaten and his fatal heart attack. Given that my uncle weighed around 220 pounds and that he had certainly enjoyed the family*

product, the question seemed a reasonable one. But my father was not particularly interested in such reflections. "No," he said. "His ticker just got tired and stopped working."

I can now understand why my father would not have wanted to consider the question. He had by that time manufactured and sold more ice cream than any other human being who had ever lived, and he most definitely did not want to think that ice cream might be harming anyone, much less that it might have contributed to my uncle's death.

To this day, there are a number of people in my family who are angry at me for mentioning any of this in public. They tell me that when I bring this up I am dishonoring my uncle's memory. But I disagree. Burton Baskin loved life and I believe he would want his story told if in the telling it might help others to be more aware of the choices they are making, and more able to live in a way that brings greater health and happiness into their lives. Similarly, it's poignant that Ben & Jerry's cofounder, Ben Cohen, needed to undergo quadruple bypass surgery in 2001, at the age of 49, due to serious coronary heart disease.

Am I saying that ice cream is going to kill you? Of course not. What I am saying though is that ice cream is very high in saturated fat and sugar; and the more saturated fat and sugar you eat, the more likely you are to have a heart attack. This is not a value judgment, and it's not just my opinion. It is a statistical reality, arrived at by

> *the most comprehensive and conscientious body of medical research in world history. What we eat does matter."*
> JOHN ROBBINS
> The Food Revolution

I'm not a diet or food expert. I'm simply trying to show that you have choices when it comes to what you eat and that those choices will, to some extent, determine how well and how long you'll live. We all need to know more about the foods we eat. There are many good books out there. Some research on your part to identify and read a few of them will likely improve your understanding of the impact that certain foods are having on your body. I certainly recommend that you read John Robbins' book, The Food Revolution. Here is a man who gave up the chance to run the highly successful Baskin-Robbins Ice Cream and instead made the choice to devote his life to helping people make better choices about the food they eat. We could all learn something from John's example as we "weigh the factors" that influence the food choices we make.

We Say, "We Exercise!"

In my research, I found numerous reports that indicate that "more than 60 percent" of Americans say they participate in some type of exercise. However, when we compare this statistic with those which clearly indicate that "over 60 percent" of Americans are overweight or obese, we quickly come to the conclusion that much of our exercise is ineffective. When we Americans respond affirmatively to the exercise question, we seldom define to what degree we exercise, how often we do so, or whether our exercise efforts are extensive or not. To simply say "I exercise" isn't enough. It's what you actually do – and the results you achieve – that determine whether you really exercise...or not.

> *"If you asked 50 different individuals what exercise means, chances are that no two responses would be the same. To some, exercise includes just about any form of physical exertion, from walking to work to planting the garden. Others, however, believe that the term exercise is reserved for vigorous aerobic activity or vigorous resistance training. Indeed, even in the scientific literature, the word exercise is used freely without qualification."*
>
> EXERCISE PSYCHOLOGY
> Edited by Peter Seraganian

If we're going to make progress concerning our exercise choices, we must start with a clearer definition of the term "exercise." For our purposes here, I'm defining exercise as an activity that has four characteristics – it raises your heart rate, it requires a reasonable effort to complete, it is done at frequent and regular intervals, and it is actually helping you achieve a specific conditioning goal. Accordingly, you can use these four tests – heart rate, effort, frequency, and effectiveness – to gauge the choices you are making relative to your current exercise habits or activities.

Test #1: Does it Raise Your Heart Rate?

If you want to burn fat and lose weight as a result of your exercise routines, you must get your heart rate up to 130 – 140 beats per minute and then maintain that rate for some number of minutes. For example, Jim works out on the treadmill every morning for 30 minutes. However, to get his heart rate up, he has to raise the grade to three degrees after 10 minutes and to six degrees after 20. Somewhere around the 23 minute mark, his heart rate reaches 130+ and he starts to burn fat. We might say that Jim does the first 23 minutes of exercise just to get his body ready for the last seven...for it's those last seven minutes that make it all worthwhile.

A simple way to determine your target heart rate for burning fat is to subtract your age from 220 and take 75% of the result. For example, an average 35 year old would have a target rate of 138 or 139 (220 minus 35 times 75 percent); an average 60 year old would have a target rate of 120 (220 minus 60 times 75 percent).

> "...the scientific data shows that in addition to those calories you burn from general physical activities, you also need about 60 minutes a week of stamina training – that is, a cardiovascular activity that elevates your heart rate to 80% or more of your age-adjusted maximum (220 minus your age) for an extended period of time."
>
> MICHAEL F. ROIZEN, M.D. AND MEHMET C. OZ, M.D.
> YOU: The Owner's Manual

Test #2: Does it Require a Reasonable Effort?

To be physically meaningful, exercise must require a reasonable and often extensive effort. In other words, your routine must push you or extend you if you are to reap the potential conditioning benefits that it can provide. I'm sorry, but walking the dog, especially one that takes "a relief break" every few minutes, does not require much effort. Granted, such walking might be good for an older person who is not capable of more extensive exercise, but for those of us who need to lose weight, we have to do something that requires us to work at it.

> *"There is no easy way out. If there were, I would have bought it.*
> *And believe me, it would be one of my favorite things."*
>
> OPRAH WINFREY
> O Magazine

Test #3: Do You "Do It" Frequently and at Regular Intervals?

When it comes to exercise, most of us tend to think that anything is better than nothing, but that's just not the case. No matter how good your genes are, exercising only one or two days a week is just not enough. On the days you exercise effectively, your body improves and you take a step toward your conditioning goal. On the days you don't, your body retreats and heads back toward its original condition. Common sense tells us that we need more steps forward than backwards to improve. Therefore, if you want to lose weight and achieve a higher level of conditioning, you should work out at least five days a week. An even better schedule would be six days a week, working a little extra on Saturday, and taking Sunday off to rest.

Studies have shown that someone who has been doing a low-level exercise such as walking every day for a year or longer will return to their original condition in approximately six weeks if they stop exercising all together. That means when you skip two or three weeks, you've lost almost 50 percent of the results it took you a year or so to achieve. Therefore, frequency is very important and every day that you skip, no matter how good the reason, is a step backward.

> *"Habit is like a cable;*
> *we weave a thread of it each day,*
> *and at last we cannot break it."*
>
> HORACE MANN
> American Education Reformer

Test #4: Is Your Exercise Helping You Achieve a Specific Conditioning Goal?

If your exercise activities are to be effective, you must have a goal by which to judge your results. Increasing your energy level, losing weight, or wearing a smaller clothing size are all examples. The easiest objective is to improve the way you feel. An effective exercise program almost always increases an individual's energy level; if it doesn't, that individual needs to choose a more extensive routine. Another objective could be to lose weight. If this is the objective you chose, it should be to lose a specific number of pounds. It may take months before the pounds start coming off, but it's important to have a specific weight target and track your progress against it on a daily basis. Whatever the goal, you need to <u>define your expected result in a specific way</u> and then work to achieve it.

> *William was a "level one" slob, well on his way to achieving a "level two" designation. He was at least 30 pounds overweight, always jumped at the chance to have another great meal, but never exercised. William was a hard worker, but he was starting to notice that he just didn't have the energy that he used to have. When he realized he was going to be 50 years old in a few months, he started to think about his physical condition and began to wonder if he should do something about it.*
> *He asked his office assistant what she thought. Sherry had been a physical education major, and her husband was both an athlete and a doctor. Sherry said, "Mr. Billings, you could cut back on some of your eating, but what you really need is a daily exercise program. If you exercise every day, really exercise, you can lose weight and increase your energy level without having to watch your food intake too closely."*
>
> *William always thought Sherry to be a smart young lady and her suggestion to focus more on exercise than on food made sense to him. As a result, he went out and bought a treadmill. William started getting up earlier every day and spent 30 minutes on his treadmill before showering and*

heading to the office. Over the next few months he and Sherry discussed his progress. It wasn't long before he noticed his weight going down and his energy level going up.

Thirteen years later, William is retired – but he still gets on the treadmill every morning for 30 minutes and, even when he travels, seldom misses a day. He's often thankful for the advice Sherry gave him, but he's even more thankful that he made the choice to heed it.

A Society of Pill Poppers

Another contributing factor to our unwillingness to eat better and exercise more is our belief that there's always a pill that will fix everything. High cholesterol...no problem, there are at least five well-known pills for that. Depression...there are lots of pills to make that go away. Excess gas or gastro reactions... what color pill do you want? More than 3.5 billion prescriptions are written by U.S. doctors each year – that's more than 12 prescriptions for every man, woman and child in America. U.S. prescription drug sales are now more than $300 billion and according to industry sources, are projected to exceed $350 billion in the next few years, an average of well over $1,000 per person living in the United States.

> "...having high cholesterol is only one of many factors that affect your chances of future heart disease. Yet it attracts a huge share of attention because it can be modified with drugs. Yet for most healthy people...improving diet,

*increasing exercise and stopping smoking are
the most obvious and well-known strategies."*

RAY MOYNIHAN AND ALAN CASSELS
Selling Sickness

Obviously, you need the advice of a good doctor in taking proper care of yourself. But, you also need to take responsibility for the day-to-day choices you make that determine the extent of your physical conditioning. You need to recognize that your food and exercise choices, over time, determine what you look like and how you feel. It's much better to think about the choices you're making today than to wait and hope the doctor can "fix it" when your health gets out of whack. We need to think about what we are doing to ourselves. If we want to look and live better, we must learn to think better…and choose better.

"The sound body is the product of a sound mind."

GEORGE BERNARD SHAW
Irish Playwright

Other "Sins of the Body"

I won't try to use a story to illustrate each of these, but there are three additional "sins of the body" that I would like to mention: namely smoking, drinking, and drugs. While there are fewer of us doing so these days, smoking is still a horrible habit and one that every one of us should avoid at all costs. Many of us look forward to the afternoon cocktail hour, but alcohol consumption is something we all need to control and practice in moderation. As for drugs, the best advice here seems to be "never, never, never" as the addictions that develop from an initial casual use are ruining far too many lives.

Smoking...

Smoking...who needs it? The answer is no one. Certainly not the one doing all the puffing, but now there are reliable secondhand smoke studies that prove that the smoker is not only hurting himself but also those around him, including his children, his spouse, his friends and anyone else unfortunate enough to be in the vicinity of his fumes. According to the American Cancer Society, smoking damages nearly every organ in the human body. It is linked to at least 10 different cancers, and it accounts for some 30 percent of all cancer deaths. Yet one in four Americans still light up. In view of all of the evidence, why would anyone make a choice like that?

> *"Smoke may be great for grilling, but you don't have to be the Marlboro Man to know what kind of damage smoking can do to your lungs. It puts you at great risk for lung diseases such as cancer, emphysema, and bronchitis. But, unlike a White House press secretary, a good damage-control plan won't bail you out. Your only option is to stop."*
>
> MICHAEL F. ROIZEN, M.D. AND MEHMET C. OZ, M.D.
> YOU: The Owner's Manual

Drinking...

Those of us who indulge in alcohol tend to let ourselves off easy on this one because we claim to drink responsibly. Many of us are quick to point out that "wine is good for you" as we look for ways to justify our afternoon cocktail routine. Granted, if you limit your intake and use the time to relax with family or friends, a drink or two may be okay. But the truth is that many of us enjoy it a little too much. As a result, it may cause you to do or say things you would otherwise never say or do. Some of us need to significantly reduce or even eliminate our intake of alcohol simply because we're not controlling it – it's controlling us. Each of us needs to make an honest assessment of our drinking habits. If you are drinking to excess, you need to make the choice to take action and correct the situation. If you allow your drinking habits to "cloud your view" of the world and the opportunities it presents, you may never even see, much less experience, the life that you were intended to live.

> *"The vine bears three kinds of grapes: the first of pleasure, the next of intoxication, and the third of disgust."*
>
> ANARCHIS
> Priest in the Order of Saint George

Drugs...

There are many well-done studies available concerning the effect of illegal drugs, so it's difficult for me to offer any enlightenment beyond what is already widely known. The bottom line is that no good ever comes from illegal drug use. The drug scene, whether using or selling, whether involving marijuana, cocaine, or other narcotics, is dotted with missed opportunities, broken lives, and even death. So to think that you can "touch it" and remain unharmed is a foolish thought indeed.

Few of us understand the implications of being addicted to a drug until we've been sucked into its influence. Typically, we don't see ourselves changing, but an addiction transforms a free person into a captive, living without the ability to make choices. That may be a good way to understand what an addiction really is: a desire that, as a result of its strength and power, takes away your ability to make other choices in your life.

The best solution for avoiding such misery is a simple, but firm, choice to never start. If a person is already addicted, it's vital to make an even tougher choice to get professional help. Drugs will kill thousands of people in the United States this year and alter the life experience of even more. Don't let your choices make you one of them.

"It's a choice only you can make, Jessica," her mother stated once again as they wrapped up their nearly two-hour conversation. Jessica had come home from school crying that afternoon, and her mother immediately recognized that something was wrong.

Jessica had always tried to be a good friend and fit in with her group at school. She wanted to be accepted and liked by both the girls and the guys in her class. As a result, she frequently held back to see what the others were doing so she could follow their lead. That worked okay through elementary and junior high school, but now as they started their first year of high school, the alternatives began to get a little more serious and she wasn't as sure about what she should do.

Luckily for Jessica, she had a great mom who had coached her through many things as she was growing up. Her mom would never make a decision for her, but always took the time to make sure Jessica understood the potential problems that could arise from a choice she was about to make.

This time, it was drugs. There was going to be a party on Friday night and several of the guys had indicated they were bringing some marijuana for everyone to try. Several of the girls were asking Jessica if she was going to join in. When she had showed some reluctance, they teased her and said she probably wasn't "mature enough" to try drugs yet. They made such a big deal about it that Jessica had become upset at the thought of losing her friends if she didn't smoke the marijuana with them on Friday night.

"Jessica," her mother explained, "10 years from now, you won't even know where most of these kids are, much less what they're doing. Their opinion seems so important to you right now, but when you get out of college and are hard at work, you won't be calling them asking what you should do. You'll be making choices on your own. You might as well

GOOD CHOICES GOOD LIFE

learn how to make choices on your own now. If you want to try marijuana, do it because you think it's a good idea, not because they do. If you think it's a bad idea, don't – no matter what they say." Jessica loved how her mother could help her see things from a different, but very important, perspective.

Jessica had already learned a lot at school about drugs and how smoking marijuana usually led to trying more addictive drugs. She had all of the background information she needed to make this choice. Her mother helped her see that it was her choice, not her friends' choices, that really mattered.

Our Choices Are Killing Us

Why do many of us die each year? What are we doing to ourselves or to each other that ultimately causes our death or someone else to die? I'm not referring to deaths from cancer, disease, or some cause out of our control, as these would increase the total. I'm talking about deaths that would have most likely been prevented if different choices had been made. We know that if we all made better choices, we would have fewer deaths and more people would be alive today...but how many people are we talking about? According to the Journal of the American Medical Association (Vol. 293) the numbers are as follows:

Cause of Death	Annual Deaths
Tobacco	435,000
Poor Diet and Physical Inactivity	365,000

Alcohol	85,000
Microbial Agents	75,000
Toxic Agents	55,000
Adverse Reactions to Prescription Drugs	32,000
Suicide	30,622
Incidents Involving Firearms	29,000
Motor Vehicle Crashes	26,347
Homicide	20,308
Sexual Behaviors	20,000
Illicit Drug Use	17,000
	1,190,277

It's pretty amazing to think that more than a million people a year could have stayed alive if they had chosen to live their lives differently. If they had not continued to do as they wanted, but instead did what was best for them, many of these people would be with us today.

"The healthiest people are not the ones who are born healthy," according to endocrinologist, Dr. Alice Lipscomb, "but rather are the ones who made a decision, even in their middle years, to start taking care of themselves." Her remarks, which were based on studies she had done in medical school, were aimed directly at my smoking habit. Thank goodness, as I walked out of her office that day with her lecture fresh in my mind, I made the choice to stop smoking. That was more than 30 years ago and, because of the power of her advice, I never smoked again.

> *Forty-two-year-old Teresa, after more than two years on methamphetamine, now can't stand the sight of herself. "I don't look in the mirror," she told*

reporter Bob McNamara. "I don't want to see...I don't want to see."

"Meth really destroys them," Portland Deputy Bret King explained. "It deteriorates their body." While booking suspects into the county jail, King spotted a grisly trend in how the mug shots of repeatedly arrested meth users changed over time. "There's life in their eyes...then you switch to the second picture and that life is gone," King said. "Look at their eyes. Their soul seems to have left their body."

CBS EVENING NEWS
April 29, 2005

Now, Three Questions for You

While each of us can be motivated to do better or achieve more, the ultimate choice to do so must come from within us. No one can make these choices for you. You can hear something that pricks your conscience, you can know that it applies to you, but the important question is will you do something about it? Almost all of us have intended to do something at some point in our lives that turned out to be just a thought...followed by no action. The important thing for you is not just to recognize the need for living a healthier lifestyle, but to make the choice to go and do something about it.

Question #1: Are you overweight?

We all want other people to cut us a little slack when judging whether we're overweight or not. Although our size is there for everyone to see, we don't always see ourselves as others see us. We have a lot of trouble being honest about our own weight, frequently admitting to being "about 10 pounds over" when, in fact, we're really 20 or 30 pounds above our ideal weight.

So, are you overweight? You have to be honest about your circumstances if you ever expect to make better choices in your life. If you can't be totally honest about "where" you are right now, you have little chance to change things for the better. And, this is certainly true when it comes to evaluating your weight. You must be honest about your weight if you want to improve your health. So, I ask you again…are you overweight? I'll leave the answer up to you. But, as you work to make better choices in all areas of your life, you must come clean about your weight. If it's a potential problem, you need to make the choice to lose weight and become a healthier person.

"Lack of will power and drive cause more failures than lack of intelligence and ability."

HARRY F. BANKS
Canadian Soldier

Question #2: Are You Getting the Proper Amount of Exercise?

Which of these seven options best describes your current exercise program?

Good _____

___ 1. I exercise 5 to 6 times a week and have a specific conditioning goal.

___ 2. I exercise 3 to 5 times a week.

Not So Good _____

___ 3. I exercise 1 or 2 times each week.

___ 4. I try to exercise each week, but do miss weeks now and then.

___ 5. I walk or do something outside almost every weekend.

___ 6. I started to exercise several years ago, but stopped for some reason.

___ 7. I don't exercise at all.

If you want to be in good physical condition and improve your mental alertness in the process, you must work your way up to the top of this list. A score of "3" to "7" just won't get the job done…you have to become a "1" or a "2." When you're in good shape, you'll be able to perform so much better in other areas of your life – as a mother who needs to keep up with young children, as a student who needs the stamina to work and study hard, as a businessman who needs to finish an important project, or just as someone who really wants to chase that dream that you've had for so long. Yes, an effective exercise program may require hard work, but it makes handling the other parts of your life so much easier.

> *"True enjoyment comes from activity of the mind*
> *and exercise of the body;*
> *the two are united."*
>
> ALEXANDER VON HUMBOLDT
> German Explorer and Botanist

Question #3: How Many Pills Do You Take?

I'm not medically qualified, so I'll tread lightly with the idea that too many of us feel that the only solution to our problems is in one of those little prescription bottles. Sure, medications, when used appropriately, do help. But <u>you</u> can help, as well. First, you should tend to your body before the need for going to the doctor even arises. Once in the doctor's office, you can ask your doctor if there are other things you can do to help alleviate a health problem besides taking drugs. Should the doctor give you a prescription, make sure to ask about the medication. You should become fully informed not only about the medication, but also about the potential side effects, as well.

> *Americans today are used to fixing problems the quick way – even when it comes to their health. Thus, they rely heavily on prescription drugs to fix their diseases. For every conceivable ailment – real or not – chances are there's a pricey prescription drug to "treat" it. Chances are even better that their drug of choice comes chock full of <u>side effects</u>.*
>
> WWW.NEWSTARGET.COM
> Article by Jessica Fraser

Like many other aspects of our lives, our physical condition is a function of the choices we make. The better our food selections and the more we choose to exercise, the better we will feel and the longer we are likely to live. In spite of how true this is, the health trends in America are all headed in the wrong direction – more people are becoming overweight, fewer people are getting adequate exercise, and there is an increasing reliance on pills to make us better. If you are contributing to these trends, maybe you should make some changes in your life. To do so, you have to start making better health choices. It's your choice – you can continue your bad habits, or you can start to take steps that create a healthier lifestyle. Which will it be?

CHAPTER 12

Establishing Goals and Taking Risks

"Our prayers are answered not when we are given what we ask, but when we are challenged to be what we can be."

Rabbi Morris Adler
The Voice Still Speaks

Lots of Ways to Live It

Becoming an exceptional person and accomplishing something meaningful seldom happens by chance. Most of the time it takes hard work and sacrifice to achieve such results. However, hard work and sacrifice alone won't do it. We also need to have an understanding of what we want to achieve. Personal goals not only guide the choices that we make, but they also energize our efforts. This chapter addresses the logic for establishing goals and reminds us that we must also be willing to accept certain risks in order to become the person we want – and were intended – to be.

Okay, another important question…when you near the end of your life, how do you want to feel about what you accomplished? Many of us believe that we will be satisfied with our lives if we simply try our best without giving much thought to our true potential. Those who think this way tend to place more value on trying than on achieving actual results. However, trying your best is seldom enough to create a true sense of personal satisfaction. It is a much better feeling to actually accomplish something, to reach a goal that you set for yourself – a goal that you not only defined and worked on, but, in fact, achieved.

> *"There's no thrill in easy sailing when the skies are clear and blue,
> there's no joy in merely doing things which any one can do.
> But there is some satisfaction that is mighty sweet to take,
> when you reach a destination that you thought you'd never make."*
>
> SPIRELLA

How are you living your life? Are you one of those who lives one day at a time, just letting things work themselves out as you go along? Or, are you a planner with long range goals and an understanding of what you want to accomplish over the next 15 to 20 years? Possibly you fall somewhere in between these two, thinking several years ahead, but not planning much further because you feel it's good to remain flexible in case some new opportunity might come along.

We have many options concerning how we live our lives. It's another choice that is ours to make. However, without well developed goals, we are likely to accomplish something less than what we are capable of achieving. Without something to stretch us and motivate us, we're likely to miss much of the opportunity our lives represent. If you want to live a special life – to maximize your individuality and fully utilize the capabilities you've been given – you need personal goals and the will to take the risks necessary to achieve them.

Sounds simple, but we all know it's not. It's not an easy task to determine what you want to accomplish in your lifetime, let alone to go out and make it happen. It's not easy to select your personal path in a world that is filled not only with many opportunities, but with many difficulties, as well. Like most, you'll probably encounter problems and some setbacks before you reach the goals you have established. Nevertheless, carefully defining what you want to accomplish with your life and making the choices that support those objectives are the keys to becoming the individual you were intended to be.

Why Establish Personal Goals?

It's much easier to live without goals, to live without any concerns about achieving something that may be difficult or just beyond our reach. We have fewer pressures, fewer disappointments, and fewer stressful moments if we don't push ourselves to accomplish something that might require long hours or an exceptional amount of work. So, if this is the case, why put yourself in the position of having to measure up to some pre-set target? Why create worries about the future, why take risks you don't have to take? Why not just sit back and let life come to you and take each day as it happens?

These are valid questions. But, choosing the easy way seldom works to our advantage in anything and certainly doesn't when it comes to deciding how we will live our lives.

The process of setting goals causes us to think through things, to determine who we want to be instead of letting others do this for us. Goal setting allows us to define what we want to do and not wait for circumstances to dictate this to us. Goal setting is the way we take charge of our lives and live according to our own plans.

Personal goals provide the guide posts by which you can judge and evaluate your choices. They put your choices in perspective and give you a context for determining the impact of a choice you're about to make. Goals stretch and motivate you to achieve something that you would never have achieved without them. Goals give you the opportunity to experience a well-deserved feeling of satisfaction as the result of accomplishing something that you set out to do.

> Bill's grandfather watched his grandson come up the front walk as he returned from his first day of fall football practice. Bill was a pretty good high-school quarterback, but his team had won only four games the previous year. And, although the prospects for his senior year were better, Bill was still very concerned about how the coming season would turn out. He sat down with his grandfather on the front porch, and they talked about the team and the coming year.
>
> "Bill, you need someone to kick extra points," his grandfather said. "You guys only made a few extra points last year."
>
> "Pop, we don't have a kicker on our team. That's why we try for two all of the time."

Establishing Goals and Taking Risks

"Bill, you can learn to kick an extra point. I know you can." his grandfather encouraged.

"You're probably right, Pop, but I don't have the time to practice and develop kicking skills," Bill retorted.

"Tell you what: I'll give you $10 for every point you can kick this year," his grandfather offered. "The only condition is that you must kick at least 10 in order to collect."

Bill, who had never been one to pass up a chance to make some money, immediately reset his thinking. "If I could make 10, that would be $100," he said. It didn't take him long to evaluate the proposition. "You've got a deal, Pop!"

The next day, Bill started working on his kicking. He kicked for 30 minutes every day before practice, and, after noticing the kicks getting higher and truer, the coach changed the practice routine to include a daily extra point drill for Bill.

As things worked out, Bill kicked 34 extra points his senior year and two of them led to his team's 14-13 win in the championship game of an undefeated season. Bill kicked 3 for 3 in the state all-star game after the regular season. He was awarded a full athletic scholarship to the university, in part, because of his kicking.

"Without that goal, I would have never kicked the first extra point," Bill thought as he walked down the aisle to get his college diploma. "And, maybe, I would have never gone to college if I hadn't been offered that football scholarship." As

> *he walked off the stage, diploma in hand, his thoughts were all about his grandfather and what an important goal Pop had helped establish for him.*

Bill's story carries an important message for all of us. Many times we won't accomplish anything at all if we don't first establish a goal that defines what we want to do. If he had not accepted the goal presented to him by his grandfather and made it his own, Bill would have never kicked that first extra point, and maybe never gone to college. As he discovered, once the goal had been established in his mind, he could start his practice sessions to achieve it. The same is true for all of us. Once you have established an important goal, you can manage the process of achieving it. You have to think about your life if you want to live it in a special way, and goal setting helps you do just that.

> *"When you determine what you want, you have made the most important decision of your life. You have to know what you want in order to attain it."*
>
> DOUGLAS LURTON
> Editor, Your Life

Goal Setting Is a Thinking Process

What do you want to do with your life? What do you want to accomplish with the time you have on this earth? What will you do for others, for your community, and for the world in

Establishing Goals and Taking Risks

which you live? How do you want to treat others, what kind of work will you do, and what will you do to maintain a healthy lifestyle? Coming up with these answers isn't something you just sit down one afternoon and do. It's not an exercise that you put on your "To Do List" and wait until you have the time to work on it. It's not a matter of patterning your life after someone else's and simply deciding that you'll "be like Mary" when you grow up. We're all unique individuals and working out the goals for our lives is something that requires a great deal of time and a very serious effort.

Goal setting is a thinking process, often extending over a period of months or even years, during which you listen to yourself in an attempt to connect the interests and motivations you have with some future objective. You must also look closely at the world around you, not only to identify possibilities for your life, but also to chart your way around potential mistakes or problem areas. The process will most likely require that you research things of specific interest so you can make informed choices for your life. Talking to others about their experiences, getting their advice and discussing your future options are all important as you work to clarify your goals. If you make a sincere and extended effort, somewhere along the way you'll instinctively know that you have found the sense of personal direction that you seek.

> Caitlan's senior year in high school was starting in just a few weeks. As a result, she had been thinking a lot about what she was going to do with her life. Since she was 12 years old, Caitlan had worked on her grandfather's horse farm. She loved everything

about horses…seeing them work out, washing them down and even the way they smelled. She couldn't imagine what her life would be like if it didn't have something to do with horses.

However, during her high school years, she acquired other interests. She joined the school chorus, loved being involved with music, and even wrote a couple of songs. She started playing tennis and won the summer tournament in her age group. She'd also developed a keen interest in environmental issues, spending hours researching global warming and wondering what she might do to help the situation.

She now had several possibilities for her life's work – horses, music, tennis, or the environment. Which should it be? During the school year she had many conversations with other people to see what advice they might have. Her folks encouraged her to follow her instincts and to "look inside yourself" to determine what would give her the most satisfaction. Several friends told her to just "do what you want to do." But, a conversation she had one afternoon with her Uncle Brett proved to be especially beneficial.

"Caitlan, you're a talented young lady so you could do lots of things well. The challenge, however, is to find the one thing that you feel the strongest about, the thing that you believe you are best equipped for, the thing that you feel you were intended to do," her uncle advised.

"I hear you Uncle Brett, but how do I do that?"

"It's not easy, but you start by visualizing yourself doing something. It might not be a clear picture but you need to develop a <u>perspective</u> of what your life would be like if you were doing one of these things. Would you enjoy doing this? What would you want to accomplish? Why is it a good fit for you? Answering questions like these will help you form these perspectives," he tried to explain.

"The problem is that I could see myself doing any of these – working with horses, teaching music, becoming a professional tennis player, or being involved in reducing global warming," she responded.

Uncle Brett continued, "I'm sure you can, but as you develop and refine these perspectives, you have to go one step further and start to determine the level of <u>conviction</u> you have for each of these. In other words, which do you feel the strongest about?"

"I always thought it would be horses, but now I'm starting to develop some very strong feelings about the others, especially the chance to help with global warming," she explained.

"Caitlan, as you work through this you must also question your <u>will</u> to work to be the best you can be in the vocation you select. For example, it might not be too difficult to gain a perspective of yourself as a champion tennis player, or to have great conviction about it. But, do you have the will to devote years of work, practice, travel, and losses it will take to achieve this goal?

> Caitlan responded, "I'm starting to see what you're talking about Uncle Brett. Your telling me to start with a perspective of my life doing something, then to gauge the level of conviction I have for it and, lastly and most important, to determine if I have the will to work to be truly successful at what I choose to do."
>
> "That's it, Caitlan, you have to consider all <u>three</u> things as you work on this decision," Uncle Brett said as he gave her an encouraging hug. "If you take some time to think about your options in this way, I know you'll make the right decision."
>
> Caitlan graduated from high school and was heading off to college in a few weeks. She had narrowed her list down to two possibilities, and one of them wasn't even on her original list. She knew that it would take her another year to confirm what she would do. She was thankful for her parents' guidance, and for her Uncle Brett's advice. She was taking an extended period of time to consider how she would spend the rest of her life, and she knew, by doing so, her final choice would be a good one.

Goal setting is like any other type of work – some days are better than others. There are days when our thoughts are inspiring, we're hitting on all cylinders, and everything seems to be going right. And, there are other days when nothing seems to go our way. There are days when people stimulate us in special ways and other days when everyone seems to be annoying. There are times when we have experiences or learn something new that causes us to reflect on the future...and other times, when we're busy, tired, or just void of any ideas concerning how we should shape the life we want to live. The point is we have to "hang in there" with our goal setting work, thinking about our possibilities until such time that we have a breakthrough moment and things suddenly become clear.

> *"The intellect has little to do on the road to discovery. There comes a leap in consciousness, call it intuition or what you will, when the solution comes to you and you don't know how or why."*
>
> ALBERT EINSTEIN

Start by Looking Inside Yourself

Whether you believe so at this very moment or not, you possess the ingredients to be a very special person. You can touch the lives of people in special and wonderful ways, and you can accomplish things that no one else can accomplish. Regardless of your age, what you've done in the past, or your current circumstances, you can accomplish important things – in your own special way – if you're willing to establish worthwhile goals and work to achieve them.

Each of us is unique. Each of us has our own special role to fulfill in our families, our communities, and in the world around us. This belief is reinforced every time I'm touched by an exceptionally gracious person, or see a child exhibit special skills or interests, or read about someone who has devoted her life to a worthy cause. The logic for setting goals is that it provides the opportunity to look inside yourself and to chart a course to accomplish something that you've determined to be important to you.

> *One of the most successful restaurants in Chicago is Charlie Trotter's. The restaurant is filled to capacity almost every night and, during certain times of the year, reservations must be made months in advance. Dinner typically includes eight to ten small courses each masterfully prepared and served with precise explanations from the capable wait staff.*
>
> *When asked why he served in this small, multiple course format Charlie explained that this was always the way he wanted to eat when he was growing up. Rather than one large course, he had always wanted and enjoyed eating many small ones...so he organized his restaurant in the same way.*
>
> *Obviously, Charlie is successful because he's a great chef. Additionally, he's successful because he followed the motivation that was inside of him and worked to utilize the gifts he has been given. He's a chef who actually felt the way he would serve his food. Charlie didn't go out and develop a restaurant like every one else...he clearly did it his way.*

For your goals to work for you they must be in concert with some feeling you have about what you should do with your life. The lad who decides he wants to be a business executive just because they make a lot of money, but doesn't have the motivation to do the type of work involved, is not likely to be a success. On the other hand, the young woman who's motivated to save the lives of others will most likely become a great surgeon even though she sits today wondering how she'll get the money to attend medical school. There must be a connection between our motivations – our purpose, if you will – and our goals. If we can "see it" and are motivated to achieve it, we can almost always find a way to make it happen.

Effective goal setting depends upon insightful and independent thinking. Being insightful requires that you take a serious look inside yourself to understand what is really going on "in there." Your interests, abilities, and motivations are all providing you with clues as to what you should do with your life. You need to devote quality time to thinking about these personal inclinations and the opportunities they represent to make your own mark on this world. Being independent in your thinking requires that you carefully filter what's happening in the world and determine just "who and what" will influence the goals you establish for your life. If you are willing to follow the feelings that flow from within you and careful to control the influences coming from the world around you, you can live a life created by your own personal vision of the future.

> *And be not conformed to this world;*
> *but be transformed by the renewing of your mind,*
> *so that you may prove what is the good and*
> *acceptable and perfect will of God.*
>
> THE BIBLE
> Romans 12:2

What Do You Want to Accomplish?

We've all thought about the question...what is the purpose of life? However, that is not the question I am trying to get you to answer here. The question I would like for you to think about is...what is the purpose of your life?" What are you supposed to do with the life you've been given? We're all different – with different looks, feelings, abilities, and motivations. What you are meant to do and what I am meant to do are two different things. So, the biggest mistake you can make in this quest to set meaningful goals is to follow the crowd and try to do what others are doing. Instead, you must work to define personal goals based on what your own life is telling or showing you to do.

When we think about goal setting, we typically associate the activity with our work or our career. The other parts of our lives such as our family, friends and free-time activities often play a secondary role. Maybe we do this due to financial reasons, believing that the sources of our incomes should take priority over other sources of our happiness. When we stop to think about this point, most of us will quickly agree that our career isn't all we want in life. Nevertheless, we seldom think about setting goals for our non-work activities. To help us prevent this, I suggest that you approach goal setting with a "total person" perspective, considering all of the major parts of your life that collectively make you the individual you are.

> *Cameron was a very talented young man with a great legal mind. He had finished at the top of his law school class and landed a great position with*

Establishing Goals and Taking Risks

the leading firm in the city. He had been working hard, putting in lots of hours, but nearing the end of his first year he just didn't feel that he was making as much progress as he should. His gut feeling was soon confirmed.

His annual performance review with one of the senior partners had been going for only a few minutes, when Jeff Geonatti got straight to the point. "Cameron, you're one of the brightest young lawyers we've ever hired and you work hard, too. But Cameron, you treat people around here in a condescending manner, like you're better or you know more than they do. You're doing some fine legal work, but you're not making many friends while you're doing it. In fact, you are turning some people off by the way you treat them."

Cameron looked up at Jeff. He knew that Jeff was right, but he never thought that the firm valued anything other than results.

"Practicing law, like life, is a team sport," Jeff said. Most of our major cases involve three or four lawyers, all working together to effectively represent our client. If you continue to treat people as you have been doing, no one in this office will want you on their team, much less work on one of yours someday."

Cameron understood what Jeff was saying, but he had never thought that "being nice" was that important.

"Cameron, you must be able to perform well in front of your associates as well as in front of the

jury," Jeff explained. *"I've read your goals for next year and none of them address working or interacting with other people. I want you to go back to the drawing board and develop some goals concerning how you will treat other members of this firm. When you have them done, come back and we'll finish this review."*

"I'm sorry, Jeff," Cameron said. *"I've been working without much regard for my associates. I do understand what you're telling me and you can count on me to set some challenging goals in this regard."*

"Good, Cameron. Some people never notice how they impact others, but it's probably the most important ingredient in a successful career. Come back to see me when you're ready." *With that, Jeff opened the office door and stepped aside for Cameron to depart.*

To assist you, outlined below are eight types of goals with associated questions to serve as a basis for a goal-setting process. When working through these, remember that few of us actually see ourselves as others see us, so some honest self-assessment is required before any real goal-setting progress can be made. As you work on your goals, take advantage of opportunities to discuss your personal feelings, development needs and potential opportunities with someone you trust because verbalizing your feelings and intentions almost always brings greater clarity to them.

- FRIENDSHIP GOALS -

What do you want to accomplish through your interactions with other people?

We live our lives in conjunction with other people. Whether it's the neighbor we wave to as we retrieve the morning paper, the interactions with our associates at work, or our daily experiences in dealing with the members of our family, we come in contact with many other people as we live, work, and play. As a result, we have many opportunities not only to touch the lives of others, but to be touched by their lives, as well. What personal goals do *you* want to establish to make sure that your encounters with other people work to the benefit of all involved?

> *"The art of dealing with people is the foremost secret of successful men.*
> *A man's success in handling people is the very yardstick by which the outcome of his whole life's work will be measured."*
>
> PAUL C. PACKER
> Educator and Chancellor

- FAMILY GOALS -

What do you want to accomplish in your family life?

Truth is…we all have opinions about various members of our extended family. Some we love and some we don't like very much. Nevertheless, our family life can be the most influential experience in our lives, teaching us important lessons in our early years and being there for us in times of need. What you learn from family members, as well as the experiences you share with them can greatly enrich your life. The examples set by a hard-working dad, a God-fearing mother, or a gifted brother or sister can stay with you for a lifetime. Therefore, regardless of your age or position in the family pecking order, you should have goals that define how you can make your family unit a more positive environment for all involved. What personal goals do <u>you</u> have that will strengthen your family and increase the importance of the role <u>you</u> play within it?

> *"Families can help their members to grow individually. The family is the place to learn and follow moral standards. It can teach fair play which leads to justice; temperance in opinion, speech and habits which frees from excess; and honesty and sincerity which lead to a disciplined, balanced life."*
>
> ANNE G. PANNELL
> Founding Trustee, College Entrance Board of NY

- CAREER GOALS -

What do you want to accomplish in your work life?

A successful career – whether working in business, raising a child, or committing yourself to a special cause – can produce great returns in terms of personal satisfaction as you give your life in devotion to something other than yourself. What you do is testimony to your choice to either work to "achieve success" or to work to become the person you were intended to be. There are great rewards if you make the right choices, if you're willing to try to understand what you were placed here to do, and if you will listen to your interests and motivations and allow them to lead you to the work you were called to do. What do *you* hear your life telling you and what personal goals will *you* establish to follow the signals that are present in your life?

> *"If a man has any brains at all, let him hold on to his calling,*
> *and, in the grand sweep of things,*
> *his turn will come at last."*
>
> WILLIAM MCCUNE

- SPIRITUAL GOALS -

What do you want to accomplish in your spiritual life?

There are over 370,000 churches in the United States. Therefore, you have lots of places you can go to obtain guidance as to what you should do to further develop the spiritual part of your life. However, it seems to me that one of the goals we all should think about, possibly more so than which church we will attend, is how we will become more willing to "listen to" and be guided by the spiritual influence in our lives. Because God's will is not forced upon you, you have to be willing to listen for God's influence within your life. More importantly, you must be willing to make choices that align your life with that influence. Therefore, the work of goal setting would not be complete if we don't devote some careful thought to how we will open ourselves to this influence. What personal goals will *you* adopt that will help *you* listen more closely to the spiritual influence within your life?

> *"Get the pattern of your life from God,*
> *then go about your work and be yourself."*
>
> PHILLIPS BROOKS
> Former Episcopal Bishop of Massachusetts

- COMMUNITY GOALS -

What do you want to accomplish in your community?

We are members of many communities – our neighborhoods, our cities, our states and our countries. Given the extent of television coverage today and the ability to connect to any place via the Internet, we're becoming active members of a world community as well. Our lives, both in terms of quality as well as the choices we can make, depend on how well each of these communities functions and support the needs of the individuals within it. There are many needs out there: reducing crime, improving schools, electing more effective and fiscally responsible government leaders, and reducing global warming are just a few. Where will you get involved to help make things better for you and those who live within these communities? What personal goals will <u>you</u> establish to help make these communities a better place in which to live?

> *"If the world is cold, make it your business to build fires."*
>
> HORACE TRAUBEL
> Founder of the Walt Whitman Journal

- GIVING GOALS -

What do you want to accomplish in helping those less fortunate than you?

It is not only "more blessed to give than to receive," but we feel so much better about ourselves when we know that we made a difference in the life of another person. Whether it is a homeless person in our town, an elderly person living alone, a young child trying to learn to read, a battered woman trying to get back on her feet, or the victim of some weather-related catastrophe, we can make a major difference in the life of someone less fortunate. What personal goals will <u>you</u> establish that will stimulate <u>you</u> to become actively involved in the lives of such individuals?

> *"Verily I say unto you, inasmuch as you have done it unto one of the least of these my brethren, you have done it unto to me."*
>
> THE BIBLE
> Matthew 25:40

- HEALTH GOALS -

What do you need to do to improve your health and fitness?

This book devotes an entire chapter to health related choices, so hopefully it will stimulate you to establish goals that will improve the condition of your body. As you may recall, over 60 percent of us are overweight so the odds are there are things that you can do to not only improve your health, but also extend the time that you will live. What personal goals will *you* establish relative to your diet and your exercise routines that will improve your physical condition?

> *"To lose one's health renders science null, art inglorious, strength unavailing, wealth useless and eloquence powerless."*
>
> HEROPHILUS

- ACTIVITY GOALS -

What do you do want to accomplish with your free time?

This may seem to be an unlikely area for goal setting work. Who needs to establish personal goals to play tennis or to work in the yard in the afternoon? Many of us might prefer to have our free time left open and unencumbered by any type of goal or objective. However, I'm not talking about all of your free time. I'm simply suggesting that you think how you can make some of this time personally rewarding. Many of us have skills and interests outside of our work that, if properly nurtured and developed, could bring much satisfaction into our lives. The lady who learns to paint, the man who becomes an exceptional gardener, and even a guy who writes a book are but a few examples of individuals who bring balance and enjoyment into their lives by using some portion of their free time productively. What interests do you have outside of your work and what goals do <u>you</u> need to establish to help you take full advantage of this aspect of your life?

> *"You were intended not only to work, but to rest, laugh, play and have proper leisure and enjoyment. To develop an all-around personality you must have interest outside of your regular vocation that will serve to balance your other responsibilities."*
>
> GRENVILLE KLEISER
> American Writer on Success and Positive Thinking

Please Note: Goals Have an Immediate Impact on Your Life

The impact of a well-developed goal is not something you have to wait to experience. At the time you establish an important goal and commit to work to achieve it, that goal starts to change your life. You don't have to wait until the goal is fully accomplished before you start to benefit from your choice to work to achieve it. An important goal, when pursued with careful thought, honest feelings, and a firm resolve, will start to change your life the moment you commit yourself to its achievement.

A transformation takes place within us when we feel that our lives have become attached to some larger goal. We even perform better and make better choices when we can see that our daily activities are steps toward the achievement of an important goal. This transformation process starts when you gain some understanding of what you want to accomplish with your life. It continues and is nurtured as you establish goals that better define that potential. When you establish goals that you believe are right for you, you experience a contentment that comes from knowing that you are "on track" to accomplish something important with your life.

> *"What we truly and earnestly aspire to be, that in some sense we are."*
>
> ANNA JAMESON
> British Author of The House of Titian

What Role Does Risk Taking Play in All of This?

A man may dream for years about his goal to fly to Europe, but if his fear of flying prevents him from going to the airport and actually boarding the airplane, he may never experience the wonders that such a trip might provide. Likewise, many of us walk around with great thoughts, great ideas, and even great goals, but due to our "fear of flying," we never activate them in our lives.

This fear can come from many sources. You may be afraid to be different or to do something different from what your friends or your associates are doing. You may be afraid that you'll make less money if you do what you feel you should do, instead of taking the higher paying job. You may be afraid that you would simply fail, that your interests and motivations are not strong enough for you to succeed doing things your way. More frequently, you may be afraid that you're not reading yourself correctly, that what you feel you should do is a false positive and that you may be doing the wrong thing. Whatever the reason is for your fear, if you cannot overcome it, you'll most assuredly never live a life of your own making.

It is important to note that we all have fears...they're a part of everyone's life. Executives who manage large companies live with fears about market changes and competition that may adversely affect the business. Doctors who perform complicated surgical procedures have to deal with the fear of unexpectedly losing or harming the patient. Even professional athletes who have played hundreds of times have fears before a game that the outcome may not turn out to be in their team's favor. It is normal to be concerned about the outcome of some important event...the living of our lives certainly not excluded. However, if we accept fear as being a normal part of living and expect it to appear at various intervals in our lives, we can deal with it in a more effective way.

> *"Life is not meant to be easy, my child; but take courage, it can be delightful."*
>
> GEORGE BERNARD SHAW
> Nobel Prize Winning Playwright

Goal setting, even when well thought out and based on the very desires of our heart, is likely to create some level of fear within us. You must be willing to deal with that fear if you're going to go out and achieve the goals you have established. The most helpful thing in doing so is to understand that fear is, in fact, an advantage. You will actually perform better when you are somewhat fearful than when you are over confident. We've all heard stories about how a man was able to lift a car that fell on his friend or moved a heavy piece of furniture in order for someone to escape the burning building. Fear can be a motivator. Expect your goals to create fears...but also expect to use those fears to your advantage as you work to achieve the goals that you have chosen for your life.

There are no secrets here – fear is a real factor in our lives and it has stopped many a man from doing what he would dearly love to do. Many of us are stuck where we are today primarily because we are scared to follow our heart in pursuit of something different. Well developed goals that you believe are in synch with your interests and motivations will, to some extent, soften those fears as you develop some level of logic and excitement for what lies ahead. But sometimes, you just have to go for it – sometimes you can't wait for things to be totally logical, for everything to be perfect or for all risks to be minimized. If you're going to do something special with your life, there comes a time when you must step out on faith and live your life as you believe it was intended to be lived.

> *"For truth and duty it is ever the fitting time;
> he who waits until circumstances completely favor
> his undertaking, will never accomplish anything."*
>
> MARTIN LUTHER

Anytime Is a Good Time for Goal Setting

Many people think that goal setting is something young people should do. That's certainly true, but goal setting in adulthood can be even more rewarding. When you're older, you have more experience, more knowledge and a better understanding of yourself. Therefore, the ultimate productivity level of goals established later in life can be extremely high. This is also when a willingness to take risks becomes a bigger part of the equation. When you're young, you have less fear and a stronger belief that you can climb almost any mountain. When you're older and settled into a safe job or circumstances, your fear starting something new may keep you from doing so, in spite of having a great idea and strong motivation. Nevertheless, some of your greatest satisfactions can come from choices made later in your life.

> *"Junior" – the name his dad tagged him with that
> first day at the hospital – was in his early 40's
> and, by any definition, considered himself to be an
> average guy. He'd graduated from the University*

of Illinois and gone to work for a bank in a western Chicago suburb. A few years later he married Olivia, a hard-working accountant he'd met while attending a Cubs game with friends. He and Olivia had two rambunctious boys, 7 and 9 years old. Over the past 20 years, Junior had worked for three different banks and, most recently, a heavy equipment leasing company.

Working in the financial industry had been okay, but he'd never felt any significant motivation to get up and go to work in the mornings. He'd always done his job but was never on the fast track. Lately, he'd been thinking a lot about what he was doing and where his life was headed. It wasn't exactly a mid-life crisis, but he'd started to wonder if he was doing the right thing and what his life might be like in another 20 years. He definitely didn't feel fulfilled, but he had a wife, a family, and a home to take care of and knew that this was no time to do something stupid.

When Junior was in high school, he'd thought he would be an artist. He loved art classes, loved starting out with blank paper and turning it into something special, and had even won awards in several state art contests. But, his dad insisted that being an artist was a good way to starve to death. "You're going to college and make something out of yourself," he'd said. Junior's dad had been so emphatic about it that Junior suppressed his interest in art and never really made another career choice.

The bank job became available, and he took it without much thought.

During the past week, he'd thought about that conversation with his dad many years before. He'd gone up in the attic and looked at some of his old art supplies as he thought about what his dad said. One evening, after the boys went to bed, he broached the subject with Olivia.

"Olivia, I've really had some strange feelings lately," he said. "I guess I'm wondering if I did the right thing giving up on a potential art career." Olivia was well aware of Junior's early interest in art and, having seen a couple of his early works, she'd always hoped he would start painting again.

"Junior, I know this is very important to you...I can hear it in your voice," Olivia responded. "Why don't you start painting again in your spare time? We'll even set a goal to sell one painting before Christmas, and I'll help you do it."

Junior felt like the fairy godmother had just touched him with her magic wand. "Sell one painting before Christmas" – just the thought of doing such a thing thrilled him. The empty feeling he felt for several years disappeared and was replaced with a strong urge to start painting again. Now he had a goal – one that was consistent with what he'd always wanted to do, and it seemed to change his life almost in an instant.

Over the next few days, Junior replenished his painting supplies. Olivia arranged the boys' schedule so that he could be with them every afternoon before dinner, but free to paint after that. As she shooed the boys to their rooms to do their homework following dinner one evening, she turned to Junior, kissed him on the cheek, and said, "Now, go enjoy your painting time...I'll be up to check on you in a little while." Happy as a little boy with a new toy, Junior hurried off to his painting room in the attic, which was quickly becoming his favorite place to be.

With six months left until Christmas, Junior decided that he would complete three paintings, roughly one every two months, hoping that one of the three would sell. Olivia, ever the organizer, prepared a list of art shops in the city and checked them out while the boys were in school and Junior was at work each day. There seemed to be four or five good galleries, and she committed to herself to get Junior's paintings in at least three of them.

The months flew by. After struggling with a few paintings, Junior had turned out three paintings that pleased him. Olivia had told him point blank, "Junior, these are great! Mr. Owens is going to be so impressed." Olivia had convinced the Owens Gallery to show Junior's work at a special pre-Christmas wine tasting and showing scheduled for the following week.

The showing turned out to be the most exciting night in Junior's life. It was great just to be there, to meet other artists, and to see his work actually on display. The patrons loved the images of Junior's outdoor scenes. To Junior's delight and disbelief,

Establishing Goals and Taking Risks

all three of his paintings sold that night. As he and Olivia sat by the fire at home later that evening, Junior, a bit choked up, said, "Olivia, you're the greatest wife a guy could have. Thank you so much for encouraging me and helping me the way you have these past six months."

"Junior, I've loved every minute of it, but we'll need to get busy if we're going to sell 10 more paintings by next Christmas. Junior's eyes lit up – there was his next goal "10 more paintings by next Christmas."

"Sounds good to me," he said as he reached out for Olivia.

Over the course of the next year, Junior turned out 16 paintings, again wanting to have more than he needed to reach his goal to "sell 10 paintings by Christmas." Olivia had convinced two other galleries to display Junior's work. During the course of the year, she delivered 3 paintings to each of the new galleries and 10 to their now close friend, Bo Owens of Owens Gallery, who had been willing to take a chance on Junior when he was totally unknown. At Bo's suggestion, they had more than tripled the price of Junior's work, with most of his paintings now priced around $3,000. All of Junior's paintings sold during the year, with the last five quickly taken at Bo's annual pre-Christmas showing.

One of the things that had amazed Junior about all of this was that in spite of working all of these extra hours on his paintings at home, things at the office seemed to pick up, too. He had closed *three major new lease accounts, finished the year in second place in business booked, and won the "most improved player" award at the company's year end sales meeting. He started to wonder if the change he had experienced as a result of his painting was now showing up in his attitude at work, as well.*

As he and Olivia sat in front their Christmas tree at what had turned out to be their annual goal setting session, Junior raised the possibility of giving up his job and painting full time. "Frankly, it scares me to death to even think about it, but it would be wonderful if I could support the people I love the most with the thing I love doing the most...that would be absolutely fantastic," he said.

Ever the level headed one, Olivia responded, "Junior, you're doing so well at work now...and you're going to earn a good bit more this coming year...do you want to risk leaving all of that?"

"Olivia, my heart is saying 'yes' but my fear factor is saying 'no.'" They both looked at each other and into the fire as they weighed the choices that were before them.

A few weeks later, Junior told her: "Olivia, I've been thinking about what I could do if I worked at my painting full time. I feel confident that I could turn out 25 good paintings a year which could be priced in the $5,000 range. Our net would be approximately $75,000 a year...what do you think?"

"I'm thinking that will be our next goal...25 paintings by next Christmas. I'm a bit scared too,

Junior, but I will do everything I can to help you achieve it."

Junior resigned from the leasing company in January and started painting full time. He found that he could turn out closer to three paintings a month, even allowing extra time to play with the boys when they came home from school. They loved going up to "the paint room" to see what their dad had painted that day. Olivia and Junior worked out a business strategy in which Olivia would work to sell two of the paintings each month and they would save the "pick of the litter" for Bo's annual Christmas showing. There were a few scary moments waiting for a painting to sell or a check to arrive from the gallery, but they kept their goal of 25 foremost in their minds and kept chipping away at it.

They were excitedly anticipating Bo's annual Christmas event which would feature 10 of Junior's best paintings…the ones that he and Oliva had selected together as the year had progressed. Bo was also very excited when he saw the work that Junior had done. He quickly recommended a price increase to $7,500 on the group with the exception of two which he deemed "the best work I have seen in a long time" as he suggested pricing "Little River" and "Big River" at $12,500 each. Bo had been a good friend and a good advisor so Olivia and Junior readily followed his advice.

Bo's Christmas show was the biggest and best ever. He was featuring seven exceptionally good *artists this year, all national "up and comers." There was a lot of talent there but, without question, Junior's work was creating the most interest. Junior's dad had begrudgingly agreed to attend the event at his wife's insistence. He'd been standing for some time in front of the $12,500 painting looking at the fine work and then at the name in the lower right corner – Henry Hall, Jr. He recalled the conversations he'd had with his son more than 20 years ago and his comments about all of those "starving artists." Looking at the painting and down again at the signature, he realized how wrong he'd been. He turned and walked directly to his son and said, "Junior, I'm very proud of you, not only because of your talent, but also because you had the guts to use it. I was dead wrong in the way I handled things. I should have been encouraging you instead of telling you what to do. I hope that you will forgive me." "Big Henry" reached out and hugged his son for the first time in his life.*

Later that evening, Junior and Olivia sat together in front of the fire as they reflected on what was happening in their lives. All of Junior's paintings sold that evening, all at record prices and Junior quickly figured that their "Christmas bonus" was going to be about $60,000. They talked about how happy they were that Junior and his dad had reconnected after all of these years. "I always wanted to make dad happy," Junior commented. They talked about how well things had worked out for their family and how their marriage and the

Establishing Goals and Taking Risks

boys had benefited from the choices they had made. And, Junior talked about how he felt so much more fulfilled as a result of doing what he truly loved to do.

They sat there silently for several minutes. Then Junior looked closely at Oliva, kissed her affectionately and said, "Just think, Olivia... it all started with that goal to 'sell one painting by Christmas.'"

It doesn't matter if you're very young and just starting to think seriously about your life, or you're much older and wondering if you're living as you should. At either point in time – or anywhere in between – the potential benefits of developing personal goals for your life can be very significant. Some of us are blessed with youthful talent which may become apparent in our early years. Others may require, as I did, almost a lifetime of experiences before we start to really understand how we should use the talents we've been given. The main point is that well-developed goals can invigorate your life and bring a new level of energy to your daily routines. It's never too early or too late for someone to experience feelings like that.

~~~~~~~~~~

Most of us would jump at an opportunity to re-energize our lives. Life has a tendency to become routine and, at times, most of us find ourselves a bit disappointed with the way our life seems to be working out. We'd like to change things, make an adjustment, and be happier, but the question is – how do we do it? You do it by setting an important goal...a goal that's not only important to you but potentially worthwhile for others…a goal that reflects an inner desire about something that you really want to do. It may be something that has been in your mind for a long time or a rather recent idea. Whatever its vintage, if you have never committed yourself to it by turning these thoughts and wishes into a specific goal, maybe this is the time to do so. If you want to have a new and renewed feeling about your life, clarify and confirm that goal… and then commit yourself to achieving it.

CHAPTER 13

MAKING THE EFFORT

"He that would have the fruit must first climb the tree."

THOMAS FULLER
Adages and Proverbs

We can make good choices and set important goals but still fall short of our intended targets if we aren't willing to make the effort our circumstances require. We can choose to do a lot of wonderful things but not accomplish any of them if our efforts are half-hearted. Our choices are very important, but we must also be willing to expend the effort that is required to turn our choices – and our goals – into reality.

Why do some people achieve so much during their lifetimes and others very little? Why do some people do extremely well in school and others barely get by? Why do some people have rewarding careers and others fail to achieve much at all? If we posed these questions to a large group of people, we would likely hear that such things as luck, family, intelligence, personality, money, or genes played the primary role in such outcomes. And, as the writer of this book, I would certainly add "choices" to this list. No doubt about it, lucky breaks, family support, and good choices are important. In fact, any of these can be a determining factor in the way our lives work out. But, looking beyond these, there seems to be a more fundamental ingredient that makes the real difference in "whether we do" or "whether we don't."

It was 1928. W. C. Leonard owned five department stores in the mid-south. It had taken him many years of hard work, but he had built a successful business and was highly respected by both customers and competitors alike. Then came the stock market crash of 1929 and many people were wiped out. He was forced to close four of his stores. Although he managed to keep one store open, he was left with an overwhelming debt.

Many businessmen in similar circumstances declared bankruptcy to get relief from their debts and to make a fresh start. But W. C. Leonard didn't believe that bankruptcy was the right thing to do. Instead, he acknowledged his debt to his suppliers and told them he would repay them when he could. This became a personal goal as he committed himself to making sure his suppliers were repaid.

Over the next 10 years, he worked exceptionally hard to rebuild his business. Often foregoing things that he needed, he made payments to his suppliers whenever he could. In 1938, after much sacrifice, he made the final payment to his largest supplier.

Shortly thereafter, the president of that supplier wrote a special letter to Mr. Leonard saying, "I have known and worked with many exceptional people in my life, but I have encountered few men like W. C. Leonard. Your effort to repay your debt to us and the integrity you have exhibited over the past

> 10 years will always be remembered and appreciated. Whatever you need in the future, this company stands ready to provide."

Few of us get all of the lucky breaks or have all of the money or intelligence we need. Almost all of us have deficiencies, handicaps, or real-world circumstances that, if we let them, would hinder us from achieving what we'd like to accomplish in life. However, "those who do" find a way to make up for these shortcomings. They do it through effort by working longer, harder, and more diligently to achieve their goals. Without an exceptional effort, few things of note are ever achieved.

> Vijay Singh has played on the PGA tour for over 19 years. He started playing in 1989, won less than $11,000 his first year and only $728 during his third year on the tour. By no means was Vijay a natural talent. However, during 2004, Vijay won nine PGA golf events, prize money totaling more than $10,000,000, and was named PGA Player of the Year. In 2008 he won the prestigious Fedex Cup compiling the most "winner's points" on the tour. He now has 34 PGA Tour victories, another 22 victories on the international circuit, and career earnings in excess of $70,000,000.
>
> So, what happened? How did Vijay, after such a poor start, go on to become such a great golfer?
>
> The truth is that Vijay has a long-standing reputation as the hardest working professional on the PGA tour. He's noted for his relentless practice

> *habits and rigorous practice routines. He puts in more hours, hits more balls, and practices his game more than any other player. Vijay is a great example of what effort can do in one's life. Making the choice to be a golfer was one thing, but it's been the effort behind that choice that has made Vijay the outstanding professional golfer that he is today.*

These two real-life examples – one, an older man working to repay his debts and the other, a younger man working to develop his golfing skills – reflect different circumstances, but the same reason for their ultimate success. Both W. C. Leonard and Vijay Singh were willing to do whatever it took to achieve something that was important to them. They made their choices, but, more importantly, they were willing to devote the effort it took to turn their choices into reality.

> *"So with slight efforts, how could one obtain great results? It is foolish even to desire it."*
>
> EURIPIDES
> Greek Thinker

Empty Promises and Empty Efforts

How many people have openly stated they were going to lose a certain amount of weight, but never did? How many millions of New Year resolutions fade from memory in a matter of weeks? How many people have made the choice to quit smoking, but never achieved that goal? How many things have we said we were going to do, but never accomplished? Unfortunately, many of us make commitments that we never come close to turning into reality.

Why do many of us fail in situations such as these? Why do we say one thing but do another? There may be lots of reasons, even some valid ones, which cause us to change our intended course of action. However, in most instances, it comes down to one of two things. Many times, our stated intentions weren't valid in the first place. We said it, but we never had any intention of doing what we said. We call these "empty promises," and they are typically made to bolster our egos or to verbally compensate for some deficiency we think we have. Sometimes we simply make promises that sound great, but have no intention of ever fulfilling them.

> *"As honest words may not sound fine, fine words may not be honest ones."*
>
> LAO-TZU
> From The Way of Life by R. B. Blakney

More frequently, we say that we are going to do something, but with little forethought concerning what will actually be required to complete it. When we set out to do the task, we find that it requires more time, work, and sacrifice than we expected (or, more precisely, than we are willing to give). Far too many of us are long on words, but short on effort. Simply stated, we are just not willing to do the work required to achieve the goal we set.

As you work to make better choices in your life, it's important for you to understand that more is required of you than just making the choice. You must also be willing to pay the price to make that choice become a reality. It's easy for someone to say "I'm going to be successful," but something else to do so in the face of no family support, the difficulty of getting a good education, and the challenge of determining what you were meant to do. It's easy to say "I should apologize for what I did" but something else to humble yourself in front of your friend and do whatever is required to mend a broken friendship. It's easy enough to say "I want our marriage to be better" but something else to actually make the changes in behavior and schedules that will make the relationship strong once again. It's your effort that turns your choices into something real and meaningful. Without the accompanying effort, your choices – as good or as important as they may be – will have little impact on your life.

> *"More undertakings fail for want of spirit than from want of sense."*
>
> WILLIAM HAZLITT
> The Round Table

Making the Effort for Others

Sometimes we consider ourselves to be in our own little world, believing that what we do is our business and should be of no concern to others. We tend to think that we have the right to do as we please and that others shouldn't worry about what we do and why we do it. "Just accept me as I am, don't try to change me, and let me live the way I want" is how some of us think. If we were alone on this earth and were not supposed to use our lives to help others achieve happiness and fulfillment, it might be okay to think this way. However, the common purpose we all share is that we're here for each other – our lives are intended to help others in some way.

Therefore, you should be mindful that your choices will have an impact on other people if you expect to create the motivation, and thus the effort, to accomplish them. For example, let's go back to the value of honesty. If you simply decide to "be honest" and view it as little more than that, you're not likely to see the potential significance of your choice. On the other hand, if you consider the impact that your honest dealings will have on how your children learn to live their lives or how your co-workers might conduct their business activities, your simple choice to "be honest" becomes more expansive, involving many more people than yourself.

Ruth had been overweight since her first child was born 18 years ago. At first it was only a few pounds, but, over time, she ate more, exercised less, and became a very large woman. She tried many diets and, in fact, did lose a few pounds on several occasions. But every time, she returned to her old habits and soon to her previous weight...plus a few pounds more.

In reality, Ruth needed to lose at least 60 pounds. She now wore a size 14, a far cry from the size 6 she wore throughout her college years. She no longer had the energy she once did and she had noticed that her poor eating and exercise habits were influencing her two somewhat overweight children.

But, like her weight problem and her lack-of-energy problem, she chose to ignore her "I'm-a-bad-influence-on my-children" problem, as well.

One afternoon she was talking with her best friend, Liz, and the subject of weight came up. "I know I need to lose a few pounds," she confessed. "But, you know, I've learned to live with it and it just doesn't bother me anymore."

Liz saw the opening and, trying to fulfill the role of a close and concerned friend, decided to go for it, "Ruth, you don't need to lose a few pounds, you need to lose a lot." Ruth looked over at her, but didn't say a word.

Liz continued, "It's not just about you, Ruth. You need to think about how your condition affects others. If you lose that extra weight, you would be setting a great example for your daughters who will probably have to fight this problem during their lifetimes."

After her discussion with Liz about how her circumstances were influencing her daughters, Ruth confessed, "I just never thought about losing weight for someone else. I never stopped to think how my overweight condition might be affecting my children. When I think about it from their standpoint, I can see how important it really is. I need to change my eating and exercise habits...as you suggest not just for myself, but for my daughters, too."

Liz added, "And, Ralph might start to act a little younger when he sees you back in a size 6."

> *Ruth smiled as she thought about her future*
> *"new look" and how it would help her children and*
> *maybe help old Ralph, too!*
>
> *Many of the people around us are influenced by*
> *what we do. Our friends and family, as well as our*
> *business associates or school mates notice the choices*
> *we make. Therefore, the choices that determine*
> *the way we live have potential significance for*
> *those around us who are trying to learn to make*
> *good choices, too. When you view your choices as*
> *having an important impact beyond your own life, it*
> *becomes easier to make the effort required because,*
> *in so doing, you not only help yourself but you help*
> *those around you, as well.*

Don't make the choice to quit smoking just for yourself. Make the choice for your family, your friends, and the environment in which you live. Don't make the decision to become a homebuilder just for yourself; do so for the families who will enjoy living in your homes. Don't make the choice to get a job for yourself; do so with the mindset that your work will help your customers and fellow employees. In other words, when you view your choices in terms of their impact on other people, you are much more likely to make the effort that will be needed to achieve something important with your life.

> *"...we'll lower the cost of living for everyone,*
> *not just in America, but we'll give the world*

> *an opportunity to see what it is like to save and have a better lifestyle, a better life for all."*
>
> SAM WALTON
> Founder, Wal-Mart

Becoming the Person We Were Intended to Be

Another important way we stimulate our efforts is to focus our lives on becoming the person we were intended to be. While you may have several goals, your most important and overriding goal should be to develop the interests and capabilities you have been given. Every one of us comes into this world pre-equipped with certain interests, feelings, and motivations. When acknowledged and understood, these qualities give your life its uniqueness and will guide you to your primary role or purpose for your life. If you can get yourself in synch with these personal ingredients, there are few obstacles that you cannot overcome in achieving your goals.

> *While attending a psychology course his freshman year, it clicked for Noel. He had become fascinated by the study of psychology, and, visualizing how he might use this knowledge to help people, he established a goal to earn his Ph.D. and work in the field.*
>
> *Unfortunately, during the following summer Noel fell from a large tree and damaged his spinal cord. Due to his injury, returning to college would be difficult, if not impossible. He had no means of transportation, limited arm movement, and getting*

in and out of the college buildings would be very time consuming. However, he really wanted to be a clinical psychologist, and after observing some other students going to school in their wheelchairs, he decided there must be a way.

Transportation was the first obstacle -- he had to get there! He talked his father into buying an old Plymouth van. No fancy lift or electronic ramp on this one, nor did it have a lowered floor or raised roof. They built a crude wooden ramp and slid it up to the back doors of the van. And with a running start each time, his father got him inside.

Learning to write was his next big challenge. In rehabilitation, the occupational therapist tried all sorts of splints and other devices. Unfortunately, they were difficult to put on and totally ineffective for holding the pen reliably. So he tried doing it on his own without special equipment. At first it was slow and his writing was hard to read, but as time went by he got faster and more efficient.

Noel spent most of his time thinking about the day he would be a practicing professional, helping people work through personal problems and find a way to live a productive life. The very idea of helping people in this way had propelled him since the day "the bug bit him" in his freshman psychology class.

It hadn't been easy, but today Noel is a clinical psychologist in private practice and works with patients every day. It took hard work, determination, and commitment to his goals to achieve this ability.

> *What advice would he give to others? "Discover your passion...find out what you really want to do... establish a goal for your life...and remain mindful that your primary purpose in being here is to help others. That will help you overcome the obstacles that will almost certainly get in your way."*

The key to making an exceptional effort is reflected in Noel's story above. It is to have an important goal or something significant that you <u>really</u> want to accomplish with your life. Noel discovered his passion in his psychology class and soon thereafter established his goal of becoming a clinical psychologist. It was the pursuit of that goal that drove his behavior, and helped him overcome the difficulties involved. And, so it is with us. We must have an important goal – and be ever mindful of it – if we can expect to get an exceptional effort out of ourselves.

We Shall Overcome...Someday

In addition to your goal, a major part of a successful effort is the choice not to give up even though it make take years, or even a lifetime, to complete your work. To accomplish something important, a single, short-term effort is rarely enough. Martin Luther King worked from the age of 17 and throughout his adult life for fair and equal rights for all people, and I'm certain that he would still be hard at it if he were alive today. Mother Teresa spent more than 70 years of her life working in the ghettos of India to improve the lives of the poor people there. The same is true for you and me. Frequently in life, we must work at something over a long, extended period of time to accomplish the goal we have established.

For as long as she could remember, Lindsey's goal had been to win the Women's National Cross-Country Bicycle Race, which covers more than 3,500 miles between New York City and San Francisco. It's a grueling race, requiring the bikers to ride over 250 miles and almost 10 hours each day to have a chance to win. Having participated in fourteen previous races, Lindsey knew that it took top conditioning, overcoming personal pain, and exceptionally good luck to win the race. In spite of the difficulties involved, she'd thought about one thing for many years...winning that race.

During the 100-day period prior to the current race, Lindsey didn't miss a single practice day. When the weather was bad and the temperatures well below freezing, she trained anyway. When the blisters caused by her new racing shoes were raw and hurting, she rode on. When she didn't feel well, she completed her practice routines anyway. Others were simply amazed at her efforts, but to her the difficulties of the hard work were more than offset by her ultimate goal to win that race.

At the end of this year's race, Lindsey arrived in San Francisco in 24th place out of some 350 entrants. It was her best finish ever. She made a brilliant effort and many of her friends and family members were there cheering when she crossed the finish line.

> *Whether she will ever win this race or not, we don't know. But this much we do know; Lindsey's goal to win this race has carried her through many years of hard training and through the ten days of this race. That goal will likely carry her for another year...and, if necessary, for many years to come.*

Anything worth having is worth working for. The challenge for us is to identify those things in our lives that are worth having. There is no question that hard work, trying time and time again, and giving it our all are instilled in many of us by our parents, our teachers, or our friends. While you may be predisposed to being a hard worker as a result of these experiences, you still need to have important goals to discover your passion and work to achieve it. It is the pursuit of these goals – which may require months, years, or even a lifetime – that will propel you and motivate you to make exceptional efforts. Make no mistake about it, achieving your goal is very important, but it is also the diligent and active pursuit of that goal that adds zest and meaning to your life.

> *"It is not the critic who counts; not the man who points out how the strong man stumbles, or where the doer of deeds could have done better. The credit belongs to the man who is actually in the arena, whose face is marred by dust and sweat and blood, who strives valiantly; who errs and comes short again and again; because there is not effort without error and shortcomings; but who does actually strive to do the deed; who knows the great enthusiasm, the great devotion, who spends himself in a*

> worthy cause, who at the best knows in the end the triumph of high achievement and who at the worst, if he fails, at least he fails while daring greatly, so that his place shall never be with those cold and timid souls who know neither victory nor defeat."
>
> THEODORE ROOSEVELT
> "MAN IN THE ARENA" SPEECH

Where Effort Counts the Most

The greater or more important the task, the greater the effort required to achieve it. It's one thing to mow the yard, but something else to develop a beautiful rose garden that the whole town can enjoy. It's one thing to learn to read, but something else to teach thousands of other people to do so. It's one thing to complete the first year on the job, but something else to devote a career to an endeavor or work that is important to you. I'm not saying that small accomplishments aren't important – in fact, they are. However, without exception, the more important the project before us, the greater the effort required to achieve it.

> *Wilson Williams was 24 years old, single, and lived at home semi-dependent on his mom and dad. Wilson had dropped out of college because he was making poor grades and had been placed on academic probation. In recent years, he'd lost two good jobs due to his indifference toward his work and a general lack of concern for the people working with him.*

The past few weeks had been a particularly frustrating time for him because his parents had told him, "Wilson, you're 24 years old...it's time for you to move out and live on your own!" He knew they shouldn't be supporting him, but there was no way he could move until he had some money coming in. At one of his low points and feeling almost worthless, he decided to drop in on his Uncle Maxwell one afternoon to talk about his situation.

Wilson didn't waste any time getting to the heart of the matter, "Uncle Max, I got fired from my last job. I've been looking for another one for several months without any luck, and now my parents have told me that I have to move out of the house within the next few weeks. I feel like a man without a country and, frankly, I don't know what to do about it."

Fortunately for Wilson, his uncle was a savvy guy who had worked hard to become a successful husband, father, and businessman. Uncle Max got up, closed his office door, and the two of them talked for several hours. "Wilson, there are really three phases of effort that are required to be successful," his uncle said. "The first is the effort to prepare yourself for the future even when you don't know exactly what that future will be. This includes learning as much as you can...in high school, in college, or in working in a field that is of interest to you. It also includes being nice to everyone you meet because you never know when one of these people will provide you with the insights that may lead you to a lifelong career. In your case, Wilson, you have been indifferent about this preparation phase...you dropped out of school, performed poorly in not one but two jobs, and weren't very nice to the people you worked with," his uncle explained. "You've made no effort to prepare yourself and that's why you're sitting here today."

"Unfortunately, you're right about all of that, Uncle Max," Wilson replied.

"Wilson, an exceptional life takes an exceptional effort. However, before you can go out and make that effort, you have to determine what you want to do. Since you've wasted the time that most people use to make this determination, you're going to have focus on this decision. What really interests you? What would you like to spend your life doing?" his uncle asked.

Wilson had a hard time answering his uncle's question because he had given so little thought to the subject. After an hour discussing various alternatives, they hit on the fact that the only work Wilson really enjoyed was writing for his college newspaper.

After thinking about it for a moment, Wilson responded, "I did like the newspaper business in college, Uncle Max. I think I would love working for a newspaper now."

"Wilson, you tell me you loved this type of work, but never pursued it. If you still feel that way about newspaper work, go over to <u>The Daily Herald</u> and tell them you don't care what you have to do... unload newspaper trucks, clean up in the press room, or fill up the coffee and coke machines... but you want to go to work for a newspaper," his uncle advised.

Wilson sat there just thinking how he would enjoy the newspaper business and how he had missed seeing this many years ago.

"Well, quit wasting time, Wilson. Get over to that newspaper this afternoon and take any job they will give you. When you get it and work for a while, come back here and I'll tell you about the other kind of effort that you will need to make if you are going to be successful in this world."

Wilson followed his uncle's advice. He went straight to the newspaper's personnel office and explained, "I just want to work for a newspaper...I'll take any job you have...I just want a chance to prove what I can do."

Impressed with his comments, the employment clerk handed him a form and replied, "Well, fill that out...it just so happens that we need an extra hand in the press room...starting tonight!"

Wilson reported for work at 10pm and worked all night in the press room. He moved large ink drums to the presses. He helped unload two trucks full of grocery store flyers. And, after the final bundles of newspapers had been transferred to the city delivery trucks, he spent the last hour cleaning up the place, readying everything for the next day's run. He'd worked exceptionally hard that night. As he was punching out, the pressroom foreman came *up and said, "Nice work, Wilson...we could use a few more like you."*

Remembering what his uncle told him about people, he respectfully replied, "Thank you very much, sir." As he drove home watching the sun come up, he could not help but think that the past 24 hours had been a very important time in the life of Wilson Williams.

After his second paycheck from the newspaper, he'd found an apartment and moved out of the house. Wilson worked hard, but waited another five months before going back to see his uncle again. He wanted to be sure that things were working out at the newspaper before he sat down for another heart-to-heart with Uncle Max.

Wilson started to feel better. He'd met a girl he liked many months ago but, being unemployed, he'd been hesitant to ask her out...now he was planning to give her a call. He'd been embarrassed about being pushed out of the house by his parents, but now he had his own place. In fact, he now enjoyed Wednesday night dinners at his parents' house telling them about "life at the newspaper." He could hardly keep his emotions in check when he told them, "I was promoted to assistant pressman last night. I'm getting a raise and tonight I get to move to the control room where all of the big presses are regulated."

A few days later, he walked into his uncle's office, gave his uncle a great big hug, and quickly asked, "Uncle Max, how will I ever be able to thank you for the advice you gave me six months ago?"

"Believe me, you already have, Wilson. Your mother telephoned yesterday and told me about your promotion. Without a doubt, it was one of the proudest moments of her life," his uncle explained.

"There are times, Wilson, when we just don't know what we should be doing with our life. It's a big mistake to waste these times. Instead, we should make the effort to prepare ourselves by going to school, by going to college, by learning how to treat other people, by working entry-level jobs, by developing new friendships, and by thinking carefully about what we want to do in life. At some point in this process, the light usually comes on and people kick their lives into another gear."

"However, if they waste these "Phase I" efforts – whether they are young or old – they are much less likely to find their way to a happy life. In other words, sometimes we have to put forth the effort to do the right things even when the future direction of our life – or even the purpose of what we are doing – is not fully known."

Looking back on his own life, his uncle's explanation of "Phase I" preparation effort made perfect sense. He had wasted this time and until his recent conversation with his uncle had been wasting much of his life as well.

"Wilson, the second type of effort – Phase II effort as I call it – is the one required to determine what we want to do in life. You have done a lot *of good things during the past six months, but the most important is the discovery of your love for the newspaper business. I may have helped pull it out of you, but it was there inside of you all the time. It had even signaled you during your college days, but you failed to pay attention,"* his uncle pointed out.

"You're still getting yourself ready for something much more important in the years ahead. You're close to committing your working life to the newspaper business. Once you make that commitment you will be ready for an even more important time...what I call preparation effort 'Phase III.'"

"Uncle Max, are you saying that we should spend our entire life making the effort to prepare ourselves for what lies ahead?"

"That's exactly what I am saying, Wilson. Think about it, you don't really know what lies ahead so you must continue your preparation efforts by learning more about the newspaper business, by continuing to develop your people skills, by working exceptionally hard at what you are doing, and by thinking about how you want to live your life. In fact, Wilson, I've been in Phase III preparation for almost 25 years and will be for the rest of my life... and so will you."

Years later, as Wilson Williams sat down to dinner with his wife...yes, the young lady he had noticed when he didn't have a job...and his two teenage children, he couldn't help but think about Uncle Max and how right he had been. Over the past 15 years, Wilson had continued his preparation efforts. He'd gone back to college, and, working around his newspaper duties, he received his degree in English. He volunteered for every newspaper seminar and conference that his paper had offered to employees. He worked in seven different positions within the newspaper, each with increasing responsibilities and each viewed by Wilson as his Uncle Max had advised – "a preparation effort" for the next. He made exceptional friendships throughout the city and the industry. And, the toughest preparation of all, he managed to attend every school event for both of his children and to help his wife around the house. He was moving right along in "Phase III," but clearly he was still in it and, as Uncle Max had taught him, always would be.

Uncle Max died last year, and it took the wind out of Wilson's sails for a month or so. But keeping his uncle's advice always in mind, he made a special effort to dwell on all the good things about his uncle and what an important influence he had been on his life. As his daughter was saying the dinner prayer, Wilson was thinking, "God bless you, Uncle Max, you made me see what making an effort is all about."

An exceptional effort always requires an exceptional goal – an objective that is of great importance to you. An exceptional effort is dependent on a strong desire to accomplish something that is of value to you. This goal or objective may be a crystal clear target that you have carefully established over time, or it may be a recent dream that excites you but needs more thought to thoroughly define. Wherever you are in process of establishing the primary goals for your life, don't hold yourself back. Don't be afraid of trying to do something that is challenging and difficult, that you would love to do, and that would be of great benefit to others. Certainly your life is worth such an effort.

So, stop and think about what you're working on here. You're working on the most important project in the world – your life. You have certain interests and capabilities, and the potential of achieving important things. You can help other people, possibly hundreds or even thousands of them, in your own special and unique way. If you can just identify your "life project," the effort required to work on it – and to achieve it – will come forth in an exceptional way.

CHAPTER 14

Your Choices, Your Life

"Life comes before literature, as the material always comes before the work. The hills are full of marble before the world blooms with statures."

Phillips Brooks

As we come to the last chapter of this book, I invite you to reflect on the choices you will be making in the days and months ahead. Will you choose to be a positive person and look for the good in other people? Will you choose to focus on the needs of others and to help someone in your own special way? Will you choose to work to identify your real interests and to take the steps to activate them in your life? Will you choose to develop personal goals, and will you be willing to make the effort required to achieve them? Think carefully about the choices that lie ahead. As you do, please remember…you are here for a purpose. Don't miss the opportunity to achieve it.

What Will You Accomplish With Your Life?

Whether you give the credit to your parents or to God, you are here. You have been given a life. You have been entrusted with the opportunity to live a certain amount of time on this earth. You have been equipped with personal interests and motivations so that you can do things in your own special way. You have been provided with the chance to make important contributions to your family, to your friends, and to the community in which you live. You have been given a place in this world, a platform from which you can contribute to those around you. So, the question for you is this…what will you do with the life you have been given?

> *Fanny Crosby was born in 1820 and blinded by a medical accident only a few weeks thereafter. In spite of her physical limitations, she became the most prolific hymnist in history. She wrote more than 8,000 hymns including <u>Blessed Assurance</u>, <u>I Am Thine O Lord</u>, and <u>To God Be the Glory</u>…all of which are still sung in churches today.*
> *"It seemed intended that I should be blind all of my life, and I thank God for the dispensation," she said. "If perfect earthly sight were offered me, I would not accept it for I might not have sung hymns to the praise of God if I had been distracted by the things around me."*

If you can start to believe in your own unique potential, you can begin to see the importance of the choices you make. If you can start to believe that your life has a special purpose, you can begin to see how important the choices are that will "get you there." If you can start to believe that there are things that you were intended to do with your life, you can begin to value every choice that you make. Life becomes a different event when you realize that your life's potential is subject to the choices you make. The pressure is on. There is a great life inside of you, but it is up to you to "pull it out" and show it to everyone.

> *"Before I can tell my life what I want it to do,*
> *I must listen to my life telling me who I am...*
> *[this] does not come from a voice 'out there'*
> *calling me to become something I am not. It*
> *comes from a voice 'in here' calling me to*
> *be the person I was born to be, to fulfill the*
> *original selfhood given me at birth by God."*
>
> PARKER PALMER
> Live Your Calling

It would be much easier if you had been placed on a well-marked path that you simply followed to realize the potential your life represents. However, you have been placed in a world that has many paths, many opportunities, and many things you can do. There are people, ideas, and information everywhere that can influence your thinking and impact the life that you are trying to live. We're exposed to thousands of such influences during our lifetimes. The important thing is to be willing to stand proud in your own uniqueness and to choose your own way in this world, allowing your life to impact this world in good and special ways that are of your own making.

> *"No one will ever accomplish anything excellent or*
> *commanding,*

*except when he listens to the whisper
which is heard by him alone."*

RALPH WALDO EMERSON
"Greatness"

Here's the question once again...what will you do with the life you have been given? Regardless of your age, the answer is important. Although young people in their high school or college years have a special interest this topic, the question applies to everyone. Many people in their 30's and 40's have "mid-life moments" when it dawns on them that they have been "going along with life" and never really thought that much about what they were intended to do with theirs. Older people, well along in their careers or possibly even retired, still have the opportunity to do something important with their lives. Each of us, no matter what our age or circumstances, is equipped with special qualities, interests, and abilities...it's never too late to put them to good use.

Don't Settle for Being Average

We go about our lives handling things as they come our way and tend to accept the highs and lows of living as the way life is. We "roll with the punches," work our way through the more difficult times, and enjoy the special moments with our families and friends as often as we can. If pressed to do so, the vast majority of us would classify ourselves as "about average."

However, there are several problems with a willingness to accept an average label on your life. First, personal values and physical well being have deteriorated so significantly in recent years that being average is not what it used to be. To think of yourself in average terms places your life in a group that has relatively poor values and lackadaisical attitudes about physical conditioning. More importantly, viewing your life in comparison to how other people are living completely discounts the potential your own life represents. We should not be so concerned about how we "average out" or "stack up" against others. Instead, the more important question for you to ask yourself is...how much of my life's potential have I really achieved?

One of the most important steps in positioning yourself for making better choices is to disregard how you compare to others and to focus on a determination of how much of your personal potential you have fulfilled. What are you doing with the interests and capabilities you've been given? Are these qualities being further developed and enhanced by the way you are living? What do you want to achieve in your lifetime and how far along are you in getting there? If you want to achieve real success, you must curb the tendency to compare yourself to others and become enamored with what your life – supported by good choices – can become.

> *The young person today would have a far easier time understanding the role of commitment in his life if he were not misled by the juvenile interpretation of "the pursuit of happiness." The storybook conception of happiness tells of desires fulfilled; the truer version involves striving toward meaningful goals – goals that relate the individual to a larger context of purposes. Storybook happiness involves bland idleness; the truer conception involves seeking and pursuing purposeful*

> *effort. Storybook happiness involves every form of thumb-twiddling; true happiness involves the full use of one's powers and talents.*
>
> JOHN GARDNER
> Self-Renewal

So, please don't settle for being average. Please don't just accept your current circumstances – if you want to change them, you can do so. Please don't let the world define the person you can become – you can do so much more by charting your own way. Please don't let your life simply go with the flow – you can live a very special life if you so choose. Your achievements depend on your choices. Make poor to average choices and you will have a poor to average life. To accomplish exceptional things you must be willing to step out and make important and difficult choices – choices that will allow you to fully develop the potential that your life represents.

A Few Choice Reminders

In the introduction to this book, I explained that <u>Good Choices, Good Life</u> was never intended to be a "how to" book. Instead, my goal was for it to be a "things to think about" book, to stimulate your thinking about the choices that, collectively, define who you are and what you will accomplish during your lifetime. In keeping with that objective, I close the book with a few reminders that I hope will further stimulate this thinking as you continue your journey toward realizing the true potential that you possess.

Almost everything you do is by choice.

Whether you stand up and shout "I'll do that!" or go quietly along with the wishes of others, you make a choice. Granted, there are some events in life that are beyond your control but, for the most part, you are where you are today because of the choices you've made. If you're overweight, it's most likely because you've chosen a lifestyle that creates this condition. If you interact with people without any real concern for their well being, it's because you've chosen to focus on "more important" things. If you don't have all of the education you need, it's because you've chosen not to work hard enough to obtain it. If you haven't accomplished much in your career, it's because you have chosen work habits that have produced such a result. You have arrived where you are today via the choices you've made. Likewise, what you accomplish in the future will depend on the choices you make from this day forward. When you accept the responsibility for your choices, you have, in effect, accepted the responsibility for the outcome of your life.

A good choice in the first place is much better than forgiveness after-the-fact.

We all have a tendency to fool ourselves at times. This is particularly true when we want to do something that, deep down, we know is not the correct or right thing to do. In those moments, our desire to participate in some activity may override our common sense and allow us to actually justify, in some false way, that "we'll be okay" even if we do the thing that we know is wrong. However, if you want to create an exceptional life, you must be able to practice honesty with yourself at all times and, therefore, remain "equipped" with the willingness to choose the course of action that is right for you.

While forgiveness – even when you give it to yourself – is an important quality within a functioning society, relying on forgiveness to erase past mistakes will not necessarily make up for a good choice you failed to make. Forgiveness may mentally "cancel out" something that occurred previously, but the recipient, although forgiven, still missed an opportunity to do something good for himself or for someone close to him. Missed opportunities can be costly. One never knows when that one time you made a bad choice will turn out to be a missed opportunity that not only would have changed your life, but may never come your way again. So, making good choices in the first place always works better than having to rely on forgiveness after-the-fact.

Don't follow the crowd. Do it your way.

James Crook, a Canadian businessman, said that "a man who wants to lead the orchestra must turn his back on the crowd." To a certain extent, this applies to each of us as we work to find our way in this world. The signals concerning what you should do with your life must ultimately come from inside of you. Although you may benefit from the advice and guidance of knowledgeable people, the choices concerning what you say and what you do remain yours to make. Even when you don't have a ready answer or don't have all of the information you need, you are still the one who makes the choice to either "go along" or to go and do your homework so you can make an informed decision. When you follow the crowd, you not only risk that the crowd may be making the wrong choice, but you also eliminate an opportunity to "search out" what your life is telling you. Your sense of direction and the choices you make should come from within you and not from an urge to do what other people are doing. If you want to realize the potential that you possess, you must make choices independently of others based on what you feel is right for you. You are the leader of your own life…act like it and make the choices that a leader would make.

Important goals and objectives can quickly change your life.

If there is one thing that can change your life in a short period of time, it is the development of goals concerning the type of person you want to be and what you want to achieve with your life. The benefits of an important goal take effect the moment you "attach" your life to it, not just when the goal has been accomplished. For example, the woman who chooses to treat her friends with more respect will see an almost immediate reaction from them. She doesn't have to wait years to experience the favor of her actions. Likewise, the high school senior who commits himself to becoming an airplane pilot will start to "think like a pilot" almost immediately – he doesn't have to wait for the wings to be pinned on him for this goal to start to change his life. Well-developed goals provide a context for living and establish a sense of direction for your daily life. By developing personal goals you gain an understanding of the type of person you want to be and how you want to live your life. If you don't have this understanding, your choices have no context and, therefore, are almost always viewed with less importance.

Further to this point, the more challenging your goals, the more you are likely to achieve. So, stretch your thinking, and listen to what your life is telling you. If you really feel you want to do something, as difficult as it might be, roll up your sleeves and go for it. You will never realize the dream you have if you don't convert it into goals for your life and then start working to achieve them. You are special, your life is special, and your goals should be special, too.

Don't let fear keep you from doing something great.

The easy choices come and go with little thought or emotion. However, some of our really important or more difficult choices – such as choosing a career, selecting a spouse, or starting a business – can create a fear of failure and cause us to make a safer choice or, in some instances, no choice at all. This can be especially true when what we want to do is something totally new or that has never been done "our way" before. When it comes to following your dream or committing yourself to an important endeavor, it's normal to think about the repercussions of the choice you're about to make… to be concerned about how your choice will impact others or what might happen if you fail. However, if you're going to do something exceptional with your life, you must expect to have these fearful moments. If you want to do something special, there will be times when you simply have to "suck it up" and go for it. In those moments, rely on the desires of your heart and the visions in your head to support your choice. Don't be scared of doing something unique and wonderful with your life – that's why you're here.

Revisit the way you are treating other people.

How you choose to treat other people will make a big difference in your life. Regardless of any perceived justification you may think you have for speaking badly or acting indifferently toward another person, your life will never be better for having done so. In spite of the enjoyment that may result from "getting even" with someone, gossiping about the mistakes of a business associate, or saying something derogatory about someone you don't like, you'll never be a better person as the result of having done so. Even when you feel you have a valid reason for your actions, you'll never benefit from hurting someone else or taking some liberty to which you are not entitled. No matter what the other person has done, your life will be "lifted" only when you treat the other person with dignity and respect. It's another one of those things in life that works differently from the way we typically think. It is only by being respectful of other people that we, in turn, develop respect for ourselves.

Take a longer-term view.

None of us knows how long we'll live or what major problems may come our way. However, using the uncertainty of the future as justification for doing whatever you want to do today will limit your opportunity to develop the long-term potential that your life represents. Doing what "feels good" today, in spite of the immediate gratification it provides, may, in turn, cause you to feel very bad at some point in the future. Short-term thinking typically confines your choices to short-term results. However, if you can consider how the choice you are about to make today supports the long-term goals you have for your life, that choice becomes more important. If you can keep looking further down the road and visualizing what you want to accomplish years from now, it's much easier to determine if the choice you are about to make will help get you there…or not.

It's all about what you give, and not at all about what you get.

Almost all of us have looked or searched for special insights into how we should live our lives. We'd all like to have a little secret, if you will, that would make our lives better, more enjoyable, and more meaningful. We live in a complex world, if we just had some way to simplify things, maybe we could do a better job of handling the choices we make each day. Well, there are a few fundamentals that have proven to be important in this regard – being honest, gaining a good understanding before you act, and letting love guide your life would be among them. However, there seems to be one more fundamental that is certainly equal to these and, in my opinion, tops the list. It is simply the fact that life works better when you focus on giving to others instead of getting for yourself. However you describe it, "it is more blessed to give than to receive."

Remember, we're here for each other.

Our lives have one common underpinning, or connection, if you will, that is frequently overlooked. It is the fact that we are here for each other. Given our different interests and abilities, it's easy to see that we were "created" to help each other – some to bake the goods, some to heal the sick, and some to care for the neighbor down the street. I believe that we were intended to use our unique capabilities to contribute to our families, friends, communities, and to the world in which we live. Therefore, those who view their life's mission as ultimately one of helping others are the people who seem to get the most satisfaction out of life.

My grandmother worked as a seamstress in a ladies ready-to-wear shop until she was 81 years old. She didn't make much money and didn't have many assets as we think of them today. But, "Granny," as she was known to one and all, distributed more good feelings during her lifetime than any person I have ever known. She was always more concerned about others than herself. As one example, she kept her own personal birthday calendar which contained the birthdays of every family member, every close friend, and most of the acquaintances she had made over the years. Each day she would sign and mail several birthday cards. She cared so much about the people she sent them to that she even underlined the parts of the birthday message that she thought particularly meaningful and then wrote her own special comments at the bottom of every card. When you received a card from "Granny," you knew it was a card from someone who cared about you. And, so it is with us...the more we live our lives for others and the less we live for ourselves, the greater and more enjoyable our life experience will be.

An exceptional choice requires an exceptional effort.

Some people make things look easy, but almost everyone who achieved something significant during their lifetime worked hard to do so. While certain things come natural to each of us, life still requires hard work and diligence to make it a successful event. "An accomplished life" is not a label that is frequently placed on young people, but is typically reserved for those who lived for many years, often to an older age, in an exceptional way.

I firmly believe that every person can accomplish important and meaningful things during their lifetime. However, in order to do so, you must be willing to accept the challenges that your life presents and focus on the possibilities that your life contains. You must be willing to listen to your "inner voice" and have the courage to make the choices that will take you where your heart wants you to go. Whatever you want to do with your life, you must be willing to make an exceptional effort and work exceptionally hard if you really want to turn your dreams and goals into reality.

Closing Comments

I hope this book has stimulated your thinking about the choices you are making and that it will help you make even better choices in the months and years ahead. Making effective choices is the fundamental ingredient in living a full, happy, and meaningful life. Good choices, good life…bad choices, bad life. It really is as simple as that.

As I stated several times, I believe that God's spirit lives in each of us and is trying to be "at work" through the lives that we are living. Your choices, therefore, are opportunities for God to touch the lives of other people and to accomplish things within the communities in which you live. That's why our choices are so important – they not only allow us to do good and meaningful things, but they allow God to do so, as well.

In closing, I urge you to take pride in being the unique person that you are. I challenge you to process the clues provided by your interests, your motivations, and the loves that enter your life to develop a fundamental understanding of the person you are intended to be. We all can accomplish important things during our lifetimes and do so much good for other people if we listen to what our lives are telling us and follow those directions. I wish you the best as you work to make the choices that will allow you to have such a life.

*Choose not the easy way,
or what other people do.
But choose that very special route,
that was designed especially for you.*

MICHAEL NELSON

My Thanks to Others

There were many people who contributed to this book. Jan Bonucci, who I worked with in Chicago for many years, edited much of my initial writing and provided some great suggestions during the early going. Carol Turkington, Susannah Williams, and Pattie McKenna did some wonderful work in making their professional edits to the book.

In addition, I would like to thank several of my family members and friends including my mother-in-law Mack Leonard, wife "Boop" Nelson, life-long friend Preston Hughes, business associate Sally Buchanan, former pastor Denton McClellan, and many others who were kind enough to read through drafts and provide suggestions that have improved the book and the message it contains. I want to add a special thanks to my mother, Buddy Arnold, whose secretarial skills were still very sharp at the age of 84 as she corrected and significantly improved the near finished draft.

So, in spite of having my name on its cover, Good Choices, Good Life was very much a collective effort. My thanks to all of these who helped me realize my goal to write this book.

~~~~~

If you have thoughts, comments, or experiences that you would like to share about making choices, please write to me at P. O. Box 770865 , Memphis, TN 38177, or send an email to mnelson234@gmail.com.

REFERENCES

Abramson, John, M.D. Overdosed America. HarperCollins. New York, NY. 2004.

Ajiake, Matthew Omayke. When God's Purpose Becomes Personal. Sonika Publishing. San Francisco, CA. 2003.

Avorn, Jerry, M.D. Powerful Medicines: The Benefits, Risks and Costs of Prescription Drugs. Alfred A. Knopf. New York, NY. 2004.

Barasch, Marc Ian. Healing Dreams. Riverhead Books. New York, NY. 2000.

Bass, Dorothy C. (Editor). Practicing Our Faith. Jossey-Bass. San Francisco, CA. 1997.

Benson, Peter L., Galbraith, Judy and Espeland, Pamela. What Teens Need to Succeed. Free Spirit Publishing. Minneapolis, MN. 1998.

Berg, Frances M., M.S., L.N. Underage and Overweight. Hatherleigh Press. Long Island City, NY. 2005.

Berg, Kris and Latin, Richard W. Essentials of Research Methods in Health, Physical Education, Exercise Science, and Recreation (Second Edition). Lippincott Williams & Wilkins. Philadelphia, PA. 2004

Berryman, Jack W. and Park, Roberta, J. Sport and Exercise Science. University of Illinois Press. Urbana and Chicago, IL. 1992

Blank, Warren. The 9 Natural Laws of Leadership. American Management Association. New York, NY. 1995.

Blanton, Brad PhD. Radical Honesty: How to Transform Your Life by Telling the Truth. Delta. New York, NY. 1994.

Block, Peter. The Answer to How is Yes. Berrett-Koehler Publishers. San Francisco, CA. 2002.

Bohlin, Karen E. and Lerner, Bernice. Great Lives, Vital Lessons. Character Development Group. Chapel Hill, NC. 2005

Brennfleck, Kevin and Kay Marie. Live Your Calling. Jossey-Bass. San Francisco, CA. 2005.

Buckingham, Marcus and Clifton, Donald O. PhD. Now, Discover Your Strengths. The Free Press. New York, NY. 2001.

Campbell, Susan PhD. Getting Real. H. J. Kramer and New World Library. Tiburon, CA. 2001.

Campbell, Susan PhD. Saying What's Real. H. J. Kramer and New World Library. Tiburon, CA. 2005.

Campbell, T. Colin and Thomas M. II. The China Study. Benbella Books. Dallas, TX. 2005.

Charland, William. Life-Work. Friends United Press. Richmond, IN. 1999

Covey, Stephen R. First Things First. Simon & Shuster. New York, NY. 1994.

Covey, Stephen R. Principle-Centered Leadership. Simon & Shuster. New York, NY. 1990.

Edwards, Paul and Sarah. Finding Your Perfect Work. Jeremy P. Tarcher/Putnam. New York, NY. 2003.

Farrington, Debra K. Hearing with the Heart. Jossey-Bass. San Francisco, CA. 2003.

Finney, Martha and Dasch, Deborah. Find Your Calling, Love Your Life. Simon & Shuster. New York, NY. 1998.

Fuhrman, Joel, M.D. Eat to Live. Little, Brown and Company. New York, NY. 2003.

Fulghum, Robert. All I Really Need to Know I Learned in Kindergarten. Villard Books. New York, NY. 1989.

Gardner, John W. Self-Renewal. Harper & Row, Publishers. New York, NY. 1963.

Goleman, Daniel. Vital Lies, Simple Truths: The Psychology of Self-Deception. Simon & Shuster. New York, NY. 1985.

Goodman, Ted (Editor). The Forbes Book of Business Quotations. Black Dog & Leventhal Publishers. New York, NY. 1997.

Guinness, Oz. The Call: Finding and Fulfilling the Central Purpose of Your Life. W Publishing Group. Nashville, TN. 1998.

Hall, Donald. Life Work. Beacon Press. Boston, MA. 2003.

Hanson, Glen R., Venturelli, Peter J. and Fleckenstein, Annette E. Drugs and Society (Seventh Edition). Jones and Bartlett publishers. Boston, MA. 2002.

Hardy, Lee. The Fabric of the World. William B. Eerdmans Publishing. Grand Rapids, MI. 1990.

Harrison, F. C. (Compiled by). Spirit of Leadership. Leadership Education and Development. Columbia, TN. 1989

Jackson, Phil. Sacred Hoops: Spiritual Lessons of a Hardwood Warrior. Hyperion. New York, NY. 1995.

Johnson, Spencer M.D. The Precious Present. Doubleday. New York, NY. 1981.

Klein, Allen. The Change-Your-Life Quote Book. Gramercy Books. New York, NY. 2000.

Ksir, Charles, Hart, Carl L. and Ray, Oakley. Drugs, Society, and Human Behavior (Eleventh Edition). McGraw-Hill. Boston, MA. 2006.

Lacy, Alan C. and Hastad, Douglas N. Measurement & Evaluation in Physical Education and Exercise Science (Fifth Edition). Pearson/Benjamin Cummings. San Francisco, CA. 2007.

Leider, Richard and Shapiro, David A. Whistle While You Work: Heeding Your Life's Calling. Berrett-Koehler Publishers. San Francisco, CA. 2001.

Leider, Richard J. and Shapiro, David A. Claiming Your Place at the Fire: Living the Second Half of Your Life on Purpose. Berrett-Koehler Publishers. San Francisco, CA. 2004.

Levoy, Gregg. Callings: Finding and Following an Authentic Life. Three Rivers Press. New York, NY. 1998.

Libal, Autumn. The Importance of Physical Activity and Exercise: The Fitness Factor. Mason Crest Philadelphia, PA. 2006.

Machen, J. Gresham. What Is Faith? The Banner of Truth Trust. Carlisle, PA. 1991

Maxwell, John C. Thinking for a Change. Center Street. New York, NY. 2003.

Miller, Dan. 48 Days to the Work You Love. Broadman & Holman Publishers. Nashville, TN. 2005.

Moynihan, Ray and Cassels, Alan. Selling Sickness. Nation Books. New York, NY. 2005.

Novak, Michael. Business as a Calling: Work and the Examined Life. The Free Press. New York, NY. 1996.

O'Connor, Elizabeth. Cry Pain, Cry Hope: A Guide to the Dimensions of Call. The Potter's House Bookservice. Washington, DC. 2002.

Palmer, Parker J. A Hidden Wholeness: The Journey Toward an Undivided Life. Jossey-Bass. San Francisco, CA. 2004.

Palmer, Parker J. Let Your Life Speak. Jossey-Bass. San Francisco, CA. 2000.

Ray, Michael. The Highest Goal: The Secret That Sustains You in Every Moment. Berrett-Koehler Publishers. San Francisco, CA. 2004.

Ray, Oakley and Ksir, Charles. Drugs, Society, and Human Behavior. McGraw-Hill. New York, NY. 2004.

Robbins, John. The Food Revolution. Conari Press. York Beach, ME. 2001.

Roberts, Mark D. Dare to Be True: Living in the Freedom of Complete Honesty. Waterbrook Press. Colorado Springs, CO. 2003.

Roizen, Michael F., M.D. and Oz, Mehmet C., M.D. YOU The Owners Manual. HarperCollins. New York, NY. 2005.

Ryan, M. J. Trusting Yourself. Broadway Books. New York, NY. 2004.

Salzberg, Sharon. Faith: Trusting Your Own Deepest Experience. Riverhead Books. New York, NY. 2002.

Sanders, J. Oswald. Spiritual Leadership. Moody Press. Chicago, IL. 1980.

Seraganian, Peter (Editor). Exercise Psychology: The Influence of Physical Exercise on the Psychological Processes. John Wiley & Sons. New York, NY. 1993.

Siciliano, Tom and Caliguire, Jeff. Shifting Into Higher Gear. Jossey-Bass. San Francisco, CA. 2005.

Simons, Janet A., Irwin, Donald B. and Drinnien, Beverly A. Psychology – The Search for Understanding. West Publishing. New York, NY. 1987

Smith, Hyrum W. What Matters Most: The Power of Living Your Values. Franklin Covey Co. New York, NY. 2000.

Towery, Twyman L. The Wisdom of Wolves. Wessex House Publishing. Franklin, TN. 1997.

Warren, Rick. The Purpose Driven Life. Zondervan. Grand Rapids, MI. 2002.

Wilson, Hugh T. (Editor). Drugs, Society, and Behavior. McGraw-Hill/Dushkin. Dubuque, IA. 2005